MIXED BLESSINGS

Routledge
New York and London

MIXED BLESSINGS

Gender and Religious Fundamentalism
Cross Culturally

edited by

Judy Brink and Joan Mencher

Published in 1997 by
Routledge
29 West 35th Street
New York, NY 10001

Published in
Great Britain by
Routledge
11 New Fetter Lane
London EC4P 4EE

Copyright © 1997 by
Routledge
Printed in the United
States of America on acid-
free paper.

Chapter 9 was originally
published in *Women and
Peace* by Betty Reardon,
Sage Publications.

Library of Congress Cataloging-in-Publication Data

Mixed blessings : gender and religious fundamentalism cross culturally
/ edited by Judy Brink and Joan Mencher.
      p.   cm.
   Includes bibliographical references and index.
   ISBN 0-415-91185-0. — ISBN 0-415-91166-9 (pbk)
   1. Reglious fundamentalism.   2. Women and religion.   I. Brink,
Judy, 1952–   .   II. Mencher, Joan P., 1930–   .
BK238.M59   1996
200'.82—dc20   96-28341
                                                         CIP

CONTENTS

PART TWO: WOMEN STRUGGLE AGAINST FUNDAMENTALISM'S RESTRICTIONS

PART THREE: WOMEN OPPRESSED BY FUNDAMENTALISM

FOREWORD

This book began as an invited session at the 1993 American Anthropological Association meeting. We would like to thank Mary Hegland for providing not only the title of the book, *MIXED BLESSINGS*, but also the overall organization of the book. We also want to thank Terry L. Brink for his invaluable help with computer applications, and F. Southworth for help with editing.

Judy Brink
Joan Mencher

INTRODUCTION

Joan Mencher

THIS COLLECTION of papers analyzes the effect of religious fundamentalism on gender roles in a wide variety of religious traditions and national cultures. The papers in this volume look at women in many different settings.
While the authors of the chapters are all social scientists, some are women
from the culture written about while others are empathic outsiders. All attempt to relate specific situations to wider socio-economic and political
processes. The book uses the term "fundamentalism" to cover a wide spectrum of situations. In some instances we include minority groups within larger societies, in others the cases refer to majority populations as seen through
the lens of a particular group in a particular place.

The systematic cross-cultural study of religious fundamentalism was begun
by the University of Chicago's "Fundamentalisms Observed" project. This
project partially addressed gender issues in the 1993 book *Fundamentalisms
and Society* (Martin and Appleby, eds.), particularly in the article by Helen

Hardacre, which makes the observation that all of the fundamentalisms emphasize women's domestic roles and restrict their roles in the public sphere. If this is the case, she asks, why do women join? She identifies seven reasons, ranging from feelings of alienation to pressures on third world countries which lead women to prefer economic dependence on a husband rather than independence.

Mixed Blessings provides women-centered answers to the question of why some women in some regions are involved in fundamentalist religions. In her excellent chapter on the impact of fundamentalism on women, Hardacre notes a shared perception among fundamentalists of powerlessness to change other aspects of society (urbanization, industrialization, poverty both rural and urban, or the nucleation of the family) and of the need to focus on change in interpersonal relations, especially within the family: "the essence of the message is a strengthening of patriarchy in all its forms . . . [and the idea of a return to a mythical ideal family in which] women are subordinate to men, and that men should rule over women in all things" (1993:138). She discusses the issue of why and how some women have become involved in such creeds, and notes that some of the women in the Islamic world were inspired by anticolonialist (including neocolonialist) or nationalist sentiments,

> that in many of these countries women have either been excluded from the labor force or relegated to lower-status jobs [which means] that in most cases they can live at a higher standard when coupled with a man . . . faced with a no-win game in the labor market, many women make conscious decisions to use the fundamentalist message to secure the husband's loyalty to and support of them and their children. . . . Fundamentalist networks also frequently assist women in their efforts to domesticate men, to bring them under the realm of life defined by the family (1993: 141–2).

Hardacre also notes that women have been restricted from discovering and exploring alternative values and ways of life in many of these groups; that in some groups women may fear reprisal for nonconformity and disobedience, including fears of loss of economic support, battery, rape, stoning, or simply abandonment; in some instances they fear supernatural sanctions and/or banishment from the group; and finally

> many women find that modernity presents them with difficult choices to make about things they were raised to believe inevitable. . . . These rapid changes have precipitated a moral crisis in conceptions of marriage. . . . Many fundamentalist women freely and knowingly decide to relinquish power and autonomy in favor of men in order to fulfill a pattern of moral action which they believe is key to the achievement of personal salvation (1993: 143).

2

MENCHER

Almost all of the groups are also concerned about the control of female sexuality. This may be seen not only in Islamic and Christian fundamentalist groups but also among Jewish, Hindu and Buddhist groups. Thus, they draw strict boundaries between good and proper behavior for their women and deride the so-called "free" western or secular women. The example by Keng-Fong Pang (in Chapter 3) of a relatively small, isolated Islamic community in China represents a radically different sort of religious fundamentalism where women and men have gained freedom to select their own spouses, but their real increase in power has come from increased interest in and reading of the Koran. These women have much more autonomy in relation to their own sexuality. In her book on women in Cairo, Arlene Macleod notes that many of the women see no hope of men altering their behavior towards women (Macleod 1991). Therefore they feel that they must accommodate their own behavior. This feeling that men will never change, especially never give up preying sexually on nonfamilial women, seems to play a part in the behavior and rationales found among women belonging to most of the fundamentalist groups.

The detailed descriptions of the lives of women provided by the authors in this volume illustrate the complexity of these issues. As the title suggests, the evidence shows that the intersection of fundamentalism and gender is quite complex and that the effect on women is mixed. Another work on this subject, *Fundamentalisms and Gender* (John Hawley ed. 1994), focuses on "the strength of the tie between fundamentalism and a conservative ideology of gender," pointing to a wide variety of situations throughout the world and noting that "we found ourselves unable to come to a consensus" (1994:4). What Hawley is refering to here is the lack of consensus about exactly how fundamentalism affects women since they are looking at both varied Christian traditions as well as varied Islamic ones. Most of the cultures they surveyed showed militantly antimodern religious groups or movements that seemed to resemble one another, and certainly for many of the examples in this book this picture seems to fit. Yet there is considerable variation between groups and societies. The case described by Brusco, for example, stands out as being quite different because here it is the women who are involved in trying to get their husbands and sons to convert. Here the women's fervent religiosity is often motivated by the lack of other options for persuading their men to become responsible husbands and fathers.

More important, given the economic, social and political upheavals in their respective societies, what the cases in this book focus on for the most part is how the women manage to carve out spaces where they do have some degree of autonomy. The chapters are grouped in terms of three types of situations: (1) where religious participation, even of a fundamentalist nature, can increase women's public roles or benefit them substantially in other ways; (2) where women are constrained by participation in fundamentalism, but are struggling to gain power and autonomy within these constraints; (3) where women are oppressed by their religious participation, but feel they have little choice.

The three cases that fit the best into category one include: (1) Colombia, where Brusco found that the redefinition of the male public role away from machismo benefits women by providing them with more income and greater family stability. (2) Sri Lanka, where Goonatilake reports on the growing women's movement to restore an order of Buddhist nuns, thus increasing women's public participation in religion in Sri Lanka. (3) And finally in a small region in China where Pang shows that increasing interest in Muslim fundamentalism in China is combined with women's active public economic roles and high autonomy in private roles. It could be argued in the first two examples here that the increased religiosity of the women is one of the only routes to greater autonomy they could take and therefore this does not indicate true autonomy, but on the whole these women are freer than their more traditional, nonfundamentalist sisters. In the case in China it could be argued that this has more to do with being a minority group, however, this freedom is not observed in other minority groups in China.

The second category, where women are constrained but struggling, is by far the largest one. It includes: (1) Stocks' chapter which shows an example of how Protestant women use an unauthorized newsletter to challenge the church's ruling forbidding women to be elders; (2) the chapter by Bennion which shows how polygynous Mormon women use female net-working to facilitate both their community obligations and their ability to work and earn money outside the commune; (3) Eiesland's chapter which shows how fundamentalism gives women in highly male-dominated professions a place to bond; (4) Hale's report on urban Sudanese women struggling to maintain active public roles despite growing pressure on them to withdraw into the domestic sector; both (5) Friedl and (6) El-Or show how despite religious leaders exhorting women to aspire to the ideal of the domestic woman secluded from the world, women manage to find areas of autonomy by organizing women in groups capable of carrying out acts on a community level.

There is no sharp break between the three categories, especially between category two where the women are struggling to category three where they are oppressed but see little option for struggle. In some ways Hegland's women belong to category two. These are women who have found a role and place for themselves. However, if the state in Pakistan becomes more overtly fundamentalist this may change. Hegland shows how gender roles defined by fundamentalists can benefit women. The Shiite women she studied on the local level have expanded women's public roles as preachers and ceremony leaders. However, she also notes that their increasing involvement in Shi'a rituals made them more accessible to preachings which include an emphasis on strict *purdah,* obedience to husbands and pollution of women. The curtailment of these women has been increasing since her visit in 1991.

Evidence of the ways in which fundamentalism has succeeded in confining women to the domestic sphere, and on how women's autonomy and public participation is restricted in many situations, is explored more in the next two chapters. Brink shows how fundamentalism in rural Egypt is stripping women of the right to participate in religious ritual, and Sen discusses the negative effects of Hindu religious fundamentalism on Indian women, and the challenge faced by the growing women's movement in India in working with women belonging to the Hindu fundamentalist parties. She also notes the relationship between socio-economic class and fundamentalism with the fundamentalists drawing most strongly on both wealthy and lower middle classes, especially unemployed or underemployed lower-middle-class youth.

Mixed Blessings differs from Hawley's *Fundamentalisms and Gender* in that it takes a feminist perspective, rather than analyzing fundamentalism from the male point of view. In the Hawley book the authors argue that the reason women's autonomy is constrained is that men feel threatened by the onslaughts of the modern world. Their response to this insecurity and loss of control, which is similar to the helplessness of infancy, is to rebel against women (i.e. the mother) and thereby gain a sense of security by dominating the women in their group. While the articles in this book do not disagree with this conclusion, noting that it may be true in some instances, we argue that fundamentalism is a much more complex issue, and that it does not uniformly result in less power for women. Indeed, the movement by the Buddhist women to reinstate nunneries founded in the early centuries of Buddhism represents a situation where women are asserting themselves by returning to the past.

The motivation for the resurgence of these fundamentalisms at the present time in diverse cultures and places around the globe appears to be rooted in similar social, economic and political processes. Some of these have to do with major global transformations in which numerous people have lost their sense of purpose, are unemployed or underemployed, and/or where there has been a displacement of former elites or higher-ranking groups. Furthermore, in many instances members of these former elites see themselves as losing out to others, often western-trained people, or women, or racial or ethnic minorities, etc. In these arenas of the disenfranchised and disempowered, fundamentalisms find fertile ground. It is only when the women are the ones who are able to use the fundamentalist sects to their advantage (see the chapter by Brusco) by using religious conversion to "tame" or "control" their husbands, or when they can use religion as an escape (see Goonatilake) from familial male dominance, that fundamentalism offers a positive escape hatch. In most instances, as Hawley notes, fundamentalists tend to be frightened of female

5

MENCHER

autonomy (1994: 5) and to use power over women as representing at least one arena in which these men can control their lives.

The organization of the articles presents the varied information in such a way that comparisons across religious traditions can be made, permitting an understanding of how fundamentalism, in all its forms, effects gender roles. Clearly the articles in this book are not totally inclusive. It would have been good to have included articles by female social scientists who belonged to each of the fundamentalist subcultures. Nonetheless, the articles do cover a wider range and more varied situations than have normally been considered under the rubric of fundamentalism.

FUNDAMENTALISM DEFINED

Almost all of the definitions of fundamentalism seem to refer to a kind of re-turn to a former "golden age" when life was more harmonious, when people knew their proper roles, and in which people are envisaged as being happy and content. Many of course refer to periods of time when women were much more completely controlled by the men in their families than they are today. On the other hand, each of the fundamentalisms has its own features. Even the different Christian fundamentalists differ from one another, as do the different Islamic groups, especially in diverse cultural or national settings. Nonetheless, they share features with the Jewish, Hindu and Buddhist funda-mentalists. Brown in her article in Hawley's book also argues that fundamen-talism arose in these diverse situations as a result of what she called a "failed promise," i.e. the failure of current policies and programs to improve the qual-ity of life for the majority of people on the globe. The failure of modern sci-ence to make life healthier or more satisfying for most people, along with the failure of both capitalism and totalitarian forms of socialism to right the wrongs of an oppressive world, and to provide meaningful employment for all, also feeds the need for a safe sure vision of the world such as that offered by a return to traditional religion.

Marty and Appleby in their various introductions (see bibliography) discuss the various meanings of the term fundamentalism from a variety of different viewpoints. In their four-volume series resulting from the Chicago "Funda-mentalisms as Observed" project, they cover a large amount of ground in showing first of all how

> fourteen detailed studies of movements within Christianity, Judaism, Islam, Hin-duism, Sikhism, Buddhism, and Confucianism . . . share certain traits. . . . Funda-mentalism appears as a strategy, or set of strategies by which beleaguered believ-ers attempt to preserve their distinctive identity as a people or group (1992: 1).

They also discuss the organizational characteristics of fundamentalist move-ments and pose numerous questions, such as why some of the movements have been more accommodating than others (1994: 3). In *The Glory and the Power* (1992), Marty notes that modern religious fundamentalisms arose concurrently with mass media of communication in the electronic era. There is a large emphasis placed on holding fast to their traditional beliefs, on the need to protect their followers from the outside, almost a belief that the followers are easily influenced and vulnerable. Therefore, protection from the general mass media is required and at the same time, use of the mass media for religious inculcation is enjoined.

This book is more concerned with some of the ways that women deal with their lives in fundamentalist groups (however fundamentalism is defined), some of the reasons why women may turn to fundamentalism, the problems confronted by secular female activists in countries where fundamentalism is growing, barriers between fundamentalists and activists, and above all, the relationship between education, socio-economic class and in the case of minority fundamentalist groups, relations with the wider society in which they are imbedded. It shows how class (Hale and to some extent Brusco), rural living (Brink), female networking (Bennion, Hegland, Eiesland, Goonatilake), political friction (Sen, El-Or, Hegland and Brusco), being a small group in a very different type of society (Pang) and personality (Friedl, Stocks) all affect the experience of women and fundamentalism. Some of the societal conditions in Section Two (which deals with ways in which women are constrained by fundamentalism, but are struggling against or working their ways around its constraints) may change, depending on larger geopolitical considerations as well as changes in the leadership in their respective countries, etc. This is discussed in many of the chapters in the book (Hegland, Hale, Brink, Goonatilake and Pang). At present in some of the societies there is a possibility that the state may turn in either direction in the years to come. This is certainly the case in Pakistan and Egypt. It remains to be seen whether women will gain or lose freedom.

REFERENCES

Brown, K. M. 1994. "Fundamentalism and the Control of Women." In *Fundamentalisms and Gender,* ed. John Hawley, pp. 175–202. New York: Oxford University Press.

Hardacre, H. 1993. "The Impact of Fundamentalisms on Women, the Family, and Interpersonal Relations." In *Fundamentalisms and Society,* eds. M. Marty and R. S. Appelby, pp. 129–150. Chicago: Chicago University Press.

Hawley, J. and W. Proudfoot 1994. "Introduction." In *Fundamentalisms and Gender,* ed. John Hawley, pp. 3–44. New York: Oxford University Press.

Macleod, A. 1991. *Accommodating Protest: Working Women, the New Veiling, and Change in Cairo.* New York: Columbia University Press.

Marty, M. E. & R. S. Appleby 1991. *Fundamentalisms Observed.* Chicago: University of Chicago Press.

————. 1992. *The Glory and the Power.* Boston: Beacon Press.

————. 1993. *Fundamentalisms and Society.* Chicago: University of Chicago Press.

————. 1993. *Fundamentalisms and the State.* Chicago: University of Chicago Press.

————. 1994. *Accounting for Fundamentalisms: The Dynamic Character of Movements,* Chicago: University of Chicago Press.

PART ONE

WOMEN BENEFIT FROM FUNDAMENTALISM

THE PEACE THAT PASSES ALL UNDERSTANDING
Violence, the Family, and Fundamentalist Knowledge in Colombia

Elizabeth E. Brusco

chapter 1

INTRODUCTION

IN 1991, Colombians drafted a new constitution, which for the first time separated church and state and declared all religions equal. For much of its history, the Colombian government had maintained a formal agreement with the Vatican, which gave the Catholic church special privileges and substantial power over the daily lives of Colombian citizens. Marriage, education, birth and death were under the control of the Church.[1]

Since the first Protestant missionaries arrived in Colombia in the mid-nineteenth century, the evangelical movement has provided an alternative religious choice for Colombians. Until the 1930s, the evangelical movement grew very slowly. Protestant converts were subject to persecution, and the Catholic clergy had tremendous power over people, especially in rural communities. In his recollections of his encounter with the first Protestant missionary to El Cocuy, Boyacá in the late 1930s, a Colombian man said, "People had heard about Protestantism, but only as something very remote. One would hear it said that there were people of other religions, but we never thought that we would meet them."

Since the 1930s, the Colombian evangelical movement has grown at an ever increasing rate. The number of denominations has proliferated, and the presence of foreign missionaries has dwindled. Colombians themselves have taken over this new religion and it has become transformed to meet their needs into something uniquely Colombian. The single largest evangelical denomination, the Iglesia Pentecostal Unida de Colombia (United Pentecostal Church of Colombia), sends its own Colombian missionaries to the United States and Canada. Pentecostal or Christian charismatic churches have been the most successful in attracting large followings. These are the denominations which emphasize "the gifts of the Spirit," that is, speaking in tongues, prophecy, divine healing and so on. Churches started by mainstream Protestant missionaries, such as the Presbyterians, metamorphose in a charismatic direction. A young Colombian pastor of one large evangelical church in Bogotá described his congregation as *"Presbi-costales"* (A compound of Presbyterian and Pentecostal which reflects both the church's origins and its current theological orientation.)

In this paper, I will examine some of the ways in which evangelicalism in Colombia addresses key tensions in the local setting and provides converts with resources for reconfiguring their social environment. My primary emphasis is on the intersection of religious belief with gender, the family, and violence in Colombia.

COMING TO TERMS WITH THE "F" WORD

For more than a decade, since I began studying the Colombian evangelical movement in 1982, I have avoided using the term "fundamentalist" to describe these diverse Protestant and Pentecostal converts. I have chosen to speak of them as they do of themselves, as *evangélicos,* or evangelicals.

There are a number of reasons for my wariness of the term, fundamentalist, not the least of which is the negative reaction the word usually evokes from academic audiences. In my discipline, anthropology, a field that prides itself on exposing bias and undermining preconceptions about the various peoples of the world, there is a surprising alacrity to prejudge and malign Christian fundamentalists. This is usually done out of no greater knowledge of the movement than what appears on the news, a generalization of Jerry Falwell, the moral majority and Jim and Tammy Faye Baker to all evangelical Christians everywhere. Recognizing this tendency, Susan Harding, who has studied the moral majority and Protestant fundamentalism in the U.S., has written eloquently about "fundamentalism as one of modernism's 'others'" (1991:393). She says that

. . . modern voices represent fundamentalists and their beliefs as an historical object, a cultural "other," apart from, even antithetical to, "modernity," which
emerges as the positive term in an escalating string of oppositions between supernatural belief and unbelief, literal and critical, backward and progressive, big-
oted and tolerant. Through polarities such as these between "us" and "them" the
modern subject is secured. (1991:374).

The task of reporting ethnographically on these religious movements becomes more involved when at each turn in the narrative we find ourselves
challenging standard representations of fundamentalists. We must then take on
the additional job of undoing explanations which "blot out fundamentalists'
realities" (Harding 1991:374). As in all representations of the Other, the category "fundamentalist" has been invented for a purpose, which, in Harding's
terms, is "to secure the modern subject" (1991:374). Undoing these polarities
can invoke much resistance.

Major new publications on the topic of fundamentalism have appeared recently, which in some ways appear to be more ethnographically grounded
and aim to detail the diversity as well as the similarities in these types of religious movements. Perhaps the most important of these is the American Academy of Arts and Sciences Fundamentalism Project funded by the MacArthur
Foundation. As editors of the three volumes resulting from this project, Martin Marty and R. Scott Appleby acknowledge that many of the contributors
were uncomfortable with the term "fundamentalism" when applied to the
movements on which they report. Despite this fact, the editors give some
compelling reasons for retaining the term as a coordinating description en-
tailing certain unifying factors or "family resemblances" of this hypothetical
family of fundamentalisms (Marty and Appleby 1991b:816).

Not surprisingly, many of the unifying factors they mention "fit" the case
of Colombian evangelicals, while others do not. The issue of tradition vs.
modernity in Colombian evangelicalism is analyzed here, with specific reference to the family.

WOMEN IN COLOMBIAN EVANGELICALISM

I began my study of Colombian evangelicals concerned about the experience
of individuals, especially women, in the movement. There was ample evidence from past studies that women were attracted to evangelicalism in Latin
America in greater numbers than men, that they often were the first to convert, bringing their husbands (and children) in later, and that they achieved
leadership roles and prominence in these churches that were unusual in organized religion, especially Catholicism.[2]

This concern led me to investigate the impact of evangelical conversion on
women and men over the course of their life cycles, in the context of differ-

BRUSCO

13

ent domestic settings. I was most interested in adult women, most of whom were married, either formally, or living in consensual unions. I talked to women whose husbands had also converted and to women whose husbands had not. In general, women whose husbands had also converted experienced a more stable family life, a higher standard of living, and improved relations with their spouses. I have argued that Colombian evangelicalism can be seen as a strategic form of women's collective action, which, like Western feminism, seeks to transform gender roles to improve women's position in society (Brusco 1986, 1993, 1995). This particular conclusion is a far cry from the received wisdom about fundamentalist Christians, and I will return to it later.[3]

LATIN AMERICAN EVANGELICALISM AND LIBERATION THEOLOGY

A new wave of literature on Latin American evangelicals based on research conducted in the 1980s has begun to challenge some of the polemics which have plagued the field for a long time. Foremost is David Stoll's *Is Latin America Turning Protestant?* (1990) and a new collection of essays edited by Stoll and Virginia Garrard Burnett *Rethinking Protestantism in Latin America* (1993).

However, the treatment of women in Latin American fundamentalism is still highly problematic. Analyses of Latin American Protestantism have tended to look at social process on the level of larger structures, a viewpoint which obscures the motivations of individual converts. A fascination with the political implications of evangelicalism in Latin America also explains the preferential focus on liberation theology as the religious movement of choice in academic writing.

In much of the scholarly conceptualization of Catholic liberation theology and Protestant evangelicalism in Latin America, liberation theology has been portrayed as the good guy and evangelicalism as the bad. Liberation theology is lauded as the foundation of the Sandinista revolution, a religious movement through which the poor and oppressed are given voice. Evangelicalism, on the other hand, has been viewed as the ideological agent of imperialism and patriarchy, mystifying the exploitation of workers and women. In this view, liberation theology is transformative and evangelicalism is conservative.

Studies of evangelicalism in Latin America which steer clear of these polemicized debates and attempt to comprehend conversion from the viewpoint of converts themselves are much needed. One example of this positive trend is Linda Green's study of Mayan widows in Guatemala (1993). Her conclusions are notable in that they return agency to the participants in the evangelical movement at the local level. She states that, "fundamentalism in these instances is not so much a religion of repression, although initially it was for many, nor the religion of advancement, as it has been for a few, but a 'religion of survival,' a refuge from suffering and a space in which the women are able to reclaim some personal control over their lives. In this way the women

14

of Chicaj are utilizing a panoply of responses to the seemingly intractable economic misery and ongoing state repression" (1993: 162).

What I would like to consider here is the transformative potential of fundamentalism in Latin America. Like liberation theology, fundamentalism aims at a radical restructuring of society. The most salient arena of change is not directly political and economic, however, but rather personal and domestic. An important issue to be considered in this regard is the following: When it comes to gender roles and the family, are Colombian evangelicals traditional or modern?

ASCETICISM AND MACHISMO

One "family trait" of fundamentalisms identified by Marty and Appelby is that they set boundaries. This is certainly the case for Colombian evangelicals. In Colombia, the most distinctive and readily identifiable characteristic of *evangélicos* is their asceticism. Drinking, smoking, gambling, visiting prostitutes, listening to or dancing to secular music, are labeled as vices and prohibited. Significantly, the above-named "vices" are all common characteristics of Colombian male social life, the kind of male subculture which goes along with that brand of Latin masculinity known as "machismo."

Conversion takes its greatest toll on machismo. The ascetic injunctions have little direct impact on the personal behavior of most female converts, for women are already ascetic if they are fulfilling the marianista ideal of the long-suffering, sacrificing mother. Indirectly, however, as dependents on a male wage earner, women stand to benefit from their mate's conversion. This positive outcome of conversion is often mentioned by Colombian women, and has been noted by other researchers on the topic. Maldonado (1993: 235) states, "Women, 'the oppressed of the oppressed'

15

> . . . find in evangelical and Pentecostal communities the space and opportunity to exercise their gifts. In practice, if not in theory, women participate as equals in the governing of their homes, their time, their gifts, and their future; their husbands are encouraged to encounter a relational and affective part of themselves denied by the traditional macho culture.

Over the past several years, as I have talked about this change in male habits which accompanies conversion and argued that it explains in part the attraction of evangelicalism for Colombian women, I have repeatedly been asked, "But what's in it for the men?" This question usually comes out of the equation of machismo with male dominance, and the perception that a man stands to lose much and gain little by converting.

To clarify this issue I would like to discuss for a moment the difference between machismo and patriarchy, which I see as thoroughly different male roles and versions of male dominance. The literature on Latin American kinship and gender reveals many contradictions and little consensus about what machismo is. Paul Kutsche (1984: 6–7) has usefully distinguished between machismo based on self-confidence and machismo based on self-doubt. The self-confident machista is the familiar patriarch, whose dominance over his family correlates with his responsibility to them.[4] In part, the patriarch's identity is derived from the status of his household. The other form of machismo, the self-doubting one, is characterized by the alienation of men from the household (including the attenuation of their roles as husbands and fathers) and their identification with the world outside rather than with the household group. This is accompanied by an extreme divergence of men and women from common goals and understandings. An exceptionally high rate of abandonment and of female-headed households results. This means that women are on the receiving end more often than not in terms of "the distribution of hardship."[5]

While the economic well-being of women and children is enhanced when the husband converts, identifying the attraction of evangelicalism for a woman as simply a way to get hold of more of her husband's paycheck is economic reductionism that does a great disservice to the religious experience of Colombian evangelicals. Such a conclusion also continues the tradition of treating Latin American evangelicalism as an ideology which serves to disguise reality rather than elucidate it. In that view, whether evangelicalism is mystifying the forces of imperialism in order to make the male convert into a disciplined and compliant worker, or provides the means by which his wife can divert more of his income into the household, the evangelical convert is a victim of false consciousness and inevitably not acting in his own self-interest.

I think it is more accurate and productive to see conversion as stemming in part from a linked set of processes which renegotiate gender and family relationships and personal identity in a climate of crisis.

VIOLENCE, POVERTY, AND MACHISMO IN COLOMBIA

Pedro and Consuelo live in the highland community of El Cocuy, in Colombia. They own no land, and Pedro provides for his family by traveling around the countryside buying livestock (pigs, goats, sheep, and occasionally cows or horses) for resale in the weekly market. Pedro has had two years of formal education, his wife Consuelo has had three. They converted to evangelicalism (Assemblies of God) twelve years ago. According to Consuelo, conversion has worked a miraculous change in their life together. Before Pedro converted, he was a cruel man who drank heavily, beat her, and was having difficulty supporting his family. She said, "When we were recently married we weren't Christians—we were unconverted. And then the home was a disaster area, because we didn't understand each other (no nos comprendíamos), there wasn't affection, there wasn't friendship, there wasn't love or anything. Everything was a disaster." Shortly before he converted, she had decided to leave him, de-

16

BRUSCO

spite her anxiety about how she was going to be able to support their four children. During a visit to Bogotá, Pedro, who was then suffering from an illness, was compelled by his converted sister to attend an evangelical church service with her. That night he was cured and converted himself. Both Pedro and Consuelo were criticized by the unconverted members of their families for converting. Pedro reports that only one brother supported his actions. When the family spoke of "ridding Pedro of these evil customs," that is, his evangelical practice, the brother replied, "But what evil customs? Now he doesn't get drunk any more, nor does he smoke, nor does he fight, and he's responsible for his home . . . what do I have to say to him?"

What crisis do Colombians face that has led them, in increasing numbers, to separate themselves from the mainstream, sometimes alienating themselves from their families and communities, and fill the Pentecostal temples?[6]

Marty and Appleby link the emergence of fundamentalisms to crises in social and personal identity. They say, "The sense of danger may be keyed to oppressive and threatening social, economic, or political conditions, but the ensuing crisis is perceived as a crisis of identity . . . " (1991b:822–823). In Latin America, it is axiomatic that the rural migrants who become the urban poor experience a sense of anomie, loss of important kin and social support networks, and so on that make them "a fertile seedbed for evangelical proselytism." (Deiros 1991: 155) What is missing from this truism is an awareness of the way such experience is a gendered one.[7]

People continue to create families and domestic groups in the urban settings. In Colombia, the three great challenges to family security are the linked phenomena of violence, poverty and machismo. The torrent of violence in Colombia goes back a long way and gives no indication of abating. Even before the drug wars and the terrorism of *narcotraficantes* made walking down the street in Bogotá perilous, Colombian journalists were reporting that the number one cause of death for males in Colombia between the ages of 15 and 45 was homicide (Pachón de Galán 1981:105). They link this fact directly to machismo and the behaviors which characterize it. The classic stance of the machista is intransigence in male-male relations and this coupled with all-male socializing centered on endless rounds of reciprocal drinks is a highly volatile combination. It is not unusual for a fight to have lethal consequence.

Evangelical teaching and preaching aggressively address the interconnected problems of machismo, violence and poverty and offers solutions. Reorienting male social life from the street to the home and the church, from all male groups to mixed male-female ones, is a major step. This can only be accomplished with powerful ideological support. What is significant is that the rhetoric and ritual, although tied closely to the Bible, cannot be said simply to invoke or revert to "tradition."

Marty and Appleby identify fundamentalists "as traditionalists who perceive some challenge or threat to their core identity, both social and personal"

17

BRUSCO

(1991a: ix). However, we might ask here, what "tradition" is in the Colombian context? I pose the question with specific reference to the "traditional" sex roles, family forms, and conjugal relations which Colombian evangelicalism seems to be so good at reinforcing.

For some time, anthropologists have spoken of the "invention" of tradition. The fluidity and flexibility of what had earlier been thought of as rigid and enduring has been established. Particularly useful to the present discussion is the following statement by Lancaster (1992:91):

> Rather than seeing tradition as the set of laws it purports to be, it would be better to see it as a certain form of discourse . . . whereby actors engage themselves in the social world, negotiate their multiple relations with others, formulate and justify their courses of action, and thereby . . . reconstruct the world every day in the light of self-interest.

This statement effectively captures the way "tradition" is involved in reestablishing the family along evangelical lines.

There is much evidence from the Colombian case to support the assertion by Marty and Appleby that "fundamentalism has proven itself selectively traditional and selectively modern" (1991b:825). The constitution of male and female identities and conjugal relations is transformed from common patterns through religious practices which are at the same time restrictive and liberating.

As a minority religion in a strongly Catholic country, evangelicals in Colombia negotiate their identity and beliefs in opposition to dominant Catholic practice.[8] In this regard, Colombian evangelical vocabulary is interesting. Evangelicals talk about when they became *"cristianos"* (Christians), but they don't mean that they were nonbelievers before. They use the term "Christian" to describe themselves and their fellow believers, and this does not include Catholics. Evangelicals do not perceive of themselves as being "religious." The words religious, and religion are used to refer to Catholic practices; they connote something that has to do with rites and rituals. An evangelical describing her nonconverted mother as "a very religious woman" might be implying something she sees as quite negative: for example, that her mother had many statues of saints around the house, she attended mass and confession regularly, and she owned and believed in the efficacy of religious objects that had been blessed by the priest. Other words that might occur in the context of such a description are *"fanatico"* (fanatic), *"idolotria"* (idolatry), and *Romano* (Roman Catholic). One of the main features of conversion to evangelicalism in Colombia is a strong rejection of what is seen as "meaningless ritual" of the Roman Catholic church. In this opposition frame, evangelicalism emerges as nonhierarchical and contemplative. The "priesthood of all believers" means that each individual is empowered to seek the truth through Bible-reading, reflection, and direct divine inspiration.

The Bible is the central symbol of evangelicalism in Colombia. Only very recently has the Catholic clergy encouraged or permitted the laity to own and read the Bible, and this Bible orientation still distinguishes evangelical practice. I might add that in the rural countryside and among the urban poor, for individuals with very little formal education, owning and reading a "book" of any kind is a rarity.[9]

Evangelical vocabulary also distinguishes two different kinds of prayers: Catholics, it is claimed *"resan"*, that is they recite prayers by rote, while evangelicals *"oran"* that is they spontaneously create prayers from their own experience appropriate to the setting.

In brief, evangelical practice encourages individuals to reflect on their situation and analyze it according to a set of principles which derive from Bible reading. Keeping aside what this means on an ideological level for a moment, on a practical level the evangelical convert cultivates an introspective attitude and the ability to articulate her or his thoughts to a group, which is quite distinctive in this segment of the Colombian population. Women regularly lead prayer and Bible study sessions in their homes (this is, in fact, the backbone of evangelical ritual in Colombia), and these gatherings and the leadership role that women take on in them constitute an extraordinary break with the common pattern in which men speak in public settings and women stay quiet at home.

Marina, a member of the Four-Square Gospel church in Bogotá articulates her experience of this process:

19

> In order to prepare a sermon you start by praying. Then you go to the Bible. You don't sit and write it all at once, the inspiration comes to you bit by bit, as you're cooking, doing things around the house and all. The Holy Spirit guides you in terms of what to write down. You have to have love and discipline. When I prepared a sermon for a service at my church, I spent all week in prayer, and the Holy Spirit gave me the message little by little. The Holy Spirit helps you get over your nervousness, helps you to forget the people in front of you.

The feminine ethos of evangelicalism in Colombia is revealed in the imagery used by women in sermons. For example, a woman's sermon during a *"culto de liberación"* (service of liberation) in a Pentecostal church evokes the daily feminine routine of cooking and cleaning:

> Some people say, my Bible is very pretty. I keep it as an adornment. Well, we may have a fine, clean Bible, but our life is not going to be as clean as the Bible, it will more likely be dirty. What is clean is the Lord's word. Really, speaking is an art. What we have to tell the world is short, small, but substantial. It's like food; it might must be a little bit, but it should be nutritious.

For male converts, too, there are reversals of common gender patterns, beginning with the ascetic codes mentioned above. In regard to ritual, the antihier-

BRUSCO

archical structure of evangelical religion is the antithesis to the system of pa-tron-client ties which have characterized the relations of male peasants with Catholic priests as well as with *hacendados*. Male converts report a "search for the truth" as a primary motivation for conversion. This search usually entails close reading of the Bible and personal interpretation. The words of a male convert in El Cocuy reveal the way in which conversion is an active choice based on a search for personal meaning:

> I would come down to town on Sundays to go to mass, and then I'd come out of mass and go to the evangelical service. Many times in both places they'd be discussing the same part of the Gospel, the same chapter. But in the Catholic church the explanations were very twisted, very different from what the chapter was trying to say. I felt that there must be something more.

At the same time, a receptivity to the diffuse power represented by the Holy Spirit is uncharacteristic for males: the image of male converts with their arms and faces upraised, inviting in the Holy Spirit, stands as a stark contrast to the impenetrable stance of machismo.

CONCLUSION

In their introduction to the Fundamentalism Project volumes, the editors se-lect the theme of "fighting" as a key feature which distinguishes fundamen-talisms (1991a:ix).[10] They step off from the following statement included in one of the contributions, that is, that fundamentalists "no longer perceive themselves as reeling under the corrosive effects of secular life. On the con-trary, they perceive themselves as fighting back, and doing so rather success-fully" (Heilman and Friedman 1991: 255). In Colombia "the corrosive effects of secular life" do not fit into a neat dichotomy between tradition and modernity. Transformed roles and identities of males and females, and a redef-inition of the relationships between them, constitute something distinctively evangelical and radically new.

That evangelicalism takes on the homely task of healing both individuals and families accounts for its tremendous appeal in societies such as Colombia. James Fernandez, in his discussion of African religious movements (1978: 220), points out that western Christian religions have given up attempts to explain, predict, and control. "In the face of the worldly power of rational-technical thought and positivistic science . . . they have come to recognize religion as communion between persons and not as an explanation of the facts of existence." He views the success of African religious movements as founded on the "fundamentalist desire for total explanation." These observa-tions also apply to the defection of Colombians from established Catholicism. The explanatory power of Pentecostalism and its this-worldly applications provide a powerful format for living, especially in terms of the intimate areas

20

BRUSCO

of gender identity and family relationships. In an uncertain and chaotic environment this knowledge is likely to be well received.

ACKNOWLEDGMENTS

I would like to thank Judy Brink and Joan Mencher for inviting me to participate in the session "Gender and Religious Fundamentalism," at the 1993 American Anthropological Association meetings in Washington, D.C., where this paper was first presented. I would also like to thank Janet Bauer, the discussant on that panel, for her insightful comments and useful suggestions. Patricia Killen in the Religion Department at Pacific Lutheran deserves special thanks for guiding me to some of the new material on fundamentalism and providing a fresh perspective.

NOTES

1. Levine (1981) describes the legal status of the Colombian Catholic church as "unusually favored." In 1887 the Colombian government signed a Concordat with the Vatican that stood as "a model of the traditional ideal of Christendom—complete Church-State integration" (Levine 1981: 70). Major junctures of the individual's life cycle were under the control of the church hierarchy. For example, Levine states, "The Church also received the predominant role in registering births, with parish records having preference over civil records. In addition, the management of death was placed in Church hands, as cemeteries were turned over to the ecclesiastical authorities. Marriage, another step in the life cycle, was also placed firmly under Church control. Civil divorce did not exist, and civil marriage for baptized Catholics was made contingent on public declaration of abandonment of faith."

2. The numerical preponderance of women in evangelicalism in both the United States and Latin America is mentioned in many texts, including Argyle and Beit-Hallahmi 1975; Blanchard 1975; Flora 1976; Garrison 1974; Harrison 1974; Sexton 1978. Women's leadership roles in evangelical churches have been noted by Flora 1976; Hardesty 1979; Hollenweger 1972; LaRuffa 1971; Ruether 1979; Samarin 1972 to name but a few. In my fieldwork I found that women are often the first to convert, bringing their husbands in later, which supports the observations of Goodman 1972, 1973; LaRuffa 1971; and Mintz 1960.

3. The experience of women suffers in the Fundamentalism Project volumes. In her essay on "The Impact of Fundamentalisms on Women, the Family, and Interpersonal Relations," Helen Hardacre concludes that fundamentalism is the ultimate patriarchal mandate. She states that "It is little wonder, then, that men are attracted to fundamentalist creeds, but the persuasive power of such creeds for women is much more difficult to comprehend" (1993: 141). In Pablo Deiros' review of Protestant fundamentalism in Latin America (1991: 142–196) the persuasive abilities of the male authority figure, be he the local pastor or the mass evangelist, eclipse the diverse contributions of women who make up the majority of congregations.

4. Micaela di Leonardo usefully distinguishes between two connotations of the word "patriarchy": the first is interchangeable with "institutional oppression," referring to "a historically changing set of social relations among men which functions to main-

21

BRUSCO

tain their power over women." The second, more precise definition, is relevant to the case of the self-confident machista, that is, patriarchy as a "family type characteristic of feudalism in which older men were household heads, controlling younger men, women, and children (di Leonardo 1984: 193). This more precise usage follows Eisenstein, 1979.

5. Lancaster (1992) uses this phrase in his analysis of the impact of machismo on women and families in post-revolution Nicaragua.

6. During the early 1980s, when I conducted my fieldwork, estimates of the number of evangelicals in Colombia ranged from 900,000 to two million (out of a population of 29 million). For the period from 1960–1985, Stoll (1990: 337) cites a growth factor of 6.2 percent in the evangelical population, projecting ahead to the year 2010 when evangelicals will comprise 15.1 percent of the Colombian population. This figure apparently does not include the fastest growing segment of evangelicals, the Pentecostals.

7. There is substantial evidence that the urban poor are quite effective at creating networks which replace whatever was lost when they moved from the countryside. In Colombia, urban-rural ties were strong and vital, and extended kin groups straddled the urban and rural locales. This is to say that the image of the lonely migrant fixing on the Pentecostal church as a substitute kin group is not a very powerful explanation.

8. People's involvement in the Catholic church in Colombia varies greatly; and identifying as a Catholic, especially for men, may essentially mean a form of folk belief and very little institutional involvement. In the non-evangelical population, Christian, like Colombian, is a characteristic that is taken for granted. It is a status, like human, that one does not have to work to achieve.

9. Evangelical families often experience upward mobility through education, and evangelicals commonly place a high value on education. Evangelical schools, such as the Presbyterian-run "Colegios Americanos" are popular even among non-evangelicals, due to their reputation as serious high quality high schools which have a proven record of preparing students for careers.

10. Colombian evangelicals certainly can be said to fight against a particular enemy. For much of the history of evangelicalism in Colombia, that enemy has been the Roman Catholic church. Freedom of religion has not been a basic value in Colombian society. In Colombia, all evangelic converts were Roman Catholics. It is important to consider the particular nature of Colombian Catholicism. Colombia was the last country in the world to maintain a Concordat with the Vatican, granting the Roman Catholic church special powers over major junctures in the individual's life cycle. Birth, marriage, and death were under the dominion of the church. Church and state were separated in Colombia as the result of a new constitution drafted in 1991. Furthermore, the Roman Catholic church has long identified with the Conservative party in Colombia, and Liberals were routinely denounced from the pulpit. During the period of civil strife known as *La Violencia*, liberals and conservatives clashed and some 200,000 people were killed. Evangelicals tend to identify as Liberals, and suffered a double persecution during that time.

REFERENCES

Argyle, M. and B. Beit-Hallahmi 1975. *The Social Psychology of Religion*. London: Routledge & Kegan Paul.

BRUSCO

Blanchard, K. 1975. "Changing Sex Roles and Protestantism among the Navajo Women in Ramah." *Journal for the Scientific Study of Religion* 14: 43–50.

Brusco, E. E. 1986. "Colombian Evangelicalism as a Strategic Form of Women's Collective Action." *Feminist Issues.* 6(2): 3–13.

———. 1993 "The Reformation of Machismo: Asceticism and Masculinity among Colombian Evangelicals." In *Rethinking Protestantism in Latin America*, eds. V. Garrard-Burnett and D. Stoll, pp. 143–158. Philadelphia: Temple University Press.

———. 1995 *The Reformation of Machismo: Gender and Evangelical Conversion in Colombia.* Austin: University of Texas Press.

Burnett, V. G., and D. Stoll eds. 1993, *Rethinking Protestantism in Latin America.* Philadelphia: Temple University Press.

Deiros, P. A. 1991. "Protestant Fundamentalism in Latin America." *In Fundamentalisms Observed*, eds. M. E. Marty and R. S. Appleby, pp. 142–196. Chicago: University of Chicago Press.

di Leonardo, M. 1984. *The Varieties of Ethnic Experience.* Ithaca: Cornell University Press.

Eisenstein, Z. 1979. *Capitalist Patriarchy and the Case for Socialist Feminism.* New York: Monthly Review Press.

Fernandez, J. W. 1978. "African Religious Movements." *Annual Review of Anthropology* 7:195–234.

Flora, C. B. 1976. *Pentecostalism in Colombia: Baptism by Fire and Spirit.* Cranbury, N.J.: Associated University Presses.

Garrison, V. 1974. "Sectarianism and Psychosocial Adjustment: A Controlled Comparison of Puerto Rican Pentecostals and Catholics." In *Religious Movements in Contemporary America*. eds. Zaretsky and Leone, pp. 298–329. Princeton: Princeton University Press.

Goodman, F. D. 1972. *Speaking in Tongues: A Cross-Cultural Study of Glossolalia.* Chicago: University of Chicago Press.

———. 1973. "Apostolics of Yucatan: A Case Study of a Religious Movement." In *Religion, Altered States of Consciousness and Social Change.* ed. E. Bourguignon, pp. 178–218. Columbus: Ohio State University Press.

Green, L. 1993. "Shifting Affiliations: Mayan Widows and Evangélicos in Guatemala." In *Rethinking Protestantism in Latin America.* eds. V. G. Burnett and D. Stoll, pp. 159–179. Philadelphia: Temple University Press.

Hardacre, H. 1993. "The Impact of Fundamentalisms on Women, the Family, and Interpersonal Relations." In *Fundamentalisms and Society.* eds. M. E. Marty and R. S. Appleby, pp. 129–150. Chicago: University of Chicago Press.

Hardesty, N., L. Dayton and D. Dayton 1979. "Women in the Holiness Movement: Feminism in the Evangelical Tradition." In *Women of Spirit.* eds. R. Ruether and E. McLaughlin, pp. 225–254. New York: Simon and Shuster.

Harding, S. 1991. "Representing Fundamentalism: The Problem of the Repugnant Cultural Other." *Social Research* 58:373–393.

Harrison, M. J. 1974. "Sources of Recruitment to Catholic Pentecostalism." *Journal for the Scientific Study of Religion* 13:49–74.

Heilman, S. C., and M. Friedman 1991. "Religious Fundamentalism and Religious Jews: The Case of the Haredim." *In Fundamentalisms and Society.* eds. M. E. Marty and R. S. Appleby, pp. 197–264. Chicago: University of Chicago Press.

Hollenweger, W. J. 1972. *The Pentecostals*. Minneapolis: Augsberg Publishing House.

Kutsche, P. 1984. *On the Lack of Machismo in Costa Rica and New Mexico*. Paper presented at the American Anthropological Assoc. Meetings in Denver, Colorado.

Lancaster, R. N. 1992. *Life is Hard: Machismo, Danger, and the Intimacy of Power in Nicaragua*. Berkeley: University of California Press.

LaRuffa, A. L. 1971. *San Cipriano: Life in a Puerto Rican Community*. New York: Gordon & Breach.

Levine, D. 1981. *Religion and Politics in Latin America: The Catholic Church in Venezuela and Colombia*. Princeton: Princeton University Press.

Maldonado, J. E. 1993. "Building Fundamentalism from the Family in Latin America." In *Fundamentalisms and Society*. eds. M. E. Marty and R. S. Appleby, pp. 214–239. Chicago: University of Chicago Press.

Marty, M. E. and R. S. Appleby 1991a. "Introduction: The Fundamentalism Project: A User's Guide." In *Fundamentalisms Observed*. eds. M. E. Marty and R. S. Appleby, pp. vii–xiii. Chicago: University of Chicago Press.

———. 1991b. "Conclusion: An Interim Report on a Hypothetical Family." In *Fundamentalisms Observed*. eds. M. E. Marty and R. S. Appleby, pp. 814–842. Chicago: University of Chicago Press.

Mintz, S. W. 1960. *Worker in the Cane, A Puerto Rican Life History*. New Haven: Yale University Press.

Pachón de Galan, G. l981. *Se Acaba la Familia: Investigacion Sobre la Sociedad Colombiana*. Bogotá: Editorial Pluma.

Ruether, R. 1979. "Introduction." In *Women of Spirit*. eds. R. Ruether and E. McLaughlin, pp. 15–28. New York: Simon and Shuster.

Samarin, W. J. 1972. *Tongues of Men and Angels: The Religious Language of Pentecostalism*. New York: Macmillan.

Sexton, J. 1978. "Protestantism and Modernization in Two Guatemalan Towns." *American Ethnologist* 5(2): 280–302.

Stoll, D. 1990. *Is Latin America Turning Protestant?* Berkeley: University of California Press.

BUDDHIST NUNS
Protests, Struggle, and the Reinterpretation of Orthodoxy in Sri Lanka

Hema Goonatilake

THIS CHAPTER discusses how the Buddhist female renunciates (*dasa-sil-matas*)[1] in contemporary Sri Lanka have successfully made their voices heard in the public debate on the revival of the *Bhikkhuni sasana* (community of fully ordained nuns). It will initially survey briefly the history of the order of nuns during the Buddha's time, for two reasons: firstly, to provide the historical context that led to the formation of the order and its growth, so as to understand the contemporary situation; secondly, to show that there are distinct parallels between the role played, and the criticism and prejudices suffered, by the nuns of the sixth century B.C. and the *dasa-sil-matas* of today.

THE FORMATION OF THE ORDER OF NUNS: A NEW PATH OF LIBERATION FOR WOMEN

In Buddhism, there is equality of all humans. The Buddha asserted, "Not by birth does one become an outcaste or a brahmin. It is by deed alone." His technique of liberation which centered around the cultivation of the mind has no formal barriers of sex, caste, race or religion. Yet the particular calling the Buddha and his followers were engaged in, namely that of homeless seekers for truth, was solely the province of men. It was men who went from mendicant to mendicant, searching for truth. There were hardly any women.

The admission of women into the monastic order by the Buddha in the sixth century B.C., therefore, heralded a new era in the history of woman's status in India. However, it was only after Prajapati Gotami and five hundred women with shaven heads and attired in saffron robes demonstrated by walking nearly a hundred miles and pleaded with the Buddha for the third time, that the Buddha agreed to grant admission. And that permission was granted only on the condition that the nuns adhered to eight *garudhammas* (special rules), in addition to the other disciplinary rules. The reluctance and the delay on the part of the Buddha, it has been argued, were due to his greater concern with the wider problems of the monastic organization (Dhirasekera 1982). It has also been argued that it was clear from the content of the rules that the primary objective of laying down the rules was the healthy continuation of the institution of the monastic community, rather than to assert spiritual domination over the nuns.

It is, however, apparent that at the time of the admittance of the nuns, the monks were looked upon by the Buddha as more mature and responsible, and thus, capable of guiding the newly established order of nuns. Yet, it should be noted that generally the monastic rules laid down by the Buddha arose from practical situations, and in his lifetime were changed as situations changed. Accordingly, some of the specially formulated moral precepts for the nuns were relaxed as the circumstances demanded, and accordingly, some of the powers were transferred to the nuns themselves.

FIRST PROTEST AGAINST MALE SUPREMACY

The first protest against male supremacy in the Buddhist order was launched by the founder of the nuns' order herself. This marks the beginning of the male/female confrontation in the Buddhist order which has continued for over 2500 years.

Prajapati Gotami asked the Buddha, not long after entering the order, through his favorite disciple, Ananda (who pleaded the nuns' cause with the Buddha) to remove the first special rule (which prescribes that even a nun of 100 years standing must show respect to a monk just ordained), to allow monks and nuns to pay respect to each other, not according to their sex but by seniority. The quick rebuff that came from the Buddha was bitter. "Not even the *Titthiyas* who propound imperfect doctrines sanction such homage of men towards women. How could the *Tathagata* do so?" (Oldenberg 1879: 258).

This episode is perhaps one of the earliest cases of female protests against male supremacy in a religious order anywhere in the world. It also illustrates that even a most liberal male committed to women's emancipation eventually succumbed to the dominant cultural norms of the times. Horner comments on the episode, "The rule (the first rule) is the outcome of an age-old and widespread tradition rather than a prudent provision to keep women in their place. . . . It is but particularisation of the current views on the relation of the sexes" (Horner 1975).

MONKS' ENVY OF THE NUNS

There is also evidence to show that the monks continued to level criticism against the order of nuns even after its recognized success (Dhirasekera 1982). Ananda was accused by a section of the monks at the First Council (meeting of all monks) held three months after the passing away of the Buddha to codify the teachings, for helping with the admission of women into the order (Saddhatissa 1915). Dhirasekara has pointed out from the Chinese version of the Mahisasaka Vinaya, a statement ascribed to the Buddha which tends to indicate that the reason for the monks' criticism of nuns was the fear of being eclipsed by the newer order. In this statement, the Buddha, says that after his death, the male and female lay devotees would have honoured the monks in many ways if there were no nuns in the order (Dhirasekera 1982). On this evidence, one could perhaps further suggest that the reason for the opposition by monks is the monks' envy of the nuns, since now the monks could not monopolize the respect of the laity.

27

SPIRITUAL EQUALITY ESTABLISHED

The strong disbelief of women's spiritual attainments held by men, even after the recognized success of the nuns' order, is beautifully illustrated by the statement made by the Buddha to Prajapati Gotami when she visited him on the eve of her death. "O Gotami, perform a miracle in order to dispel the wrong views of those foolish men who are in doubt with regard to the spiritual potentialities of woman" (Lilley 1925: 535).

Before long, however, equality of nuns with the monks in intellectual and moral eminence was well established. In fact, the spiritual attainment of the nun Bhadda Kapilani was equal to that of one of the intellectually highest in the order of monks, namely Maha Kassapa, who was elected by the monks as the head of the whole order to succeed the Buddha himself.

THE HISTORY OF SRI LANKAN NUNS: A CASE OF NEAR EQUAL PARTICIPATION

The order of nuns was founded in Sri Lanka by India's King Asoka's daughter, Sanghamitta, in the third century B.C., just five years after the establishment of the order of monks there. It grew in such strength and eminence that the fourth century Sri Lankan chronicle Dipavamsa makes reference to nuns in the same vein as it does to monks (Oldenberg 1879). (For this reason, it has been argued that the Dipavamsa is a compilation of the Buddhist nuns. The later chronicle Mahavamsa totally ignores the story of the nuns and provides only a 'male' history of the Theravada[2] fraternity). By the eleventh century, after the Chola invasion from South India, however, the order of nuns had disappeared.

No order of nuns, therefore, exists in Sri Lanka today. The only female renunciate religious group found among Buddhists today is the community of those who observe the ten precepts (the Theravada tradition has 311 precepts for nuns and 227 for monks), known as *dasa-sil-matas,* who may be equivalent to the ancient *samaneris* (novice nuns with interim ordination waiting to be fully ordained) who observed ten precepts and *sikkhamanas* (disciplinary rules observed by novice nuns).

RESURGENCE, STRUGGLE AND PROTESTS: THE PRESENT PHASE

Buddhist resurgence in the latter part of the nineteenth century in Sri Lanka led by Anagarika Dharmapala brought an awakening among the women devoted to a religious life. In 1891, Anagarika Dharmapala arrived in Burma for the first time with a view to promoting close religious links between Sri Lanka and Burma. However, it was the personal dedication and commitment of a single woman that created the *dasa-sil-mata* movement and gave it recognition to remain a living force up to the present times.

A young Christian-born Sri Lankan affluent woman had embraced Buddhism, and had requested her village monks in Bentota to ordain her as a nun. When she heard from the monks that they could not do so since there was no such practice in Sri Lanka, she left for Burma in 1894. After a training period of three years there, she became a *dasa-sil-mata* by the name of Sudharmacari. She returned to Sri Lanka in 1905 and formed the Sudharmadhara Samiti in Kandy for the promotion of the movement of *dasa-sil-matas*. With the help of the wife of British Governor Blake and two other local officials, the first nunnery was established in Kandy and was named The Lady Blake Aramaya in 1907. This marked the beginning of the *dasa-sil-mata* movement.

Most of the *dasa-sil-matas* who were ordained for the next thirty years received their training at the Lady Blake Aramaya (*aramaya* is a dwelling of one or more *dasa-sil-matas*). Some Burmese *dasa-sil-matas* also resided in this nunnery and helped the ordination and the promotion of Sri Lanka *dasa-sil-matas*. Many Sri Lankan *dasa-sil-matas* who had the means went to Burma and spent some time there.

Several nunneries were soon built by prominent Buddhists in many parts in the country. By this time, quite a few educated women from middle-class background had been ordained. A Burmese *dasa-sil-mata*, Mavicari, had come to Sri Lanka in 1928 and began teaching *dasa-sil-matas*. Thus, the *dasa-sil-mata* movement had gathered some momentum by the late 1930s.

In the course of the subsequent decades several others followed suit. The early disciples have included a principal of a school, writers of religious tracts and several educators. Since then, the movement has grown strongly, and at present there are nearly three thousand *dasa-sil- matas*.

SOCIAL PROFILE OF THE *DASA-SIL-MATAS*

To understand the present status of *dasa-sil-matas*, it is useful to sketch a social profile. For this, we draw on a survey of *dasa-sil-matas* conducted by the Department of Buddhist Affairs in the Ministry of Cultural Affairs in 1984, the only comprehensive survey done to date. A questionnaire was sent to approximately 2,500 *dasa-sil-matas*—all those who could be contacted. Of the 1175 responses received, only 478 questionnaires were completely filled out. An analysis of some of the information in these responses, however, throws some light on the contemporary situation of *dasa-sil-matas* in the country, although this sample may be biased.

As to educational qualifications, a proper assessment of education cannot be made from a questionnaire, since many of the respondents had renounced household life at an early age and had not followed the formal school system. (Sri Lanka as a whole has had high literacy rates for nearly three generations, and the literacy rate for women at present is 90 percent.) Almost 50 percent (238) of the respondents had studied beyond Grade Six. Some half of this number had passed *dhamma, vinaya* and *abhidhamma* examinations (those based on the Buddhist canon). Yet, even those who were barely literate could understand Pali (the language of Buddhist scriptures) through constant practice of reciting the scriptures.

Almost 70 percent of the respondents had entered the religious path before they reached the age of 30 years. The biggest single age category (153) consisted of those who entered in their twenties. Personal interviews with *dasa-sil-matas* confirmed that even if the girls develop an interest to renounce household life quite early, they are not permitted by their parents to do so until after they reach maturity. Only 15 have been able to "break through" before the age of 15. The youngest to have entered the path had done so at the age of four. Only one respondent out of 110 who entered before the age of 20 had married before she entered the path. Only ten respondents out of 153 of the group who entered in their twenties had married, and six of their husbands were still living. Only nine out of 67 respondents who entered in their thirties had married, and only six had their husbands living. (It is also possible that "for fear of losing respect," some avoided stating in the survey that they had married.)

About one third of the sample (156) entered the religious path after the age of 40. Many of this group had joined after fulfilling their family obligations (such as children's education, marriage of daughters) or when widowed, although they claimed they had developed the religious urge much earlier.

A reason that has led a small minority of elderly *dasa-sil-matas* to enter the religious life is social marginality— either extreme poverty or the absence of anyone to take care of. Becoming a *dasa-sil-mata* is perhaps the best survival strategy open to them. This category has the least number, but is perhaps the most visible, for they wander about begging for a living and often subsisting on food given to them by pilgrims. Some of them are even mentally unsound in a medical sense, and have become an easy target of contempt and ridicule.

Dasa-sil-matas shave their heads and wear robes with a long sleeved blouse, of saffron or ocher colour. They live a life of celibacy in an *aramaya*. A well established *aramaya* has a shrine room, a Bo (pipal) tree, a preaching hall, living quarters, a toilet and, if in a village, a well. Generally such an *aramaya* is built with financial help from lay supporters who live in the neighborhood. A *dasa-sil-mata* usually has very few possessions—a bed, a table, a chair, a begging bowl, a few changes of clothes, a pair of slippers and books. When food is not supplied by lay supporters, they cook their own food. (The food for monks is regularly supplied by lay supporters, and the practice of begging for food rarely exists in Sri Lanka today.) The *dasa-sil-matas* are well known for their simple and frugal food and living, unlike some of the monks who live comfortable lives.

The activities of *dasa-sil-matas* cover religious, spiritual and social aspects. Religious and spiritual activities include daily Buddha *puja* (offerings to the Buddha), reciting devotional *gathas* (verses), meditation, special *pujas* for particular occasions and persons, conducting monthly *sil* (eight precepts) campaigns, preaching on such days and teaching younger *dasa-sil-matas*. They confer merit on those who offer them alms. (These activities are very similar to those performed by monks.) It is sometimes said that the poor neighbors prefer *dasa-sil-matas* to monks to offer alms to, since the former consume less and are not particular about the menu.

In the way of social work, their activities are wide and varied. Activities include conducting classes in Buddhism for children, chanting *pirit* (blessings) for pregnant mothers for easy delivery, nursing the sick in the neighborhood, and organizing and helping societies for social work for the poor. One of the most useful social functions performed by *dasa-sil-matas* to women is the informal advisory service given on occasions when women run to the village *aramaya* after being assaulted by their husbands, physically and/or verbally. Sometimes, they go into the *aramaya* for refuge even with their little babies and spend a night. They confide in the *dasa-sil-matas* and get advice on family disputes. The oppressed women find a feeling of solidarity in the *dasa-sil-matas*, and thus, the *aramaya* provides comfort and solace.

It is significant that the factors that motivate *dasa-sil-matas* to renounce the lay life are in sharp contrast to those that motivate some monks. *Dasa-sil-matas* themselves invariably take the initiative to give up household life, whereas in the case of monks, it is often the parents who take the initiative.

When a boy's horoscope has a particular planetary combination, it is believed that he will not be successful in household life and the parents are keen to see that he enters the order. In the case of a girl, the parents make it a point to discourage her from renouncing lay life, for the most fulfilling role for a woman is believed to be a wife and mother. In the case of a boy, the parents give all encouragement since it is believed that if a boy enters the order, relatives from four sides (father's father, father's mother, mother's father and mother's mother) will attain nirvana (release from the cycle of rebirths). Another strong reason that motivates a boy is the aspiration for more mundane gains or a leadership position. It is a practice sometimes that a Buddhist monk who is head of a temple with substantial land and wealth is tempted to persuade a close relative to join the order in order to succeed him. Another motivating factor for the boys has been the initiation ceremony of grandeur. The comfortable life certain monks continue to have with cars, televisions and refrigerators could also be a motivating factor. The life of a *dasa-sil-mata*, in contrast, is a life of simplicity and often, one of deprivation. Perhaps, they are the most marginalized religious group in Sri Lanka. Thus, it is clear that it could be the external factors that sometimes motivate a boy to take to monkhood, whereas it is more often the inner spiritual awakening that motivates a girl to renounce lay life.

THE CRY FOR THE RESTORATION OF THE ORDER OF NUNS

A Buddhist society consists of four groups: *Bhikkhu* (monks), *Bhikkhuni* (nuns), *Upasaka* (laymen) and Upasika (laywomen). The first two are called *Mahasangha*. Today, Sri Lanka is devoid of the second component of a Buddhist society, the nuns. The restoration of the order of nuns became an issue in Sri Lanka over fifty years ago. Arguments for and against the revival of the order of nuns have been put forward by Sri Lankan Buddhist monks as well as by the laity. We would like to review here the main arguments.

The disciplinary rules for regulating the life of nuns were formulated five years after the formation of the order of nuns and twenty years after the formation of the order of monks. The rule was that the precepts of entering the order were conferred by ten nuns first, and confirmed or reconfirmed later by ten monks. The question did not arise then as to what the rule should be in a country, or during a period, where nuns are not available.

The main objection today against the revival of the order of nuns is that in the lineage of the Theravada, the order of nuns has been broken, and until a Buddha is reborn and reestablishes the order of nuns (the next Buddha, according to the Theravada tradition, will be born after millions of years), there is no possibility of reviving the order of nuns. The order of nuns cannot be revived, according to the opponents, because the Theravada tradition has it that the women should be first ordained by the nuns, and then by the monks. But the Theravada order of nuns no longer exists in any Theravada Buddhist country. The order of nuns exists only in Mahayana countries, such as China, Taiwan or Korea. If the order of nuns is introduced from a Mahayana country, it is the Mahayana tradition, it is argued, and not the Theravada tradition that will be introduced. In fact, the only Theravada country where the order of nuns ever existed was Sri Lanka.

Sri Lanka had, however, on earlier occasions lost the lineage of higher ordination of monks, but received it back from the countries where the higher ordination had been earlier introduced by Sri Lanka. When the order of monks became extinct in Sri Lanka after the Chola invasion in the eleventh century, King Vijayabahu brought monks from Burma to give the higher ordination to Sri Lankan monks. There was no mention of the restoration of the order of nuns at the time. Again from around 1580 to 1773, Buddhism declined and only novice monks observing ten precepts were found in Sri Lanka. At the invitation of King Kirti Sri Rajasinghe, a delegation of monks from Thailand came to Sri Lanka and reintroduced the higher ordination to Sri Lankan novice monks (Paranavitana 1959–60). If the same rule applies for nuns, then, those who argue for the restoration say that the order of nuns which exists in China can be brought back to Sri Lanka. The higher ordination of nuns was introduced to China by Sri Lankan nuns in 433 A.D. Opponents argue that China belongs to the Mahayana tradition, and that the validity of the lineage is questionable because it has not been transmitted continuously.

32

VOICES SILENCED

The question of the restoration of the order of nuns has also become a subject of debate in the mass media from time to time during the last fifty years or more. The usual scenario was as follows: A person of standing who feels a genuine need for the restoration comes up with a strong plea for the restoration. A member of the monks' hierarchy replies in the mass media opposing the restoration. The issue then dies down and emerges again after another couple of years. It is useful to review some of these episodes in recent history.

As early as 1934, Gunapala Malalasekera, the president and founder of the World Federation of Buddhists, advocated the restoration of the order of nuns through conferring of ordination by Sinhala monks without the participation of nuns. He cited the injunction issued by the Buddha to confer higher ordination on nuns, as is recorded in the Cullavagga of the Vinaya Pitaka. The text reads, "I permit you monks, to confer higher ordination on nuns" (Malalasekera 1934: 24).

In 1952, Pundit Narawila Dhammaratana Maha Thero, who led a delegation to an international Buddhist conference in China, wrote, "The absence of the Bhikkhuni order is a great loss to Sri Lanka. The Bhikkhuni order was established in China by Bhikkhunis from Sri Lanka. The Bhikkhuni order there exists in its purity and unbroken line of succession. Therefore, it is most fitting that we restore the Bhikkhuni order in Sri Lanka with the assistance of Chinese Bhikkhunis" (Dhammaratana 1952: 36).

More recently, this question again came up in 1980 when three members of Parliament (all male) were in the process of preparing proposals for the promotion of Buddhism to be presented to the Parliament. One proposal included the restoration of the nuns' order. This created an uproar among the Buddhist community, both lay and clergy. This proposal for the restoration of the nuns' order was then abandoned.

The heads of all the three chapters of the order of monks in Sri Lanka are said to be opposed to the restoration of the order of nuns. Only one such head, however, has made public announcements periodically on the issue, and continues to maintain that it cannot be granted within the Theravada tradition. It should, however, be noted that generally the heads of chapters have been cautious on lay social matters too. But more junior monks, especially since the 1940s, have been in the forefront of social change in Sri Lanka defying their elders. In the mass media, some monks of the older generation speak disparagingly about *dasa-sil-matas* saying that they bring disgrace to the country for they are not properly educated and go begging at street corners. Some strongly protest that they should not be allowed to claim the same status as nuns, wearing yellow and patched robes, and that they should not accept alms in the particular ritual form in which the monks accept alms, which confers more merit to the givers. Some bitterly remark that they are frauds, and even mock the *dasa-sil-matas* by saying that they have joined the order to run away from problems of household life.

A new awakening occurred in 1983 when the Department of Buddhist Affairs in the Ministry of Cultural Affairs initiated a programme of action for the promotion of *dasa-sil-matas*. A programme was launched to provide educational facilities at district-level monastic institutions to *dasa-sil-matas* to prepare them for Pracheena examinations (on Buddhism and oriental languages), a facility that was available only to Buddhist monks up to that time. Identity cards were issued to *dasa-sil-matas* as a first step of recognition. A federation of *dasa-sil-matas* was formed with representatives elected from the *dasa-sil-mata* organizations at the district level. This federation began to meet in Colombo to discuss and decide upon the country level activities.

In September 1984, I visited China as part of a study tour of Buddhist nuns in Asia, for the purpose of doing a comparative study of the tradition of nuns. I was especially fortunate to be the first foreign guest to reside in some of the nunneries in Beijing, Nanjing, and Shanghai, that were just being opened up at that time after the Cultural Revolution. On this occasion, I made a comparison of the Vinaya (disciplinary codes) of the Theravada with the Vinaya of the Dharmagupta which is followed by the nuns of China to date. According to the Sri Lanka chronicles, among the eighteen Vinaya schools prevalent in the Third century B.C. during the time of King Asoka (who introduced the

33

GOONATILAKE

order of monks and nuns to Sri Lanka), the Dharmagupta school was a sub-sect of the Theravada school. The Dharmagupta Bhikkhuni Vinaya rules as they function in China today are the same as the Theravada Bhikkhuni Vinaya rules, except for the addition of a few minor rules in the former, which reflect the local needs of a social and climatic nature (Goonatilake 1993). (Although interpretations of doctrine and modes of practice differ between Theravada and Mahayana traditions, there are only minor variations in the Vinaya of the two traditions.) I also found that, in spite of political turmoil, some Chinese nuns had continued the practice under very difficult circumstances at a time when many disrobed. Some others fled to Taiwan and continued as nuns (Goonatilake 1994).

In 1985, a delegation of Buddhist scholars was led to China by the Minister of Cultural Affairs, to explore the possibility of restoring the order of nuns in Sri Lanka. The report of the delegation was never released, although one member of the delegation mentioned in an article that an unbroken lineage of nuns still exists in China (Wickramagamage 1985).

Subsequent to the Minister of Cultural Affairs' visit to China, I was requested by the Department of Buddhist Affairs to draft a memorandum stating all arguments, from my experience and knowledge, for the restoration of the order of nuns with assistance from China. I have not been informed of the fate that befell the memorandum I drafted. It is well known, however, that leading establishment Buddhist organizations such as the All Ceylon Buddhist Congress, Young Men's Buddhist Association, Maha Bodhi Society and Buddhist Theosophical Society had all passed resolutions against the move.

CHALLENGES TO AUTHORITY

Nevertheless, the interest generated during the period 1984–85 on the issue of the restoration of the order of nuns continued to gather great momentum. The debate and discussion in the mass media did not die down as before to surface after another couple of years. The issue now turned into a continuing public discourse. For the first time, a documentary was made in 1986 by the State Television Corporation on the *dasa-sil-mata* movement presenting arguments for and against the restoration of the order of nuns with interviews from advocates as well as from opponents. A weekly Sinhala newspaper on Buddhism ran a series of articles for twelve months in 1988–89 on the controversy between a senior monk and a strong male advocate for the restoration. Kantha Handa, a feminist group, organized several seminars to discuss the issue.

The state patronage lent to the *dasa-sil-matas* even on a small scale also helped them in the process of gaining self-confidence and self-esteem. In addition, the strong resentment of the monks' hierarchy to the restoration of the order of nuns had encouraged some of the younger *dasa-sil-matas* to better equip themselves with more education and greater disciplinary strength. The

34

fact of marginalization itself had apparently given them a spirit of militancy that could build up to challenge the order of monks in the future (Goonatilake 1985). Up to this time, there were only a few young militant *dasa-sil-matas* who had the courage to challenge the order of monks. During the last decade, many more young *dasa-sil-matas* were seen voicing strong sentiments in the mass media in support of the restoration of the order of nuns.

As illustrative of this tendency, we quote below a poem written in 1985 by *dasa-sil-mata* Ambala Rohana Gnanaseela which reflects the spirit of militancy that has kept the struggle alive in recent years.

LIBERATION NOW ?
Let us have back
The lost inheritance
Our freedom and rights
The spiritual equality
Denied to us
By our Brothers Big
The educated gentry
Who wage battles
Hold forth
On equality and justice
"Equality for all
Justice for all"
Is their slogan.
But, none
For their little sisters.
We seek no favour nor fervour
Let us have back
our lost inheritance (Gnanaseela 1986: 15).

Another sign of hope in the last decade is that *dasa-sil-matas* have been building alliances with scholars from universities and monastic institutions, both lay and monks, and thus a critical mass of advocates for the restoration has emerged. Articles by these scholars often appear in daily and weekend mainstream newspapers and magazines, both in Sinhala and English.

An annual magazine devoted to the issue of the restoration of the order of nuns called Meheni Udawa (Dawn of the Nuns) initiated in 1989 by *dasa-sil-mata* Ambala Rohana Gnanaseela has been able to harness the support of many Buddhist monks and lay men and women. A monthly version of this magazine called Siri Lak Meheni Udawa (Dawn of the Nuns in Sri Lanka), sponsored by a group of lay men and women and published by Janopakara Buddhist Society, Kandy, which was established in 1989, has also attracted a great deal of attention to the issue. Booklets published in Sinhala and English in support of the issue by the Society have been widely disseminated. The Society also had several interviews with the Ministry for Buddhism on the issue of the revival of the order of nuns. The office bearers and advisory board members of the Society are persons of standing in the country. The latter consist of seven scholar monks, nine greatly respected *dasa-sil-matas* and fifteen lay men among whom are seven university professors. In the published pamphlet, *dasa-sil-matas* are referred to as *sikkhmanas* (nuns with interim ordination waiting to receive full ordination). This term is used for the first time in Sri Lanka to refer to *dasa-sil-matas*, and is a notable step forward on the road to the revival of the order of nuns.

The annual Buddhist publication of the Sri Lanka Government Printing Department called Nivan Maga (Way to Nirvana) has devoted its 1994 publication to women's liberation. A picture of a serene nun entering a shrine room with a bowl of flowers adorns the cover. This issue has a galaxy of monks, *dasa-sil-matas*, laymen and women contributors advocating the revival of the order of nuns from their different perspectives.

Several European and American *dasa-sil-matas* as well as those women who have been ordained as nuns in the Mahayana tradition have also been active in the campaign for the revival of the nuns' order. Their writings have brought the issue to the international arena. They have provided considerable support and strength to the *dasa-sil-matas* in Sri Lanka. Another factor has been that many Sri Lankan monks running Buddhist centers and temples in the West have become increasingly open-minded towards the issue. Some have even conducted *samanerika* ordination (interim ordination before full ordination) in the United States. In addition, educated Sri Lankan monks who travel frequently outside the country have been exposed to the questioning of the rationale for excluding women from the Buddha's order.

A serious effort was made in 1993 by the Sri Lankan monk, Ven. Kamburugamuwe Chandananda Maha Thero, the Bharata Sangha Nayaka (chief prelate of India), to canvass support from the monks' hierarchy to revive the order of nuns in Sri Lanka. This was a genuine need he faced in his missionary activities in India. This suggestion was opposed by the hierarchy. There is a move again being initiated by the same prelate of India with the support of some leading monks in Sri Lanka to arrange for a group of Chinese and Korean nuns to confer full ordination to a group of Sri Lankan *dasa-sil-matas* at the beginning of 1997. This is to be done in India at the very place where the Buddha founded the order of nuns, namely the Jetavan*aramaya* where this monk is presently the chief abbot.

OFFICIALLY MARGINALIZED

The contradictions in the current situation, and the sense of movement as well as of frustration, is illustrated by the third Sakyadhita International Conference of Buddhist Women which was held in Colombo in October 1993. The Sakyadhita organization was formed in 1987 in Bodhgaya, India on the last day of the International Conference of Buddhist Nuns. An underlying theme of this conference was the restoration of the order of nuns. One of the stated objectives of the Sakyadhita organization was, "It will assist women who wish to obtain ordination and will work toward establishing full ordination for Buddhist women in countries where it is not currently available" (Tsomo 1989: 36). His Holiness the Dalai Lama who graced this occasion said, "Speaking personally as a Tibetan Buddhist, if an authentic *Bhikshuni* lineage like this (the Chinese) could be established within the Tibetan tradition, this would truly be something to be welcomed" (Tsomo 1989: 44). The president of the Sri Lankan branch of Sakyadhita said in her presentation in India: "It is indeed a heartening fact that the present Minister of State for Cultural Affairs in Sri Lanka has fully understood, in all its complexity, the value and crucial necessity for the resurrection of the *Bhikkhuni* order in Sri Lanka and is supporting this cause in every possible way. And we may hope that this epoch-making gathering in the sacred precincts of Bodhgaya will spearhead a renaissance movement toward establishing *Bhikkhuni Sangha* in the four corners of the world" (Devendra 1989: 215).

When the office bearers of the Sri Lanka branch of Sakyadhita applied to the Ministry of Buddhism for permission to hold the third conference of Sakyadhita in Colombo, they were requested to get the recommendation from one of the three chief prelates (Weeraratne 1994). The recommendation was given by one of the three chief prelates on one condition, that the conference should not take up the issue of the restoration of the order of nuns. The conference was opened by the Executive President of Sri Lanka, and an English daily newspaper carried a special supplement with messages from the three chief prelates. However, the official agenda released to the press did not mention the presentation on *The Order of Nuns: Its Revival, Arguments For and Against* which was, in fact, made by a university academic who is a well-known advocate for restoration.

At the small group discussions in the conference devoted to the issue of the restoration of the order of nuns, Ambala Rohana Gnanaseela, president of the Hambantota District Dasa-sil-mata Association, moved a resolution that the conference request the government of Sri Lanka to take steps to improve the educational and other essential facilities for *dasa-sil-matas* and take action to confer the status of nuns to them. It was duly seconded by Mitra Gnaneswary, the president of the Dasa-sil-mata Federation. After a lengthy discussion, the group which consisted of foreign Buddhist nuns, the president of the International Sakyadhita and local *dasa-sil-matas* unanimously adopted the resolution. After the resolution was passed at the group meeting, however, the president and the secretary of the Sri Lanka branch of Sakyadhita pleaded with the *dasa-sil-matas* not to press for the restoration, since they claimed much needs to be done before restoration in the way of improving educational and other amenities. Consequently, the resolution that was ultimately presented to the plenary was different from the one initially passed unanimously. The final resolution only called upon the government of Sri Lanka to help and promote the *dasa-sil-mata* activities, such as in education and other amenities. The pressure of authority had had its temporary victory.

CONCLUSION

Over the years, the *dasa-sil-matas* have made great strides in their struggle for the revival of the order of nuns. It is clear that they recognize the importance of approval and acceptance by monks, and therefore they have been proceeding carefully in seeking the right to receive full ordination in accordance with the Theravada tradition. More and more monks are increasingly becoming sympathetic to the issue. The alliances the *dasa-sil-matas* have built with scholar monks, and lay men and women have today greatly enhanced recognition and legitimacy of the issue. A parallel to this movement is seen in the intransigence of the hierarchy fifty years ago against the young monks who stood for radical social reforms. Just as these militant monks eventually prevailed, so will, probably within the next decade, the movement of the nuns' order after nine centuries.

NOTES

1. *Dasa-sil-mata* means literally "ten-precept mother." This refers to a woman who follows partial renunciation by observing ten precepts. A fully ordained nun observes 311 precepts while a fully ordained monk observes 227 precepts.

2. This is the oldest school of Buddhism which spread to Sri Lanka, and later to Myanmar, Thailand, Cambodia and Laos. Mahayana is the form that is practiced in China, Korea, Japan and Tibet.

REFERENCES

Devendra, K. 1989. "Establishment of the Order of Buddhist Nuns and Its Development in Sri Lanka." In *Sakyadhita: Daughters of the Buddha*. ed. K.L. Tsomo, pp. 215–266. New York: Snow Lion Publications.

Dhammaratana, N. 1952. *The Future of Sri Lanka: Buddhism or Marxism?* Colombo: M.D. Gunasena.

Dhirasekera, J. 1982. *Buddhist Monastic Discipline*. Colombo: Ministry of Higher Education Research Publication Series, Sri Lanka.

Gnanaseela, A. R. 1986. "Liberation Now?" In *AWRAN Newsletter of the Asian Women's Research and Action Network*. ed. H. Goonatilake, pp. 15. Colombo: Asian Women's Research and Action Network.

Goonatilake, H. 1985. "Dasa-sil-matas of Sri Lanka: Integration or Marginalization." In *The Proceedings of the Annual Sessions of the Sri Lanka Association for the Advancement of Science*. pp. 86–7. Colombo: Sri Lanka Association for the Advancement of Science.

———. 1993. "Women and Family in Buddhism." In *Buddhist Perception for Desirable Societies in the Future*. ed. S. Sivaraksha, pp. 224–243. Bangkok.: Inter-Religious Commission for Development Sathirakoses-Nagapradipa Foundation.

————. 1994. *Pi-chiu-ni-chuan Caritapadana : Translation of Biographies of Chinese Buddhist Nuns into Sinhala*. Colombo: Lake House.

Horner, I. B. 1975. *Women Under Primitive Buddhism*. Delhi: Motilal Banarsidass.

Lilley, M. E. , ed. 1925. *Apadana*. London: Pali Text Society.

Malalasekera, G. P. 1934. "The Restoration of the Order of Buddhist Nuns." In *Ceylon Daily News Vesak Number*. Colombo: Lake House.

Oldenberg, H., ed. 1879. *Dipavamsa*. London: Pali Text Society.

Paranavitana, S. ed. 1959–60. *History of Ceylon*. Colombo: University of Ceylon.

Saddhatissa, Thera, ed. 1915. *Cullavagga (Vinaya)*. Alutgama: Pali Poth Prakashakayo.

Tsomo, K. L. 1989 "The First International Conference on Buddhist Nuns." In *Sakyadhita: Daughters of the Buddha*. ed. K. L. Tsomo, pp. 31–44. New York: Snow Lion Publications.

Weeraratne, D. A. 1994. *Buddhist Nuns in Sri Lanka*. Kandy: Janopakara Buddhist Society.

Wickramagamage, C. 1985. *Young Buddhist*. Singapore: Buddhist Society.

ISLAMIC "FUNDAMENTALISM" AND FEMALE EMPOWERMENT AMONG THE MUSLIMS OF HAINAN ISLAND, PEOPLE'S REPUBLIC OF CHINA

Keng-Fong Pang

THIS ESSAY[1] focuses on Islamic "fundamentalism" in a community of Austronesian-speaking Muslims near Sanya on the southern end of the island of Hainan. Part of the People's Republic of China, Hainan is located in the South China Sea across the Gulf of Tonkin from Vietnam. The Hainan Muslims call themselves Utsat when using their own Chamic language, Tsat, but they are better known in China as Hainan Hui.[2] Although their historical origins have always been somewhat of a mystery to the Utsat community, they believe that they have always been Muslim.[3] A brief historical background of this enclave of Muslims and their connection to a larger diaspora is necessary in order to understand the nature of Utsat religious practice and the revivalism of Islamic practice between 1981 and 1994, as well as the impact of these changes on gender relations in the community. This essay is based primarily on data from my long-term fieldwork with the Utsat which began in 1986.[4]

I argue that Utsat Islamic religious revivalism, or fundamentalism in the very basic sense of "returning to the fundamentals of Islam," did not have the same type of consequences Islamic fundamentalism had elsewhere in the Muslim world because of the different and specific historical circumstances in China and locally in Hainan Island. As we shall see, the nature of the revival of Islamic teaching and practice among the Utsat and the manner in which the emphasis on stricter Islamic practice was received by the Utsat community were also different. Instead, I will argue that Utsat women were able to empower themselves through a better understanding of Islam via the attainment of religious education by three Utsat women (who were themselves educated during this period of religious revivalism) and through Utsat women's own labor in exploiting the economic niches found in the Hainan Special Economic Zone.

The empowerment of Utsat women was most dramatic during this period of simultaneous engagement in the new political economy in the Hainan Special Economic Zone and in the religious revivalism. Utsat women's empowerment, an example of what I call "indigenous feminisms,"[5] evolved out of a complex set of factors which included the transformation of certain gender-based cultural institutions indigenous to the society. These cultural institutions and the cultural practices surrounding them had encouraged gender solidarity among the Utsat in the past, and they nurtured feminist actions and ideas in the late 1980s and early 1990s. It is significant to note that the religious revivalism or fundamentalism during this period did not negatively affect the feminist practices of Utsat women which were beginning to be acknowledged by Utsat men by mid- to late-1980s.

UTSAT IN A HISTORICAL CONTEXT

The Hainan Muslims, or Utsat, number about 6,000. They primarily live in two villages near the southern coast of Hainan island.[6] These Utsat, however, are more widely known as Hui by Mandarin-speakers. The Utsat were officially designated as a Hui minority nationality during the minority identification exercise of the late 1950s, even though their historical, linguistic, and cultural origins are quite different from those of mainland Hui Muslims.[7] Linguistic evidence strongly established that the Utsat were part of the ancient diaspora of the Kingdom of Champa, which was centered in what is today Vietnam. Champa was a maritime power which flourished between the seventh and ninth centuries before succumbing to Vietnamese forces in the fifteenth century.[8] The Utsat are additionally known as "*Huan-nang*" by the local Han Hainanese.[9] The community may have successfully maintained an Islamic identity over the six to nine centuries it has been in Hainan, despite generations of discrimination and periodic persecutions by the Han Chinese as well as assimilative pressures to become Han culturally.[10]

A sea-oriented population, many ancestors of present-day Utsat sojourned

42

to Southeast Asia with the Han Chinese before the 1930s. Seeking adventure, riches and Islamic knowledge, some Utsat and their descendants in Malaysia were recognized by local Malay communities as devout Muslims who were knowledgeable about the Quran. In my Malaysian research on the social and cultural history of the Utsat and their descendants in Malaya, I found that several Utsat were revered Muslim leaders in their local communities and were admired for their religious piety.[11]

By various accounts, the pre-Communist Hainan Utsat community of the 1940s—numbering fewer than 3000 at that time—was led by a small number of respected Utsat religious leaders, including an *Imam* (prayer leader and leader in the mosque hierarchy), and scholars (*ahongs*, "religiously educated people"). The moral authority of the religious leaders and scholars was largely unquestioned. Together with a small number of landowning Utsat families who were wealthy and educated, religious Utsat were part of the "ruling" elite other Utsat looked up to. At that time, the majority of the Utsat men were not religiously educated and Utsat women were even less educated.

All over China religious practice was curtailed somewhat after the Communist Revolution in 1949 and was expressly forbidden after the beginning of the Cultural Revolution in 1966. In Hainan, despite the official prohibition and regular persecution by zealous local political cadres (both Han Chinese and Utsat), many Utsat attempted to practice an Islamic way of life—praying behind closed doors, and fasting during the month of Ramadhan whenever possible. Almost all their religious leaders and scholars were detained for political reeducation and reportedly tortured. Many Utsat were forced to denounce the existence of God (*Allahu*), and "nonclergy" men who tried to lead communal prayers were sent to reeducation camps. It was not until 1981, fifteen years later, when religious instruction and religious practice were once again officially sanctioned, that the Utsat began to reaffirm communally their Islamic faith and revitalize their Quranic learning. Having lacked any systematic means of teaching the Islamic faith in the community for about fifteen years, the Utsat accelerated the revivalism of Islamic knowledge by inviting two elderly religious teachers from Gansu Province in Northwest China to reside in their two villages for over a year in order to instruct or re-educate the Utsat about Islam and Quranic learning.[12] It should be pointed out that an entire generation grew up during the Cultural Revolution practically unschooled about Islam, even though many older Utsat prayed privately and tried their best to fast during the month of Ramadan. The years of religious persecution, when almost all religious leaders and scholars were jailed for refusing to publicly renounce their belief in Allah, strengthened the community's desire to return to proper Islamic practice at the fundamental level. It is in this sense of "returning to the basics," taking into account the local history and political conditions, that I use the term "Islamic fundamentalism."[13]

PANG

43

Thus, the revival of religious education and reaffirmation of religious practices were both desired and welcomed by the entire community. The fact that the very core of their cultural identity as Muslims was threatened and questioned for a decade was not just a motivation for a revival of religious practice and understanding, but also a psychological reaffirmation of their self-hood as a people quite distinct from the Han Chinese or the formerly "aboriginal/ tribal" communities of Li and Miao.

REVIVING ISLAMIC KNOWLEDGE, PRACTICE AND INTERNATIONAL BROTHERHOOD

Starting in 1981, when two religious teachers from Gansu Province arrived to educate the Utsat on Islam as a way of life, men of all ages sought to learn under these two mainland *ahongs*.[14] While school children focused on mastering the secular curriculum during the school year, school vacations were spent focusing on Islamic learning at the mosque. Many Utsat boys took seriously the task of being religiously educated. This included learning the Arabic script, even though the Chinese script was often used on the board to explain Islamic concepts. Verbal instruction about Quranic teachings primarily took place in Tsat, the Utsat's indigenous language. Utsat women and girls learned about Islam and its teachings during their evening classes after work. The women's religious teachings emphasized less reading and writing Arabic and more on reciting Arabic verses and learning certain Islamic morals (in the Tsat language) which especially pertain to women. Utsat women learn about the Quran and Islamic teachings in the two village *nihok* or "female schools."[15]

Attaining a religious education soon regained the level of importance it had in the pre-Communist days. Families viewed it as very important for at least one boy in the family to be well-educated in Islamic matters and many send their sons to Yunnan Province at the mainland's southern border to study further with religious teachers in Hui villages. Completing a four-year education at a mainland mosque with an *ahong* also culminated in the attainment of a graduation certificate. Young men with these certificates become highly eligible bachelors in the community, and receive the honor which comes along with being known as young *ahongs*.[16] Among the Utsat young men who are now certified religious scholars, a few went on for further Islamic education in Beijing's Islamic Center or to other parts of China where advanced Islamic religious teachings were available. Many of these religious scholars later were given scholarships by foreign Muslim governments with embassies in China and were able to go abroad to continue their Islamic education. Today, over ten of these young men are still abroad in countries such as Saudi Arabia, Iran, Pakistan and the United Arab Emirates.

One of the most dramatic and visible changes in the Utsat community as a result of the teachings of the two mainland religious teachers from Gansu province is the requirement that Utsat women cover their hair with some sort of cloth. Utsat women, both young and old, adopted the practice of covering their heads, in varying degrees of tightness, with towels purchased in the town. These towels are colorful and are normally used as face or (bath) towels.[17] Some girls as early as nine began to cover their hair, modelling adult behavior.

A second significant social practice suggested by the Gansu *ahongs* was in reaction to the fairly common occurrence of premarital sex and premarital pregnancies. Unable to reform a cultural practice long established in the community, they suggested that a young couple intending to have premarital sex should make a witnessed statement in front of two male friends or one male and two female friends that they intend to marry each other.[18] Unlike the performance of *nikah* by the Imam, which solemnizes a marriage publicly, this practice of making a witnessed statement of intention to marry (*ngau chuo zheng*) is a private ritual and is intended primarily to insure that any resulting foetus from the sexual union will not be illegitimate in the eyes of *Allahu*. When I first conducted longterm fieldwork in 1987–89, most young people and elderly estimated about 40 to 50 percent of marriages were preceded by this practice of *ngau chuo zheng,* although some young and more conservative women felt it was closer to 30 percent. In 1993 and 1994, the percentage had gone up to almost 100 percent in the estimation of the community. These changes in morality must be understood also in terms of negotiating with two sets of outside factors. One is the increasing contact with foreign Muslims and the internationalization of Utsat's Islamic discourse. The other is the more immediate changes in Hainan's political economy which had a direct impact on the way the Utsat view their own increasing modernity.

A fairly isolated community in Hainan Island during the past five decades, the Utsat community strengthened its renewed international connections after the mid-1980s. More Muslim visitors arrived on the island and sought the Utsat out for communal prayers in Utsat mosques and for *halal* (ritually slaughtered) food. With increased religious education and actual contact with foreign Muslims, the Utsat community became more caught up in public discourse about Islam and about being proper Muslim men and women. This Utsat discourse about the practice of Islam took on international dimensions not only through the hosting of foreign visitors to Hainan Island and organizing "lectures" by Muslim visitors to the community, but also through the financial support canvassed by Utsat scholars abroad. Support from Muslims abroad also took more concrete forms such as large cash donations. I once witnessed a donation of US $6,000 in cash by Iranian visitors.[19] The most recent and dramatic foreign financial aid is to build an entire mosque and related complex, which was being constructed in 1994. The financing came largely from Muslim supporters from the United Arab Emirates. The arrival of

Muslim visitors to Hainan, however, must be viewed in the larger context of Hainan's dramatic economic development in the last ten years.

Hainan Island became China's largest Special Economic region in 1984, and China's newest province in 1988. The island's promise as an experimental economic paradise, where socialist economic practices are increasingly replaced by more capitalist practices, attracted tens of thousands of mainland Han Chinese to the island seeking riches and Hainan's relatively "freer air."[20] Overseas investment in the island was also encouraged by the new provincial government, which offered preferential taxes and profit repatriations to foreign investors. These dramatic changes in the local political economy brought about rising real estate prices, increased tourism, and a jump in Hainan's cost of living. The Utsat are particularly successful in the tourist industry. Many Utsat men drive minivans which offer one-day tours of tourist attractions around the town of Sanya, which is eight kilometres from the nearer of the two Utsat villages. More recently, they have begun operating boat rides for tourists at popular beaches near Sanya. At the same time, many Utsat women began to peddle tourist items such as cultivated pearls or exchange foreign currencies. Widespread Utsat experimentation in business began in about 1982, after the abolition of the commune system and after Utsat were no longer required to be vegetable farmers or fishermen in their respective brigades. At about the same time, as I shall explain later, increasing numbers of Utsat women started to become independent income earners.

46

UTSAT GENDER RELATIONS AMIDST ISLAMIC FUNDAMENTALISM

Socially confident among friends and assertive in their familial contexts as wives, daughters, and sisters, Utsat women now derive significant prestige from their roles as important economic contributors to their families. An emphasis on being" more strict" Muslims did not change that. I argue that Utsat women have been empowered by this Islamic fundamentalist trend. In a society where women previously had no serious formal Islamic education, three Utsat women, encouraged by their families, pursued religious education on the mainland in 1988 and graduated as certified religious teachers in 1992. This enabled Utsat women to understand Quranic teachings through female religious instruction and interpretations—an important milestone indeed. How did these developments come about? To answer this question, we need to examine the local contexts in which the privileged position of males in Islam has been somewhat buttressed by Utsat women's greater ability to earn and save money, and the agency of Utsat women and men in changing some cultural traditions and establishing new ones.

Scholarly literature on Islamic resurgence generally indicates that Muslim men, as religious leaders and as fathers, brothers, and husbands, assume moral authority in defining the limits of female Islamic propriety and in curtailing Muslim women's freedom of movement (see other chapters in this book).

This literature would not lead us to anticipate the rather different and complex dynamics of Utsat gender relations after 1981.

Hainan Utsat's experience is different because during the twenty years of economic collectivization, when Utsat men and women were organized into work-teams, Utsat women became aware of the value of their physical labor. Women proved as capable as men in the vegetable growing work-teams. When the commune economy was restructured in 1983, nuclear families were allocated land for agriculture and for residential purposes. With each family being responsible for its own economic survival, both husband and wife typically worked in the fields with their grown children. However when adult children married and had families of their own, the initially allocated farming land was often too small to be divided. With no remaining communal lands being released, and private land prices increasing in anticipation of both inflation and Hainan becoming a province, most families in the mid-1980s began to look for other sources of income. Vegetable prices, now left to economic forces, became unstable. Furthermore, the annual summer drought limited the amount of vegetables the Utsat could grow. In addition, with the central government's directive that Hainan's economy be quickly restructured into China's largest free economic zone, Hainan attracted many mainland tourists as well as mainlanders who wanted to reside and work in Hainan. Hainan, hailed as "China's Hawaii," provided many new economic niches which the Utsat could exploit.

As mentioned earlier, Utsat women succeeded in peddling items to the local tourists and in becoming unofficial money changers of foreign currencies. They dominated the latter trade early because they were aware that the Public Security agents generally allowed them to openly peddle because they were an economically depressed minority. Han money changers, on the other hand, had to be more discreet. Other Utsat women, however, felt more comfortable buying vegetables from Han growers and reselling them in city markets. Working from dawn until dusk, both kinds of work were tedious enough that Utsat men considered them to be women's work. Utsat men preferred to seek work in the state-owned sectors when they could, or to start small businesses. Many purchased moped-driven trishaws and, later, taxis and small vans, and became drivers. However, other young men without capital or social connections remained unemployed. By 1986, when I started my research, and clearly by 1988, more Utsat women—from 14 year olds to women in their 50s—were peddling in the city than were working in the fields. They had in effect become independent income earners. Very often their monthly incomes were more stable than men's, and certainly their personal expenditures were lower than men, for the latter spent more on clothes and entertainment. Generally, it is fair to say that unmarried Utsat women who are independent income earners definitely earn more money than unmarried Utsat men and, very often, more than their fathers. Most married women who are independent income earners also earn more than their husbands unless their husbands are exteremly successful in their careers.

With increased economic power, Utsat daughters and wives became significant contributors to the household economy, often providing cash for construction of new homes. Unmarried daughters often paid for their brothers' education. Not unexpectedly, Utsat women increasingly wielded more influence in family decisions and more political clout. Public articulation of sentiments such as "Women are smart at earning money" or "The more daughters one has, the more money there is in the family" pointed to a definite shift in Utsat gender relations. Utsat women succeeded in changing the community's perceptions about the value of having daughters and the power of women. Independent income earning women were most sought after as brides.

Child-minding responsibilities not infrequently fell on village-bound husbands who saved "face" by occasionally going on business trips or operating a small shop out of their homes. Other women worked outside the village and paid their younger siblings or grandparents to mind their children while they worked outside the village. Utsat women in clearly unsatisfactory marriages increasingly took action by moving from their marital homes back to their natal homes or by initiating divorce through secular state family courts. This was a clear threat to men, who had always had the prerogative of divorcing their wives through *talaq*—publicly repudiating their wives three times.

Young Utsat women of marriageable ages were also able to exercise some control over whom they married even though they still had to wait for a man's proposal. Some daughters refused so many suitors that their parents worried because the gender balance would favor males who usually preferred younger women as spouses. At least one woman married her suitor without her divorced father's permission by arranging her ceremonial departure from her paternal aunt's home. Yet another woman threatened to commit suicide to protest their parents' opposition to their choice. Utsat women, with their independent careers, were able to change certain cultural practices and force the community to recognize their value and power as individuals and as a gender.

These economic and social developments occurred after the Utsat began to observe a stricter practice of Islam. Religious reaffirmation by Utsat women took the form of the symbolic act of covering their hair with store bought towels, learning about Islam at night religious classes, and practising Islam with greater understanding. Despite the visits of Muslims from Iran, Saudi Arabia, Pakistan, and the United Emirates, who often donated huge sums of money and Qurans to the community, religious fundamentalism did not lead Utsat women to assume Middle Eastern ideals of female seclusion and veiling. (Incidentally, the Iranians presented white and black veils to the Imam's wife but the practice of veiling was not adopted by the Utsat.) While Utsat men and women implicitly subscribe to the Middle Eastern ideals of female seclusion when they

48

PANG

say that Utsat women have to work outside to support their families and do not have the luxury of being secluded, no women have ever suggested that they would prefer not to be working!

Prior to the visits of Middle Eastern Muslims, but after the arrival of the two Gansu religious teachers, elderly Utsat women had started wearing a black one-piece head-and-neck covering. Most Utsat women wear the earlier mentioned brightly colored, casually tied towel over their heads, securing it under their chins or tying it bandanna-style around their heads. The increased emphasis on Islamic awareness did not hinder their daily economic dealings with non-Muslims and tourists, nor prevent them from being away from the village for most of the day. However, some Utsat women clearly stated their preference for vegetable selling over peddling foreign currencies or tourist items because they viewed vegetable selling to be straightforward selling in a circumscribed environment. Exchanging foreign currencies and selling tourist items required a significant amount of public cajoling and persuading of male non-Muslim tourists in order to be successful.[21]

EMPOWERMENT OF UTSAT WOMEN IN THE RELIGIOUS DOMAIN

One aspect of Islamic fundamentalism actually empowered Utsat women. Utsat women were encouraged to learn more about Islam, whereas previously religious study had been considered important only for men. Previously, educated individuals of the community, literate either in Chinese or Arabic, tended to be sons (not daughters) of families who could afford to send their children to school. Only one woman over the age of 40 had completed high school, while her cohorts had not gone to school at all or had gone for only a year or two. Only in the last ten years have more girls completed five years of primary school education—the majority still drop out before that. Among girls who can qualify for high school, some still choose to follow the footsteps of independent income-earning Utsat women, who have become powerful role models. That Utsat women could master religious knowledge and read Arabic was thought inconceivable until the three earlier mentioned 18 year old Utsat women decided to study at a mainland mosque in Yunnan Province. In due course all three were certified as religious teachers. Until this event, most Utsat women had considered themselves incapable of mastering Quranic knowledge in the same way that men could. These three women religious teachers, incidentally, are vegetable sellers by day.

The need for women religious teachers to educate women about Islam had long been desired by the male Imams because those Imams felt awkward teaching a room full of elderly Utsat women and some younger women in the *nihok*. In my observation, they spent most of their time just orally reciting Arabic verses, and the Imams felt more comfortable looking away from the women. In contrast, when women were taught by female religious teachers, more real learning took place in a congenial atmosphere. Even when the

49

PANG

three women were still studying in Yunnan, they sent audio-tapes about Islamic teachings back to the village, where the tapes were eagerly listened to by groups of women. The eventual return of the three women to the village was marked by three nights of public lectures in the courtyard of the main mosque by each of them in turn. These lectures were not just to women but to the entire community. The respect and pride, and the extent of communal celebration in the forms of dinners hosted in the women's honor, surpassed any demonstrated for Utsat male scholars.

The domain of religion in Utsat life had been a male preserve until these three women were qualified as religious teachers. Even the mosque grounds had been carefully avoided by most adult women, who were socially conditioned to walk around the mosque. Now, Utsat women were able to understand Islam through the women *ahongs'* interpretations. More importantly, these women instilled confidence in women to regard Islamic knowledge as accessible to any woman who wished to learn.

PRAGMATIC ISLAMIC PRACTICE AND MALE RELIGIOUS DISCOURSE

Increased religious knowledge did not lead to any level of fanaticism in Utsat society. The Utsat adopt a very pragmatic approach—they recognize that Utsat women need to continue their economic activities. More significantly, male religious leaders have not tried to discourage Utsat women from any type of peddling business. In my view, Utsat women are now too independent and pragmatic to bow to any social pressures from male religious leaders. In some respects, women tended to regard male religious discourse with a certain level of disinterest. Although women kept publicly silent in religious discourse, they did have opinions about various male religious leaders and their followers. In particular, they disdained the level of religious factionalism in their community, which had divided the community for almost a decade and have resulted in fathers and sons affiliating with different mosques and boycotting some wedding dinners.

It was not until 1994 when I spent some time with young Utsat women who had ventured on their own to peddle currencies in the provincial capital city of Haikou, 260 kilometres north of their villages, that I began to hear Utsat women's personal opinions of certain male religious scholars, particularly the younger ones who had studied Islam on the mainland and abroad. Young women, mostly unmarried and as young as fifteen, travel back and forth in small groups of between two and four, and stay in rented quarters which sleep about eight to a room. Most women return to their homes near Sanya city once a month, a journey that takes about five hours by taxi. The consensus among these young independent women was that it did not matter where you had studied Islam and how good you were in reciting the Quran;

50

what was most important was how you conducted your own life and how you led by personal example. Male religious scholars have long been considered the most eligible males, and they know it. But a group of them went too far when they made a pact among themselves to give only 800 yuan for bride-price when the going rate was 1,250 yuan. Although one woman did accept one of their proposals, the community at large felt that these young men were simply too arrogant. However, it is generally agreed that the costs of having weddings (especially bride-price and the primarily bride-generated "dowry") have gone up both because of inflation and because these young women with independent incomes have been able to save much more for their "dowry."

RELIGIOUS FUNDAMENTALISM VERSUS MODERNIST DESIRES

Throughout the decade of Islamic "fundamentalism" and "modernization," younger Utsat women experienced a tension between their desire to remain "properly" Muslim in attire and to be outwardly modern. For the most part, the conservative forces prevailed; and most women over 25 maintained their traditional attire and grew their hair long under their towels. The only woman in the village who cut her hair and dressed like a modern Han woman was considered, probably correctly, to be a prostitute. Younger women who attend school preferred to wear long pants with long-sleeved blouses except on special occasions such as when they become involved in wedding celebrations. More recently, I observed a young Utsat woman dressed in a fashionable ankle-length skirt with a long-sleeved blouse. She worked with Han people in the state-owned sector and usually did not cover her head. The latter practice of not wearing a headcover when working with Han people had always been acceptable to most pragmatic Utsat. Nevertheless, her fashionable and modest clothes made quite a stir when she walked through the village.

The desire to appear modern is largely due to the influence of television, now a common possession in most households. When I began my fieldwork in 1987, only two television sets were available in the village for news and entertainment. At that time, Utsat were largely heeding the *Imam*'s call not to watch entertainment-oriented television programs or big-screen cinema movies. Most Utsat did not want to be publicly seen watching these programs. However, since the television set became part of a bride's dowry in the 1990s, television-viewing in private has become entertainment for the entire family, who regard television as their window to the outside world. The *imams* know that although their moral authority has eroded, the Utsat's belief in Islam as a guiding principle in life has not. This is clearly demonstrated when Utsat women money changers frequently stress their honesty by telling doubtful customers that "we do not cheat people, because we are Muslims."

51

PANG

CONCLUSION

In today's social climate of the Hainan Special Economic Zone, where making money and becoming rich is the dream of most people, including male religious scholars, the type of religious conservatism one might expect in Utsat society with the return of Utsat religious scholars from abroad simply did not materialize. Ever since the Communist Revolution and the rise of secular authority, Utsat religious leaders had felt powerless to control or influence the behavior of Utsat. Nevertheless, most Utsat consider themselves to be proper Muslims in their praxis. The few young Utsat women who wanted to dress in more modern attire and yet not be ostracised for failing to be proper Muslims found support from one Saudi-trained religious scholar who publicly stated that the Quran did not forbid women to cut their hair.

But what of the veil? Would Utsat women one day adopt the veil and still continue their economic activities? The influence of more radical Islamic ideas has been mitigated by women's personal success as independent income earners. It is conceivable that Utsat gender relations would be more drastically affected by a more radical form of Islamic fundamentalism if Utsat women were homebound and economically dependent on men.[22] But, in the context of Hainan, Utsat women continue to be economically independent and enjoy the attendant benefits. Among these benefits, unusual in a Muslim community, are: (1) Utsat daughters, sisters, and wives have gained greater social prestige and have been better regarded and socially valued as a gender class since the 1980s. This is because of their economic independence, money-earning abilities, and their ability to contribute significantly to the household wealth as well as to their natal households; (2) Utsat women clearly have economic freedom, including freedom of movement and considerable choice of careers and workplaces; (3) Utsat women are free to refuse marital offers and also have greater sexual autonomy, including the freedom to decide whether or not to have pre-*nikah* sexual relations; (4) Utsat men do not begrudge women's economic success. Instead, Utsat women's economic success is both welcomed and enjoyed by their parents and husbands. As one proud husband of an enterprising independent income earner wife said to me, "My wife did not have a single year of education, but she is the number one woman, the smartest woman in the village." Finally, and most importantly, (5), religious fundamentalism or revivalism in Utsat society resulted in the demystifying of Islamic knowledge and teaching as an inherently male preserve and privilege. This clearly empowered Utsat women in the religious realm, a development enhanced by their increased social confidence brought, in turn, by their economic success.

NOTES

1. This essay is a revised version of a paper originally prepared for the invited session on Gender and Religious Fundamentalism Cross-Culturally at the 92nd Annual

Meeting of the American Anthropological Association Meeting, Washington D.C., November 17–21, 1993. For this essay, I would like to thank both Judy Brink and Janet Bauer for their patience and editorial suggestions.

2. Utsat have at least three ethnic identities, each of which is mediated by the language of interaction and the historical evolution of that identity. For a detailed examination of these simultaneous and multiple ethnic identities, see Pang (1995a). From a linguistic perspective, the word "Utsat" can be shown to mean "people who speak Tsat" (see forthcoming a). But being Muslim is so central to Utsat lives that they translate the term "Utsat" to generically mean "Muslim." Thus, American Muslims will be called by Utsat as "Utsat Meikok."

3. Considering the veracity of Chinese accounts of the clearly Muslim practices of the Utsat recorded during in the 13th century, the Utsat must have become Muslims before their ancestral Cham community in Vietnam converted en masse in the sixteenth or seventeenth century (see Pang 1992:431–435, Appendix D). A manuscript on the historical origins of the Utsat which considers Western, Chinese, Japanese and miscellaneous sources of information on the Utsat, is in progress (see Pang n.d.a). See Benedict (1941) for one of the earliest western sources which identified the Utsat as a Cham colony.

4. After my initial research trip in 1986, I conducted sustained long-term fieldwork between 1987–1989 for my dissertation on the dynamics of gender, ethnicity, and the state (see Pang 1992). I wish to acknowledge the two-year research funding I received from National Program on Advanced Research in China administered by CSCPRC and a grant-in-aid from Wenner-Gren Foundation for Anthropological Research (#4867). Subsequent shorter field-trips were made in the spring of 1993 and fall of 1994.

5. My working definition of "indigenous feminisms" is "local feminist ideas and practices which evolved independently of any Western or nationalist feminist movements." See Pang 1992 and 1993 for my argument for the structuring of gender solidarity among Utsat women, and Pang (n.d.b.), a manuscript in progress titled "Beyond 'Western' and Third World Feminisms: A Consideration of Utsat Indigenous Feminism" for a more detailed examination of the concept of "indigenous feminism."

6. My field data derived mostly from my research within the smaller and more exclusively Muslim village which I refer to as Piai (not the name by which the village would normally be identified). However, I have visited the second larger village on numerous occasions. Many of my informants in the city of Sanya and Haikou live in the second village.

7. See Dru Gladney (1991)'s Muslim Chinese for a broader perspective of the mainland Hui, and Pang (n.d.c.) for a delineation of differences between Utsat and Hui of the mainland

8. See Maspero (1928) for an early authoritative account of the Champa of Kingdom and Pang (1992: 431–435, Appendix D) for my comment on Utsat's Chamic origins. My current transnational research with the several refugee Cham communities who now live in the United States also establishes that the Utsat and the Chams still share many basic cultural ideas and Cham words. The transnationally-oriented Cham nationalists are very interested in reaching out to the Utsat and the Utsat are delighted to be "found" by their fellow Chamic-speakers (Pang 1995a). See also Pang (1994a) for details on Cham nationalists, Maddieson and Pang (1993) and Thurgood (1993) on

53

PANG

linguistic analysis of Tsat language, and Benedict (1941) for the earliest suggestion that the Muslims of Hainan was a colony of Chams.

9. For a more detailed exploration of Utsat's simultaneous multiple ethnic identities which are both linguistically mediated and historically-significant, see Pang (1995a). Hainanese-speakers sometimes call the Utsat "Hui-tok," a direct translation of the Mandarin term for Hui-zu (Hui nationality).

10. Even today, Utsat parents are still concerned about their daughters and sons marrying non-Utsat who would have to become Muslim converts. One father spoke of not allowing his daughter to enter the "big doors of university" because she would be more influenced by Han ideas. Unsaid is the fear of daughters becoming culturally Han and losing or submerging their Islamic identity.

11. See Pang 1989 and 1994b for an analysis of multiple views on the Utsat migrants in Malaya, who were known as Orang Kwangtung and the assimilation of their descendants as Malays of Orang Kwangtung descent. For contrasting cultural experiences of border-crossings during two historical periods and their reception by Malays and Chinese in Malaya (1930–1940s) and Malaysia (1980s), see Pang (forthcoming b).

12. Although the Utsat consider themselves to be Sunni Muslims, some religious teachings by the two Gansu religious teachers might be Shiite in origin, such as their prescription of the practice of "ngau chuo-zheng" mentioned later. See Lipman (1989) on Islam in the Gansu province.

13. My use of the concept "fundamentalism" in Islam in terms of "returning to the basics of Islam" accords well with several views of Islamic fundamentalism espoused by several Muslims in the final chapter of a book published by two Muslims with Ph.D.s, Karm B. Akhtar and Ahmad H. Sakr (1982), simply titled *Islamic Fundamentalism*. For example, Abbas O. Jibril writes on page 147 that "Islamic fundamentalism is a constant reference to basics so that Islamic teaching becomes a guidance in searching for better things, higher levels of knowledge and the elevation of the dignity of mankind. . ."

14. For accounts of the introduction of Islam into China, see Gladney (1991), Leslie (1986), and Pillsbury (1973; 1989). For an overview religious policy and practice in China, see MacInnis (1972, 1989).

15. These *nihok* are buildings within the village set aside specially for women's religious education. One of them has three separate classrooms complete with blackboards. In the other *nihok*, a separate room serves as a prayer room for women who might choose to pray communally with other women. Utsat women do not pray in the men's mosques which are called *sang piok* which literally translates into "big houses."

16. See chapters 2 and 3 in Pang (1992) for an analysis of gender relations, marriage and courting practices.

17. In the 1990s, some Utsat women began to use specially-made head-covering cloths, usually presents from relatives in Malaysia or purchased by male Utsat scholars in other Islamic countries. It has been remarked to me that in the 1990s, some Utsat women are less concerned with the need to cover their hair. I have noticed more and more women, especially those working in the city, being less careful about covering their heads. Those money-changers in Haikou city, far from their village, actually take off their hair towels in the evenings on their journeys to their lodgings to avoid being recognizably Muslim and being robbed since these women are known to carry substantial amounts of cash with them.

18. I have long suspected that this practice might have been derived from Shiite teachings which are believed to have influenced a sect of Chinese Muslims in the Gansu region known as the Twelvers. There is a possibility that the two Gansu religious teachers might have been from this sect. I have not yet been able to locate these teachers in Gansu to clarify their teachings to the Utsat. This practice appears to be an idiosyncratic interpretation of the Gansu *ahongs* and should be distinguished from *mut'aa* marriages (temporary marriages which are often of a specific temporal nature) as viewed among Shiite Muslims.

19. Utsat who are knowledgeable about Islam are aware of Shiite-Sunni differences. However, as a fairly isolated Muslim community, all foreign Muslims were welcome in the Utsat community.

20. For an analysis of the changes in social relations between mainlanders and Hainanese Han and a discussion of intra-Han ethnicity see Pang, 1995b.

21. While most Utsat women and men without any formal education can usually speak Hainanese, the island's lingua franca, those who have a few years of education usually speak some Mandarin. Although English is taught at middle high school, most educated Utsat do not have enough verbal practice to be comfortable using English. Utsat women money changers are braver than most Utsat and most can articulate, in English, phrases such as "changing money?" with foreign tourists. With or without any formal education, Utsat women's mental arithmetic skills are quite formidable.

22. It seems to me that Utsat women have been very successful in changing Muslim male perceptions of women, compared to the difficulties faced by many women of the Arab world who remain economically dependent on their husbands (see Toubia 1986).

REFERENCES

55

Akhtar, K. B. and A. H. Sakr 1982. *Islamic Fundamentalism.* (privately published with ISBN D–911119–02–7).

Benedict, P. R. 1941. "A Cham Colony on Hainan Island." *Harvard Journal of Asiatic Studies* 6:129–134.

Gladney, D. C. 1991. *Muslim Chinese: Ethnic Nationalism in the People's Republic of China.* Harvard East Asian Monographs, no: 149. Cambridge, MA: Council on East Asian Studies.

Leslie, D .D. 1986. *Islam in Traditional China: A Short History to 1800.* Canberra: CCAE.

Lipman, J. 1989. "Sufi Muslim Lineages and Elite Formation in Modern China: The Menhuan of Northwest China." In *The Legacy of Islam in China: An International Symposium in Memory of Joseph F. Fletcher,* compiler Dru Gladney, Conference Proceedings Volume, Harvard University, April 14–16.

MacInnis, D. E. 1972. *Religious Policy and Practice in Communist China.* New York: MacMillan.

———. 1989. *Religion in China Today: Policy and Practice.* Maryknoll: Orbis Books.

Maddieson, I. and K.-F. Pang 1993. "Tone in Utsat." In *Tonality in Austronesian Languages,* eds. Jerold A. Edmondson and Kenneth J. Gregerson, pp. 75–89. Special Publications of Oceanic Linguistics no. 24. Honolulu: University of Hawaii Press.

Maspero, G. 1928. "The Kingdom of Champa." Chapter 1 of *Le Royaume de Champa* (Translated in 1949) New Haven: Yale University Southeast Asia Studies.

Pang, K.-F. 1989. "The Muslims of Hainan and their Southeast Asian Connections: A

PANG

Preliminary Analysis." In *The Legacy of Islam in China: An International Symposium in Memory of Joseph F. Fletcher*, compiler. Dru Gladney, Conference Proceedings Volume. Harvard University, April 14–16.

———. 1992. *The Dynamics of Gender, Ethnicity, and the State Among the Austronesian-speaking Muslims (Hui/Utsat) of Hainan Island, People's Republic of China*. Ph.D. Dissertation in Anthropology, University of California, Los Angeles. Ann Arbor: University Microfilms International.

———. 1993. *The Structuring and Practice of Gender Solidarity Among Austronesian (Chamic)-speaking Muslim (Utsat) of Hainan Island*. Paper presented at the Annual Meeting of the Association of Asian Studies, Los Angeles, California, March 25–28.

———. 1994a. *Neither Vietnamese nor Cambodian: History, Identity, and Transglobal Networking Among Nationalist Chams*. Paper presented at the Annual Meeting of the American Anthropological Association. Atlanta, November 30–December 4.

———. 1994b. *How Orang Kwangtung from China became "Melayu": The "Malayization" Process from Four Communal Perspectives*. Paper presented at the 46th Annual Meeting of the Association for Asian Studies, Boston, March 24–27.

———. 1995a. "Being Hui, Huan-nang, and Utsat Simultaneously: Contextualizing History and Identities of the Austronesian-speaking Hainan Muslims." In *Negotiation of Ethnicities in China and Taiwan*, ed. M. Brown. Berkeley, CA: UC Berkeley's East Asian Studies Institute.

———. 1995b. *The Structuring of New "Hainan-ren" Boundaries in the Hainan Special Economic Zone*. Paper presented at the Association of Asian Studies Meeting, Washington D.C., April 6–9.

n.d.a. *Paul Benedict's A Cham Colony in Hainan Island Revisited: Assessing the New Evidence for the Chamic Origins of the Utsat* (Hui). Manuscript in progress.

n.d.b. *Beyond "Western" and Third World Feminisms: A Consideration of Indigenous Feminisms*. Manuscript in progress.

n.d.c. *Articulating Differences: Utsat as Hui*. Manuscript under revision.

Forthcoming a. "Chamic Ethnonyms in Hainan." In *Chamic Studies II*. ed. D. Thomas. Camberra: Australian National University.

Forthcoming b. "Chamic-speaking Utsat of Hainan Island and their Experience of Border Crossings." In *Borders in Southeast Asia*. Singapore: Institute of Southeast Studies.

Pillsbury, B. L. K. 1973. Cohesion and Cleavage in a Chinese Muslim Minority. Ph.D. dissertation Department of Anthropology, Columbia University.

———. 1989. "Transformation of Hui Identity in Taiwan and China." In *The Legacy of Islam in China: An International Symposium in Memory of Joseph F. Fletcher* compiler, Dru Gladney, Conference Proceedings. Harvard University, April 14–16. Cambridge, MA: Fairbank Center for Chinese Studies.

Thurgood, G. 1993. "Phan Rang Cham and Utsat: Tonogenetic Themes and Vaiants." In *Tonality in Austronesian Languages*. eds. J.A. Edmondson and K.J. Gregerson, pp. 91–106. Special Publications of Oceanic Linguistics no. 24. Honolulu: University of Hawaii Press.

Toubia, N. 1986. *Women of the Arab World: The Coming Challenge*. London: Zed Books. (Translated by Nahed El Gamal)

PART TWO

WOMEN STRUGGLE AGAINST FUNDAMENTALISM'S RESTRICTIONS

VOICES FROM THE MARGINS
Evangelical Feminist Negotiation in the Public Debate of a Small Denomination in the United States

Janet Stocks

IN THE auditorium of a small denomination-affiliated college representatives have gathered for the denomination's yearly Synod meeting. The Synod is the highest court of the church and is responsible for the continuing reformation of the church in maintaining the subordinate standards of the church in harmony with Scriptural truth and order (as stated in the denomination's Constitution).[1]

Synod is made up of two elders from each congregation. Since the office of elder is open only to men in the denomination, most of the faces seen in the auditorium this morning are male. There are rows of tables and chairs making up most of the meeting space, and chairs around the circumference of the room where some delegates and observers are sitting. It is in these chairs around the edges that the faces of women are seen. In all there are approximately 150 people in the room, about 15 of whom are women.

This morning, after a discussion of pensions for retired elders, the participants turn their attention to proposed changes to the denomination's Constitution. The amendments were introduced at last year's Synod, with the aim of clarifying the church's position concerning the place of women. The essence of the debate this morning is whether or not the term "head" (*kaphale*) in scripture is meant to imply authority of husbands over wives. The men participating in the debate have very different opinions about this, and about the implications of the church explicitly stating that husbands have authority over their wives in the church's Constitution. Never once in this public discussion is the voice of a woman heard.

I am sitting next to Grace, a woman in her fifties who has been successful at bringing the question of women's place in the denomination into the public debate. She has had to do this through indirect means since, as a woman, she is not allowed to represent herself or her congregation in this, the highest court of the church. I lean toward Grace to ask her about several of the speakers this morning as men flip through the Bible, step up to the microphone, and support their various positions with passages from scripture.

This chapter tells the story of a small, conservative, evangelical Christian denomination in which there is an ongoing debate about the position of women, both within the church organization and within the family. This debate can be traced back at least 100 years in the denomination. Current discussions include the authority of husbands over wives, the practice of not allowing women to be pastors, and the question of whether a small group of women should be allowed to continue publishing a newsletter which challenges the denomination's interpretation of the place of women.

Issues of power and authority are central to the feminist struggle for equality. This study looks at how power is exercised and resisted within the context of overt structural barriers to women's participation in positions of authority. Although women are often constrained by power within institutions, they also exercise agency (Giddens 1984; Davis 1991). They have the ability to make choices about their actions, and the actions they take can serve to reinforce or challenge the existing relations of power. By exercising the power they do have (even if limited), women have an impact on what is considered "appropriate" gender behavior, and "orthodox" religious practice. Through the study of a group in which these issues are currently being debated, we can see the process by which boundaries are set and shift, and both gender and religion are constructed (Scott 1985, 1990; Genovese 1969, 1972).

Evangelical Christian groups provide an effective microcosm for studying gender and authority for two reasons: 1) gendered authority has been central to the structures of Christianity throughout its history (Lerner 1986), and 2) feminists within Christian organizations have recently been struggling to change these gendered authority structures (Davidman 1991; Neitz 1987; Ammerman 1987; Stacy 1990).

Women struggling for change in society have sought to define and voice their own issues, relying on their own experiences and points of view. This paper analyses the ways in which feminists within one small, conservative denomination have successfully made their voices heard in the public debate over women's place. Although women's voices have been structurally marginalized in this denomination, women have negotiated a space for themselves in the discourse.

METHODS

Three sources of data inform this study: 1) observation of worship services and meetings within the denomination; 2) in-depth, open-ended interviews with a variety of members (e.g. feminists trying to bring about change, people trying to resist that change, people in positions of authority within the group, and people knowledgeable about the debate but who are not taking sides); and 3) documents: church historical documents, newsletters published by individuals and small groups expressing a variety of opinions about the issues under discussion, and official church documents (e.g. minutes of meetings, the church Constitution, proposals to be discussed at Synod).

STRUCTURE AND HISTORY

Location and Origins

This small Protestant evangelical denomination has its seminary and denominational college in a midwestern city, with its most concentrated cluster of congregations in that part of the country. There are congregations throughout the U.S., except in the South because the denomination took an abolitionist stance early in the nineteenth century. The theology of the group comes out of the Reformed tradition and theological discussions in the denomination center on understanding the correct meaning of God's word as found in the Bible. Discussion of women's place in this group is a debate about the most scripturally sound way to interpret certain passages, most of which are found in the letters of Paul, concerning women's place both in the church and in the family.

Women's Place

Women are not allowed to be elders or pastors in this denomination (pastors are teaching elders), but they are allowed to be deacons.

> The Diaconate is a spiritual office responsible for the ministry of mercy and stewardship of the congregation. It is neither a ruling nor a teaching office. Its exercise, like the whole life of the church, is under the oversight of the session and its function is administrative (Constitution D–25)[2]

Deacons do things such as visit the sick, oversee the finances of the church, and organize church social events. In those congregations I visited, these functions are further divided along gender lines with men doing more of the financial tasks and women doing more of the social ones.

The rationale for women's exclusion from the position of elder are Paul's statements that women should not exercise authority in the church, and his description of the perfect pastor as a man:

> 1 Timothy 2: 11–15: Let a woman learn in silence with all submissiveness. I permit no woman to teach or to have authority over men; she is to keep silent. For Adam was formed first, then Eve; and Adam was not deceived, but the woman was deceived and became a transgressor. Yet woman will be saved through bearing children, if she continues in faith and love and holiness, with modesty (Revised Standard Version).

> 1 Corinthians 14: 33b–35: As in all the churches of the saints, the women should keep silence in the churches. For they are not permitted to speak, but should be subordinate, as even the law says. If there is anything they desire to know, let them ask their husbands at home. For it is shameful for a woman to speak in church (Revised Standard Version).

> Titus 1: 5–6: . . . appoint elders in every town as I directed you, if any man is blameless, the husband of one wife, and his children are believers and not open to the charge of being profligate or insubordinate (Revised Standard Version).

Women are not literally expected to be silent in the church. They can take part in discussions in Sunday school classes, can pray aloud in mixed groups, and can make announcements and ask for prayers during church services. But women are not allowed to be in any position that could be interpreted as having authority over a man, or teaching a man.

Occasionally, women are permitted to teach adult Sunday school classes. This usually occurs when she is part of a husband-wife team, or when she is a co-teacher along with an elder (a man). The necessity of having a man oversee a woman's teaching (especially when she is teaching other adult men) is to be sure that her interpretation of scripture is correct. There is no mechanism like this in the organization to specifically oversee the teachings of other men to make sure their interpretation is correct, although dialogue and disagreement does take place between men on various occasions regarding exegesis and hermeneutical principles. This dialogue, when it occurs among men, is seen as a legitimate struggle to understand the true meaning of God's word. On the occasions that women attempt to enter the dialogue, questions of motive quickly arise.

The formal decision-making structure of the denomination is all male. At the congregation level a group called the session is made up of all the elders of the congregation. The session is "the court having original jurisdiction over the members of a congregation" (Constitution D–29), and is charged with such duties as admitting and dismissing members of the congregation and caring for the "spiritual interest of the congregation and of each member" (Constitution D–30). The session is the body most open to women. Women, as well as men, vote within their congregations in the election of elders and pastors. Session meetings are supposed to be open to the public, and women can bring questions and grievances to their elders if they would like an issue to enter the formal decision making structure of the church. Beyond the session, though, women have little power over how and where discussion goes. Two members from each session are chosen each year to represent their congregation at the Synod meetings, the highest court of the church.

The denominational practice concerning women's place is actually more conservative today than it was 50 years ago. At that time, lay men and women had relatively equal opportunities to participate in different aspects of the life of the church. From the mid-nineteenth to the mid-twentieth century women gained some small ground in their ability to have authority in the church. During this time it was not uncommon for women to teach adult Sunday school with no formal restrictions, or to chair committees. There were women superintendents of Sunday school programs who sometimes addressed congregations on spiritual matters. Many single women served as foreign missionaries. In the latter part of the nineteenth century, women in the denomination were very active in the Women's Christian Temperance Union, the Abolition movement, and in the Sunday School movement.

But during the years following World War II, a small group of young pastors, some of whom joined the denomination from other denominations they considered too liberal, began to question the practice of allowing women to be in any position that might be interpreted as having authority over men. These men were heavily influence by the general move in society at the time to encourage women to return to their homes, after having participated more in public life during the war. Gradually their stance on women became accepted throughout the denomination and avenues of involvement that were once open to women were then closed.

Twice in this century the denomination has taken up the question of women's role in the church. In 1939, two separate papers were submitted to Synod recommending that women be allowed to be elders. After a discussion that was heavily influenced a young pastor who had recently entered the denomination from a more mainline (and more liberal) denomination, and who argued against allowing women to be pastors, Synod rejected these papers, reaffirming the status quo. In the late 1980s, a number of papers came to Synod regarding a book written by a woman in the denomination urging a more expanded role for women. The result of these papers was a report entitled "Report of the Committee on the Role and Service of Women" released in 1990. The many men who worked on this report had different opinions about expanding women's roles in the church. The document reflects these differences of opinion. In the end, the committee that wrote the report was dissolved with no change in the denominational status quo regarding women's place. The report, with its different opinions, was made available to those within the denomination who might want to study the matter.

At present, women are structurally limited in their ability to make their voices heard, and particularly to challenge the church's doctrine and practice regarding women's role. While allowed some positions within the church, their voices are officially marginalized. Public forums in which decisions are made (on the congregational level the session, on the denominational level the Synod) do not allow women to speak (literally), so women can initiate grievances with their elders, but cannot take them through official church channels for themselves. Nevertheless, by making noise on the margins, women have managed to have their grievances heard.

CHALLENGES TO AUTHORITY

Women Find a Voice

One casualty of the growing conservatism of this denomination during the 1960s was Grace, whose family has been part of the church for many generations. As a young woman, Grace was fortunate enough to marry a man who was able to support the family and so she expected to use her considerable energy and intelligence in the service of the church. At this time, however, the doors to women's participation in various positions of real responsibility started closing. Although she was upset by these changes, she found a place for herself on the Women's Association board which oversees the denominational retirement home which at the time was involved in a major building project. She was also raising three boys. Grace exercised real authority in her work on the board of the retirement home (including negotiating a mortgage for several million dollars). This experience sharply contrasted with her experience in her congregation, where her position of chair of the social committee had been taken away from her because she was a woman. As her boys grew, and the building project was completed, Grace decided to turn her energies to studying the question of the place of women within the church. The result of her studies was a book.

In this book, Grace carefully looked at what the Bible has to say about the place of women, and argued that the denominational interpretation preventing women from occupying positions of authority was wrong. Grace met with much resistance when her book was published. She faced calls for discipline, even to the point of excommunication. Her book was sent to the Committee on the Role and Service of Women to study its scriptural soundness. The report issued by this committee focused on the positive things women can do to serve the church (while never being very specific about

64

STOCKS

what these are), while affirming the church's stance on structural barriers to women's participation in positions of authority.

As a result of writing this book Grace came to identify herself as a feminist. She is careful to draw a distinction, though, between Christian feminism, with which she allies herself, and secular feminism, which she distances herself from, largely due to the movement's focus on abortion and homosexuality, both of which she opposes.

Eight years ago, together with a small group of other women who support her position, Grace started a quarterly newsletter to keep discussion of "the woman question" alive. The newsletter typically has a central article, written by a woman, about some aspect of the interpretation of scripture that has an impact on the question of women's place. It also frequently has book reviews, reports of meetings within the denomination that affect women in some way, and letters expressing diverse opinions. This newsletter is sent to people who subscribe and to each pastor within the denomination, whether or not he subscribes.

One of Grace's initial purposes in publishing the book and the newsletter was to initiate a dialogue within the denomination on these issues. Since formal channels were not open to women who wanted to challenge the denomination's position, Grace and the other feminists in the church chose to publish written documents of their own. These women were criticized by some for taking this issue into their own hands, studying scripture without male tutors, and coming to their own conclusions. Nonetheless, they have managed to get their document into the hands of a large number of people within the denomination, and their voices heard on their own terms.

There are two ways in which feminist challenges have affected the public discourse. The largest part of the debate has concerned process and has focused on whether or not women have a right to be part of the discussion at all in a direct way (instead of through their elders representing them at Synod). But these women have also been successful at entering debate on at least one issue of substance, that being the meaning of "head" (*kephale*) and whether or not the concept of headship implies authority.

Men Attempt to Silence Women's Voices

Many times during the past decade questions have arisen about the propriety of women engaging in public dialogue about the place of women in the denomination. Two recent examples of this will illustrate how the arguments are constructed, and how the women involved in this debate continue to successfully have their voices heard.

During the Synod meeting of the summer of 1993, four different papers were introduced that in one way or another dealt with the "woman question" in the denomination. All four papers were a response to issues that the feminist newsletter had stirred up in the denomination. One paper was specifically directed to the question of whether or not the newsletter should be allowed to exist. The paper called for the Synod:

a) To appoint a committee to study and make determination whether the teachings that have been promoted by the editorial staff of [the newsletter] are generally "in harmony with Scriptural truth and order" (Directory for Church Government, Chapter 7, Paragraph 1), and if not, whether they should be allowed to disseminate their teaching throughout the denomination; b) If it is determined that the teachings are not in harmony with Scriptural truth and order, and they should not be allowed to disseminate their teaching throughout the denomination, that synod instruct the editors of [the newsletter] to work through the courts of the church to address their issues of concern.

Debate on this paper was spirited, with some taking the position that it was not the denomination's "place to censor or even examine every publication entering the homes of the members," and others pointing out that this "heresy is being mailed out to our wives and daughters; it is very important that it be stopped" (both quotes from a newsletter report of the Synod meetings). The outcome of this paper was the appointment of a judicial committee that met during the year and reported back at the 1994 Synod. The committee found many positive things about the newsletter. Among them: it generally frames its articles within a Christian world view and "makes a number of positive contributions to informed Christian discussion" such as sensitizing some men to use more inclusive language when appropriate, and it acknowledges the contributions of women to the church.

Nevertheless, the committee noted two areas, one specific and one general, in which the newsletter "has departed from harmony with Scriptural truth and order as understood and taught" by the denomination:

The specific area of departure is [the newsletter's] promotion of the ordination of women to the office of elder . . . By advocating the ordination of women to the office of elder, the editors of [the newsletter] have departed from the doctrine of [the denomination], and are advocating a position contrary to the law and order of the Church.

The second area in which [the newsletter] has departed from harmony with Scriptural truth and order as understood and taught by the [denomination] is found in the sometimes subtle but often explicit underlying hermeneutic assumption that vernacular translation and ecclesial confessions are flawed because of androcentrism, or "male bias." This leads particularly to the conclusion that the historic Christian understanding of the Biblical teachings on headship, submission, authority, and the relationships between men and women, both in the home and in the church, is tainted by a dominant male culture, rather than simply being defined by God . . . This hermeneutic assumption drives many of the articles in [the newsletter] . . . Thus, the journal carries articles attributing to the church's teaching a range of negative effects, from frustrating gifted women to contributing to marital violence.

The assumption that traditional creedal positions, especially as they relate to the role of male and female in the home and church, have a male bias is contrary to the interpretative assumptions in the standards of the church. The results of the [newsletter] assumption is to lead these writers away from the teaching of the church, to a view that the church is being unfaithful to the Lord of the Scriptures, and unbiblical in its treatment of women. (Quoted from the report of the judicial committee to Synod).

The report from the judicial committee to the 1994 Synod was accepted by the Synod, but the consequences are unclear. Some representatives of Synod interpreted the outcome to mean that Grace's session should direct her to cease publishing the newsletter. Others understood it to mean that she could continue under the guidance of her session.

Not only has there been a move to silence the feminists by abolishing their newsletter, but there has also been a theological argument put forth that questions the ability of women to participate in serious discussions about scripture and scriptural interpretation altogether. James, a pastor from Kansas, has engaged in the debate through a newsletter of his own, and there has been a series of letters and responses going back and forth between him and members of the feminist newsletter staff.

In his newsletter James makes an argument based on two passages in Genesis: 3:16 and 4:7 that talk of desire:

67

God said in the garden long ago that one of the results of the fall within the family would be the rebellious attitude of wives regarding the concept of submission. Because of the presence of sin, wives would rather buck and challenge the headship of husbands. Their desire is for their husbands. That is, their desire is to dominate and manipulate their husbands.

James asserts that this desire of women to dominate over their husbands has led to the feminist movement, and in turn to the kinds of family problems we see in our society today:

And so we have this startling result of sin within the first family. Instead of working together as a husband and his helper, the wife seeks to gain control. She wants to 'wear the pants in the family.' On his part, the husband puts the screws on his wife and becomes the dictator. There is a struggle for power and leadership. Here we are given a preview of the modern feminist movement which is not content with equality but seeks dominance!

He also questions the motives of an author in the feminist newsletter who argues that "head" (*kephale*) in scripture does not imply the authority of husbands over their wives.

> She is perverting the doctrine of the Trinity to meet her aversion to the biblical concept of authority. She attempts to show there is no authority structure within the Trinity. She errs. She embraces this error in order to elude the divinely ordained authority structure within the family and the church.

James thus questions women's motives for engaging in this debate, and their ability to engage in serious biblical interpretation (especially if it concerns authority relations between women and men) because they, by nature, desire to dominate over men and therefore cannot see clearly enough to interpret the true meaning of God's word.

Not all of the elders in the denomination agree with James' position, although there are many who do. There have been no papers introduced to Synod questioning James' ability to publish his newsletter and his interpretations of scripture. Although there is disagreement concerning some of James' exegeses, the dialogue around this is seen as the normal, healthy, legitimate debate that elders (and other male members) in the denomination have engaged in throughout its history in an honest attempt to understand scripture. His motives are not questioned.

James questions the ability of women to engage in serious dialogue on these issues, yet he himself is engaging in a dialogue with these women. Grace sees this as at least a minor victory. James is given an authority by the denomination that is not available to women, but women have found a way to enter the public debate from the margins.

FEMINIST IMPACT ON SUBSTANCE: HEADSHIP AND AUTHORITY

While the majority of the discussion that has been aroused by the work of the feminists in this church has concerned process—whether or not women should even be allowed to engage in this public debate—these women have been successful in engaging the denomination in at least one issue of substance: the question of the meaning of "headship."

> In Ephesians (5: 22–24; RSV) Paul states: Wives, be subject to your husbands, as to the Lord. For the husband is the head of the wife as Christ is the head of the church, his body, and is himself its Savior. As the church is subject to Christ, so let wives also be subject in everything to their husbands.

Carol, a frequent contributor to the newsletter, and another woman who traces her family roots back many generations in the church, published a series of articles in the newsletter entitled "Applying the Major Themes of Scripture to Women." One of these articles dealt with the meaning "head" in the Bible when describing the relationship between husbands and wives. Carol argues that "head" is used metaphorically in two ways in scripture by Paul, one meaning "authority over" and the other meaning "source of." She further argues that the passages regarding the relationship between husbands and wives should be interpreted as "source of," emphasizing the unity and oneness of husband and wife and the loving nourishment they receive from one another, and that authority is not implied. Central to the governing structure of the denomination is the concept that all people have a direct, personal relationship with Christ, therefore no complex formal hierarchy is necessary to mediate between Christ and the members of the church (the priesthood of all believers). Carol concludes her arguments by stating:

> If women are not allowed, invited, and encouraged to participate in every aspect of the life of the church; if positions, responsibilities, and tasks are elected, appointed, and apportioned on the basis of sex, rather than on the basis of fruitfulness and giftedness, then we do not completely reflect the oneness of the body or the servanthood of all.

In addition to publishing this article in the newsletter, Carol also delivered it as a talk at a denominational conference during the summer of 1992. A great deal of controversy surrounded Carol's presentation of this paper. Several elders made a motion to cancel the workshop although it had been approved on the program—the newsletter people had been given permission by a program committee to organize three presentations at this conference. The Synod passed a motion to cancel Carol's workshop, then reversed its decision and instead resolved to send a committee of five elders (men) to the presentation to listen and respond to it. This committee then wrote a highly critical report for the 1993 Synod meeting. The report took issue with Carol's interpretation of "head" and authority. It went further to comment on the feminist newsletter (a task not originally given to them) stating that the newsletter "has disseminated (and continues to disseminate) doctrinal material in opposition to our Church's standards" (quote from committee report to Synod).

While a portion of the discussion of this issue continues to focus on these women's right to publish and distribute their newsletter (process rather than substance), another portion of it is devoted to interpretation of scripture, and of the meaning of "head" in husband–wife relationships, a particular concept that has bearing on the treatment of women in the denomination. During all the public discussions that have taken place (at the 1992 Conference and Synod meeting, at the 1993 Synod meeting, and at the 1994 Synod meeting) a small number of elders (men) have supported the arguments women have made, raising them to the status of legitimate discussions concerning biblical interpretation. It is because of this support that attempts to completely silence the feminists have failed. There are other elders in the church who uphold these women's right to publish their newsletter and otherwise engage in debates, even though they disagree with many of the feminists' positions.

Women themselves, through study, have advanced their own arguments, and because these are in writing and can be read by any member of the denomination, their voices have entered the public debate.

CONCLUSIONS

Women in this small denomination, while being constrained by the structures which deny them a voice in the official public debate, are by no means victims. They have taken the initiative to study scripture and publish their views concerning the interpretation of scripture. This is an activity which is considered normal and positive when men in the denomination practice it, but is interpreted as subversive and dangerous by some church members when women do, especially if their interpretation does not match the "official" version of the denomination. Even though these women have drawn a great deal of criticism for taking these matters into their own hands, they have successfully negotiated a space in the public debate, making people aware of their experiences, in their own words.

These women do not have much control over what happens with their interpretations and ideas once they are published. The fact that communication of their ideas occurs on the margins, and in written form, means that the verbal debates and compromises in which men in the denomination engage, the more fluid forms of negotiating meaning, are not available to them.

They also do not have much control over changes in the denominational "boundaries" which constrain them. If Synod decides, at some point, that the feminists should not be allowed to publish their newsletter, their choice will be either to cease publication, or to continue publishing and risk excommunication. At present, it appears that the more the feminists attempt to challenge the limits placed on them by the denomination, the more clearly those limits are set.

NOTES

1. Pseudonyms are used throughout.
2. To preserve anonymity identification of church documents is deliberately vague.

REFERENCES

Ammerman, N. T. 1987. *Bible Believers: Fundamentalists in the Modern World*. New Brunswick, NJ: Rutgers University Press.

Davidman, L. 1991. *Tradition in a Rootless World: Women Turn to Orthodox Judaism*. Berkeley and Los Angeles: University of California Press.

Davis, K., M. Leijenaar, and J. Oldersma 1991. *The Gender of Power*. London: Sage Publications.

Genovese, E. D. 1969. *The World the Slaveholders Made: Two Essays in Interpretation*. Middletown, CT: Wesleyan University Press.

————. 1972. *Roll, Jordon, Roll: The World the Slaves Made*. New York: Vintage Books.

STOCKS

Giddens, A. 1984. *The Constitution of Society*. Berkeley and Los Angeles: University of California Press.

Lerner, G. 1986. *The Creation of Patriarchy*. New York, Oxford: Oxford University Press.

Neitz, M. J. 1987. *Charisma and Community: A Study of Religious Commitment Within the Charismatic Renewal*. New Brunswick, NJ: Transaction Books.

Scott, J. C. 1985. *Weapons of the Weak: Everyday Forms of Peasant Resistance*. New Haven and London: Yale University Press.

———. 1990. *Domination and the Arts of Resistance: Hidden Transcripts*. New Haven and London: Yale University Press.

Stacey, J. 1990. *Brave New Families: Stories of Domestic Upheaval in Late Twentieth-Century America*. New York: Basic Books.

STOCKS

A SEPARATE UNITY
Female Networking and Status in a Contemporary Mormon Polygynous Commune

Janet Bennion

chapter 5

INTRODUCTION

THIS CHAPTER analyzes the place of fundamentalist women in a contemporary Mormon polygynist commune. It illuminates the strategies by which plural wives achieve a surprising degree of political, religious, and social power through their contributions to subsistence, ritual, and the worship of a female deity. It shows that polygynous Mormon women, like their male priesthood counterparts, are social actors seeking recognition, security, prestige, and a sense of worth and divine direction.

In seeking answers about women's roles and status in Mormon fundamentalism, I have been guided by the explanatory framework of two anthropologists: 1) Peggy Sanday's correlation of increased female status and contribution to subsistence, ritual, and worship of female deities (1973: 1683, 1981: 25–7), and 2) Nancy Leis's correlation of women's role in society with a) polygyny and b) the formation of female groups and networks (1974: 223–242).

Sanday hypothesized that women who engage in 1) subsistence activities vital to the community's welfare (such as was found among the Iroquois women, who controlled the mode and means of production), and 2) who include in their creation stories a female, or at least an androgynous deity (such as found among the Semang who worship the "grandmother of the primeval sea"), will enjoy a higher level of prestige and socio-political influence in society (1973, 1981: 55). These two factors apply to Mormon fundamentalist women's activities and beliefs and suggest the same correlation. Leis, in refuting Lionel Tiger's claim that only men are capable of forming strong vital bonds, stated that based on her observation of two Ijaw societies in Africa the formation of female groups is related to several features, which I believe can be extended to account for increased female status as well: virilocality, patrilineality, polygyny, and economic interdependence (1974: 241–2). I suggest the latter two in my hypothesis as factors determining a higher status for women in the Mormon polygynous community. I argue that a woman's place in society is not solely a factor of living in her husband's territory with his kin, but may occur in bilateral kin groups where residence is "matrifocal." In other words, virilocality does not always mean low status for women because it allows women to be thrust into close-knit groups segregated from the formal male authority structures. In short, I suggest it is a combination of many features that determines female status, the strongest in Mormon polygyny being: plural marriage, economic contribution, female deity worship, participation in ritual, female kin networking, and the prolonged absence of men from the community which forces women to engage in all of these activities in the first place.

The next section briefly describes life in the Mormon fundamentalist commune which supplies background to the analysis of fundamentalist women's strategies for temporal and spiritual survival in a patriarchal society.

MORMON FUNDAMENTALISM

In "Harker" (pseudonym of research community), a town of 700 people (50 men, 150 women, and 500 children),[1] a hierarchy based on male authority is established. Children obey their mothers and fathers, women obey their husbands (priesthood heads), and men obey the male council members who rule the community and the group. In turn, all members sustain the authority of the leader and prophet, Owen Allred, who then in turn defers to Christ, who defers to "Father Adam." This is considered to be the "eternal" political organization for the community on earth and in heaven.

The community was organized in 1961 by the current prophets' brother, Rulon Clark Allred. The group, however, originated with other Mormon fundamentalists more than 70 years ago, around the 1920s, when the schism from the official Mormon Church occurred.[2] Members of the Harker community belong to the Allred Group, which numbers approximately 11,000

74

BENNION

members in 21 branches in the Intermountain West and parts of the Netherlands, England, Canada, and Mexico. The total number of Mormon fundamentalists is approximately 60,000 (Cannon 1996).

This community is run religiously and economically by the Allred Group's larger ten-member priesthood council (all males), and civilly by the Harker branch's seven-member male board. A general board, made up of every priesthood head (50 males), meets once a month to discuss and review community problems and major decisions. Each member has a stewardship which is their duty and jurisdiction in the communal order (or "united order," as it is formally known). One man's stewardship is the bishops storehouse, a large home where food and household goods are stored for those who need them. Another man's stewardship is the cattle herd, another's the water pump, and so on. Women have stewardships in the home, as mothers of their children, and often, in the community, as teachers, nurses, and stewards of specific communal distribution, such as milk, honey, eggs, flour, and other necessities. One woman is the steward over the general store; another, over the delivery of all babies.

Women form supporting systems among themselves. Since the men are so seldom at home (approximately 35 percent work in another state during the winter, and others travel to different towns and territories to visit their other wives or search for work), the women are forced into an economic, emotional, and social interdependence. The average number of wives per man is slightly more than three thus, one wife will feed and bed her husband approximately twice a week, at the most. Essentially, the wives are forced to raise their own children, teach them in the community private school, or at home (all teachers are mothers who rotate their schedules with each other), and budget their own incomes. (Often one man cannot supply enough food and clothing for three or more wives so 75 percent of the women work outside either part-time or full-time.) The women also provide a social support network among themselves which allows them more leisure time and more time for visiting. They form alliances in childcare, bulk shopping, healthcare, home maintenance, and even reproductive strategies. Each plural wife has a regular night with her husband based on a fairly rigid schedule ideally set by the husband and his wives. I was often told that when one wife wanted some respite from her husband on "her night" with him, she would telephone another wife to replace her. Thus, the wives had a large measure of control over this scheduling. Co-wives who are lactating, pregnant, menstruating, or past childbearing age relinquish nights with husbands to those who are more impregnable.

Though married to both the husband and her co-wives, a new wife often builds stronger bonds with her "sisterwives" through day-to-day contact with them. The ideological structure which lies at the helm of the community suggests to the women that they cannot be fulfilled without ties to their priesthood heads, who give them council and guidance.[3] Likewise, the patriarchal order is sustained by the female alliances formed in the community. One could argue that without the order and authority of the male heads of household, though these heads are seldom actually in the home, the women would lack a foundation, or a framework (Wagner 1976, 1982). The male position in this sense is attached to prestige and political mechanisms, while the women attach themselves to their kin groups, their households, and the affective relations with their children and their sisterwives. In many ways, the patriarchal order could be seen as a formal "symbolic" power, while the female networking, which controls the children who comprise the largest membership, is the informal "real" power (Schlegel 1972, Rogers 1975). The one, priesthood, cannot function in this particular cultural setting without the other, the cooperative alliances of sisterwives and community women, and the rigid institutionalization of interrelationships among these main actors of the family helps to prevent conflict (Clignet 1970).

Life on earth for both mainstream and fundamentalist Mormons is said to be a replica of life in heaven, and so members place emphasis on order and "covenants." Sealings, the ritual of binding individuals together for eternity, are the tools used to achieve this cohesion, and are enacted through the priesthood powers of males. Through the sealing powers, a man can be bound to his wife or wives, and children can be bound to their parents. Even deceased relatives, and adopted children, can be bound in this same manner.

To Mormons, the creation and union of Adam and Eve is the ultimate model for a Mormon man and wife—a union that reflects the one existing between their heavenly parents (Doctrine & Covenants 121: 32).[4] This is further expanded in some Mormon camps to embrace a belief that Adam and Eve were created from a God that was in fact a two-gendered couple, a male and a female. The difference in belief between mainstream and fundamentalist communities is that the former do not actualize this belief in a two-gendered couple, while the latter more often do (Cannon 1993). The concept of "oneness" in a God sheds light on the principle of female priesthood participation, as found in fundamentalism. Since every male priesthood holder must be made "one" with a spouse, on the model of Adam and Eve, then the females will hold the priesthood more equally with them, having no division or separation to this oneness.

Stories taken from the bible about Abraham, Isaac, and Jacob, and doctrine about the character and nature of God (Adam), provide mythical justification for the kinship-based covenant order—an order which affects mainstream and fundamentalist women in two different ways. For both, the celestial human family pattern is to be replicated by all the righteous, to eventually be a perfect chain from Father Adam to his latest posterity. Priesthood power operates to seal the ordinance; sealing ratifies the covenantal promise. For a fundamentalist woman this means accommodating the increase of her husband's

76

kingdom through acceptance of a co-wife and her children as her own sister, and her own children.

The constant emphasis fundamentalists place on family kingdom translates into a different environment for polygynous women than for mainstream monogamous women. During one of the many sermons on covenant in one fundamentalist Sunday meeting, I recorded the words of one of the ruling patriarchs:

> Our Father in Heaven organized the human family, but they are all disorganized and in great confusion. Joseph [Smith] taught us that the premortal familial organization included specific husband-wife and parent-child bonds. Our Father made a covenant with one of the queens of heaven, and male and female spirits got their bodies from that union. You can, on this earth, find that person who you chose as a kindred spirit—for the women, you must find the right male to be your head, stay, husband, and protector on earth and who will exalt you in eternal worlds. Women, as wives of their king, in turn, will be sovereigns of their children in these kingdoms.

Covenant making in both types of Mormonism thus establishes a complex network of asymmetric and symmetric relationships. The formal structure of inequality within the fundamentalist Mormon household resembles that of God over Abraham, Abraham over his wives and children, and so on. The inequality within the fundamentalist hierocracy sets the prophet and his council at the top from which position all the sacred priesthood keys and economic resources are distributed. Household and hierocratic inequality are formed by the consecration covenant between the household head and the bishop or councilmember. Yet, symmetrical relations do exist in Mormonism. The baptismal covenant unites all members and separates them from the world; the consecration covenant creates a separate group of the more dedicated, who seek to achieve spiritual unity and ultimate salvation. Women, however, are formally subservient to men in both mainstream and fundamentalist societies and it is the way that women achieve some increase in status that differentiates the mainstream women from the women of Harker.

It is my premise that Mormon women, especially fundamentalist women, live in a world much broader than the formally defined world of male priesthood bearers. These women are strategists and decision-makers, organizers and instructors, producers and providers of food and goods, and are expert manipulators, as evident in church testimony meetings, in their financial dealings with the larger towns and businesses, and in their combined opposition to their husbands when they need something.

ANALYSIS OF STATUS AND WOMEN'S GROUPS

In order to understand the factors that determine women's social status and account for the differences in women's position in Mormon fundamentalism,

I collected information on 75 women living in 25 households in the northern branch of the Allred Group. Women were interviewed with reference to their daily activities, beliefs, family life, relationships, and experiences as wives, mothers, and "sisters in the gospel." I lived and worked personally with these different polygynous families, first with my daughter, Liza, and then with my second daughter, Frances, over a period of four years, observing and participating in the activities of the women of those households extensively.[5]

The following analysis is designed to test Sanday's hypothesis that female status is determined by economic, religious, and mythological factors, and Leis's premise that the formation of female groups is determined primarily by polygyny and the economic interdependence of women.

Economic and Social Production

The law of consecration and stewardship (D&C 72: 24–26) requires Harker believers to consecrate all their properties to the Lord with a covenant and deed that cannot be broken. These properties are to be laid before the bishop and/or council and subsequently not to be returned. Each consecrator, however, is then appointed steward over sufficient property or economic means to maintain his family, while the group uses surplus property to help the poor and buy land and goods. Members who sin and do not repent are to be "cast out" and do not receive the properties that they had consecrated (EMS 1:2:9). This is the essence of the "united order."

The Harker united order displays five characteristics: 1) consecration of tithes and offerings, as mentioned above, 2) consecration of time and energy, 3) communal distribution, 4) storage and rotation of new and used goods, and 5) provision for the poor and needy. The united order is controlled by the priesthood, yet is generated by the production and distribution activities of females and their networks. For example, one of the most valuable benefits of the order and the most practical uses of cooperative female labor is the Harker Academy, which schools children of ages 2 to 18.[6] The school runs on a budget of $48,000 per year, including all labor, supplies, library, film, and instructional materials, all of which come from community/family surplus and donations. (The school in the neighboring community of Corvalis, a secular public school with fewer children, is budgeted at $350,000 per year.) The Harker library, containing a large assortment of religious and academic materials and films, runs on $50 per month. The school board has successfully collected an average of $20 per month per child from nearly every household (96 percent), and is saving for new supplies and video material for their recently purchased television and VCR equipment.

A network of women cooperate to run the school, revising their schedules quarterly. Teachers are given a stipend of $20 to $40 a month to cover some expenses, but no one is paid for her time. An excellent example of how the network in the school works is the nursery program, which is held in a large

BENNION

room within the school/church complex in the center of the community. One nursery instructor has two preschool-aged children. She is currently teaching her sisterwife's child, while that sisterwife tends the teacher's younger children at home. The virtual motto in this arrangement is, "if you'll babysit my kids, I'll teach yours."[7] Another woman in the nursery teaches her sisterwife's two children in exchange for supplying her family with bread. While one teaches, the other bakes. I was told by one informant that the female network at the school is a "family" of women caring and teaching their own children or those of their sisterwives, which are, essentially, their own.

In addition to the school, women run the church bazaars held in the fall, where goods and foods are made and contributed for sale to the rest of the community. The money goes to the Relief Society or priesthood for future projects and benefits. There are also fairs, carnivals, and dime-a-dip dinners held, for example, to pay for large medical bills, or to help a wife whose husband is out of town and does not financially support her. These projects are all initiated by the female network, which is also the "Relief Society" of Harker. Where the formal male priesthood projects fail to aid the hidden needs of community members, the female networking projects succeed in reaching those in need of economic, social, and to some extent, emotional support.

Further, much of the united order's strength lies in the informal arrangements among sisterwives and community women to manage their household needs with limited finances. The allocation of family economic resources is based on the number of children per wife per husband. Ideally, each male head of a family is responsible for assuring that all of his wives and their children are cared for. In reality, because of his frequent absence from home, it is up to each individual wife to manage her household and provide her children with food and clothing. In order to manage this task, the wife relies on the female network that exists to insure that survival.

Because of the united order's provision of basic economic materials, such as land, buildings, water, and wood for heating, Harker women are less reliant on outside services, and thus spend less monthly than the average housewife in the Bitterroot Valley. If, for example, there is a financial emergency, such as an accident where an individual must be hospitalized, the female network holds a potluck dinner to pay for expenses. In Harker there is no health insurance to pay, no central heating bills, virtually no housing construction costs, and few commercial debts of any size. There is a communal garden (organized in plots by clusters of sisterwives), a wheat mill, ample lumber, and free use of goods and household appliances donated for rotation in the bishop's storehouse.

For the most part, Harker's sexual division of labor follows that of mainstream American society. The differences are accounted for by the fact that in Harker there are three women to each man. By nature of their large numbers, more women are employed in the workforce than men—a ratio of more than 2 to 1.[8]

BENNION

Harker male and female earning power is quite different, but complementary. As mentioned, 75 percent of the women work in some context or other, including caring for other's children and managing their own household. On average, Harker women work 25 to 30 hours per week on either community type or marketplace work. On average, a Harker man works 40 to 55 hours per week at his job and 5 to 15 hours per week on community and church-related jobs. These numbers show two things: 1) women have more leisure than men, yet 2) because of their large numbers, women also spend more time, collectively, in community, home, and wage labor.

In general, these women are responsible for all aspects of domestic economy, including housework, cooking, washing, tending the garden, and so on. Women are also responsible for learning any skill that may enhance the life of their children or themselves, such as higher education, art, music, literature, drama, nursing, midwifery, as well as tradework such as carpentry, electrical work, herbalism, and auto repair. Often women will go to the nearby community college or even the state university 40 miles north of Harker for their education. They need not get permission from anyone if they have adequate funds; but if they need a loan from their husbands or the Priesthood, then permission must be obtained.

In this way, Harker women follow a pattern found among early Saints—doing a little bit of everything. In the words of early Prophet Brigham Young, women were:

80

> useful not only to sweep houses, wash dishes, make beds, and raise babies, but that they should stand behind the counter, study law or physics, or become good bookkeepers and be able to do the business in any counting house, and all this to enlarge their sphere of usefulness for the benefit of society at large. In following these things they but answer the design of their creation (Widtsoe 1939: 335).

Harker women, because of the pronounced absence of their husbands, also perform home and yard maintenance jobs normally performed by men. One woman said that because her husband was gone so often she had to put on her own front door, fix the sink, and repair mechanical devices in the home by herself. She said this was common among Harker women.

In order for women to join ranks in any society, they must find commonalities. In this case the bond among the women has arisen in large part from common interests and common needs.

Religious Ritual, Power, and Influence

While in the mainstream Mormon Church, women are forbidden to participate in vital "priesthood" religious and social rituals, fundamentalist women, because of their "forced independence," often bless one another and their children, prophesy, heal, preside autonomously over their organizations and auxiliaries, and serve, to some extent, in gender-blind administrative positions, such as city recorder, city judge, adult Sunday school teacher, naturopath/midwife, and village doctor.

Harker's ideology, for example, focuses on female strength, as it subscribes to the belief that there will be wars and famines that will destroy many men in the near future. One of the purposes of polygyny, in light of this apocalyptic prediction, is to assure that the species will move forward at a healthy pace during the scripturally acclaimed "last days." Women will be so numerous that it will be common to see seven righteous women (usually thought of as sisters who have been raised by a righteous patriarch) cling to one righteous man:

> In that day seven women shall take hold of one man, saying we will eat our own bread, and wear our own apparel: only let us be called by the name, to take away our reproach (Isaiah 4:1).

In other words, wives will be expected to subsist independently of their husbands, relying on each other for economic, social, and spiritual sustenance. Occasionally, the male-priesthood head will annoint, bless, and give counsel to the wives and the children, but most of the time these women are to be on their own. Thus, they have prophetic warrant for their polygynous situation and their independence; it is not merely a social anomaly that is divinely permitted but is an essential part of God's plan for his children to survive the Apocalypse.

Further, there is some evidence that fundamentalist men allow a larger degree of latitude for women in the "priesthood partnership" than do LDS men, because of their long absences and lack of presence in all of their wives' dwellings and homes. In general, among the LDS population, women are much more separated from the priesthood powers. In Harker, because a woman is sealed to a priesthood bearer, she holds certain priesthood powers herself that are said by the group to supersede those of unmarried women, and even those of unmarried men who have not received the ultimate priesthood blessings which come only with celestial marriage. Women who have once been sealed to a priesthood bearer are able to bless and annoint their own children and the sick. The conditions under which a mother would bless her child are many. She might find that there are no male priesthood bearers in the vicinity, so she conducts the blessing herself. Or, she might make it a regular practice to daily bless the health and welfare of her children. I am familiar with both types. But there is a difference between these types and the more serious use of the Melchezedek Priesthood—a priesthood that is formally only used by men and highly respected women.

The community midwife, for example, often uses the Melchezedek Priesthood when she annoints with sacred oil and blesses her patients who are having difficulty in a birth, invoking the power and forms of the priesthood to do so. This "informal" use of priesthood powers is not permitted among LDS women. The fundamentalist women have not been "ordained" officially to the priesthood, but they are still considered to be empowered generically by virtue of their being sealed to an ordained husband. Further, because Joseph Smith authorized women to bless their children and perform many priesthood-related tasks, fundamentalists believe they have the right to do so.

The Relief Society structure itself is a powerful source of influence among Harker women. It and the all-encompassing female network are one and the same—a strong, quasi-autonomous organization that is vital to the economic, social, and spiritual welfare of the community. Within it, women participate in the laying on of hands, the anointing of sacred oil, massage therapy, the "mothers" blessing that is unique among the fundamentalists, herbalism, folk medicine, midwifery, and prayer and fasting. A regular annointing is basically comprised of dripping some holy priesthood oil on the sick one's head, laying ones hands on his/her head and speaking, "In the name of the Holy Melchezedek Priesthood, I annoint thee . . ."

Although secular hospitalization and medical services are accessible in a neighboring area, because of the direct costs involved in using them for polygynous households, these facilities and services are a last resort. Further, very few families have health insurance, so women use home herbal remedies and prayer to heal the sick. Women often gather these herbs at the community's ranch, or order them from a naturopathic supply company in Idaho. From them they concoct teas, salves, and poultices to treat most medical problems.[9] Many cures are passed down from mother to daughter and from sisterwife to sisterwife, involving an extensive network of medical information and experimentation. Between these home remedies and the healing powers of the priesthood, there are few occasions to call on a doctor.

Further evidence for Harker female influence and unity is manifested in Sunday meetings where women regularly outnumber men in bearing witness of the "truthfulness of the gospel." These testimonies state an individual's view of their own personal rebirth and affirmation of the validity of fundamentalist lifestyle. Some speak of trying to live the gospel or about ones sins to overcome, or of efforts at recruiting others.[10] No matter what is said, it is the women who more often stand and express spiritual and emotional bonds to each other and of their commitments. In this way, informally, women can gain spiritual strength without the official laying on of hands by the priesthood; the act is purely female—her testimony, her voice. This, more than any other ritualistic factor, contributes to the increase in female status and influence by providing a collective voice in a public setting and by providing a story-telling communion of common interests, desires, tragedies, beliefs, and sentiments.

According to Mernissi (1978), religious sanctuary for women, both physi-

82

BENNION

cal and psychological, provides an opportunity for the expression of female solidarity in the face of a male dominated system. Harker women who participate in rituals and religious activities benefit through the exchanges they derive from these activities. By sheer force of personality and number, women can fit comfortably into religious rituals and positions ordinarily held by men. But it is precisely these characteristics that separate them from other, outside, women.

Kinship, Marriage, and Female Networking

As discussed, women draw upon certain egalitarian concepts in fundamentalist ideology that lend support to their participation in the female network. Because women are taught much of their lives to work together, to share, and to love each other as "sisters," whether related biologically or not, their very psychological makeup is geared to female solidarity. Their salvation is dependent on how well they work together and how well they prove their love for each other. In fundamentalist society, nurturing relationships among co-wives is every bit as important as, if not more important than, the husband–wife relationship.

This is not to say that conflict and quarreling is absent in this community. On the contrary, women are often competing for their husband's attention, for limited resources, and for living space. But in the overall scheme of things, the women participate in sharing and cooperative activities far more than the males do. They work their conflicts out amongst themselves in order to deal with the greater demands of day-to-day survival.

Sisterwife Kinship

It is common for women to be related by blood prior to their marriage to the same man. The most common form of this type is sororal polygyny and cousin polygyny. Because women have an affiliation with each other prior to marriage, their bonds of love and friendship are already established. There is a spiritual predominance of the sister in Harker culture that strengthens women's status and position in relation to men in society. Women are bonded by nature of their birth and their large numbers, to the disadvantage of men who are relatively small in number and, with the exception of only the most elite family kingdoms, have small numbers of relatives in the immediate family. These biological relationships between wives are, for the most part, a product of sisters marrying the same man, yet, the union of cousins, and aunts and nieces, is also common. The significance of this kinship among sisterwives is that women living in the same proximity as their female relations reinforce each other and protect each other's interests, whether they be emotional, economic, or religious.

Further evidence of the importance of female bonding is found in the courtship and marriage customs of Harker. While a man interested in adding another wife to his family must go through exhaustive, elaborate steps from the "matchmaker" to the father or brother of the bride, and to the bride herself, the procedure for the woman is much simpler and quicker. More often than not, an unmarried female simply gets to know another man's wife extremely well, finding some commonality or bond between them. The wife then recommends strongly that the girl or woman who she has been "courting" be sealed to her husband for all "eternity". In this way, the bonds between women are often stronger than the bonds between a husband and wife.

Miriam is a beautiful red-haired, slender 17 year old, who has straight A's and is a member of the track team in the Silverton High School. She is a native to polygyny, having grown up in a prominent established family where four women shared one husband. She said she longs to marry a boy her own age, but also sees the advantages of marrying an older man who is "strong in his priesthoods." She looks forward to "rewarding sisterwife relationships," and is anxious to be a mother and teach her children the gospel. She is currently being courted by two different males. One is a rather skinny, bare-faced 18 year old boy who is also on the track team, who converted to the group with his family last year. His family lives in the basement of another member's home until they can build their own home, which may take some time because his father is a salesclerk at an autoparts store. She is also being courted by a 55 year old man who she claims had bad breath and hairy arms who she does not like. She is certain she will "straighten him out" at the soonest possible moment, letting him know she has no interest.

She is fond of a 40 year old man who has just built his two wives a beautiful home in the woods near the north creek, and feels certain he returns the sentiments. She has not yet told her father or the town's matchmaker about it, because she is also interested in continuing her education. She told me she will have to do a lot of praying and accept what "the Lord has in store for her." In the meantime, because of the informal sect rule against marriages before 18, she will bide her time, and enjoy the process.

"It is so different being courted by Harker men than it is when dating high school boys from the larger town," she said. "Here every man, both young and old, is fair game. For men seeking women, it is harder because there are only so many women to choose from. I am lucky because I get my pick."

Betsy, a 23 year old second wife, mother of two children, recalls her courtship days when she, her husband-to-be, and his wife would go to the movies together as a threesome. She loved that type of courtship system because she was equally fond of her co-wife and her husband to be. She said it was the period in her married life when the three of them were the closest, and she longs for the time when they can get out together again.

The Harker marriage ceremony takes place in an unpublicized spot chosen by the priesthood. I was never told specifically where these weddings occur, as they are sacred. The location seems to be less important than the authority of the man who blesses the marriage. During the ceremony, the husband is presented with the new wife by the latest wife in what is known as the "holy grip," a form of sacred handshake which symbolizes covenants and promises. Her hand is placed in his hand by his other wife as part of the Law of Sarah. In the bible, Sarah gave Abraham her handmaiden, Hagar, to marry because she herself was barren. Though the senior wife, or latest wife, may not have full choice in who her husband ultimately chooses to marry (although it is often the case that she herself arranged the marriage), in the ceremony, she gives him the new wife—a gesture of commitment to the bride and to the principle of plural marriage. All the other wives (if present) then place their hands on top of the wedding couple's clasp and are all sealed together for eternity. In this way, not only is the husband sealed to the new wife, but each wife is "married" to her as well.

Goddess Worship

Another crucial factor in determining female status is the existence of a female deity. In another study (Cannon 1990), I found that the concept of the Mormon Mother varied depending on the era and the current sex roles in the mainstream Church, and that fundamentalist and "liberal" Mormon women both use, and historically have used, the Goddess symbol more than mainstream women.

In Harker I found numerous female empowerment stories that translated into social behavior (Cannon 1990). Women and men both spoke often of women's "sovereignties" and their status as potential goddesses. For example, during a Sunday school lesson, the female instructor mentioned the capacity for plural wives to be like "sovereign satellites" circling their husband in their "kingdom galaxy." She related this stellar arrangement to planet Adam who had his wives (Eve, Mary, and so on) "upon thrones of glory surrounding him."[11] These wives of Adam-God are true goddesses, having received their second annointings and exaltation from the previous world. Harker women told me that they were strengthened by focusing on their own spiritual and physical powers and relating it to celestial figures such as Eve and Mary, or even Hagar, Abraham's plural wife. Some use the wives of Christ—Mary Magdalene and Martha—as role models in their progress toward goddesshood.

Harker women often idealize the early Mormon Church where women, it is claimed, often participated directly in priesthood duties, being one-half of the priesthood, in giving annointings, bestowing blessings, and praying in the name and power of the Melchezedek priesthood (a right formally designated for males only). For example, on one occasion a group of male priesthood holders came to Joseph Smith complaining about a particular woman who

85

BENNION

was performing anointings. They told Joseph that they were unhappy that she was using a power that was rightfully theirs. Joseph scolded them and told them that she was far more worthy to participate in this work than they (TPJS, Smith, 1938: 120–121).

Harker informants provided additional stories about the community midwife and her powers of healing. The midwife, having delivered more than 700 babies, often asked one of the brethren to offer a priesthood blessing on behalf of both the mother and the unborn child; yet, when no male was available she herself would give this important blessing. If the mother was in some danger, the midwife would give additional blessings and annoint with her husband's holy oil, whether a man were present or not. I heard one man tell a story about the birth of his second wife's first child. Her labor had been perilously long, and the child was crowning when the contractions stopped. The husband asked the midwife if they should take her to the hospital. But she said no, they should give her a priesthood blessing and the mother would be all right. The husband's hands were shaking and he felt unable to give the blessing, so the midwife gave the blessing and annointed the mother with the oil. The child was born without trouble.[12]

Harker women also spoke of the nature of creation, and how it works. They asked, "can any animal be formed in the womb and born with solely a male god at work? No! A female god must be present for any type of creation to take place." They said they are promised, if they endure to the end, they will be rewarded with "thrones, kingdoms, principalities, powers, dominions, glory, immortality, and eternal life" (see D&C 75: 5; 128: 12; 132: 19, 24; Moses 1: 39).

Discussion

With the aid of Sanday's model of economic and ritual contribution, and Leis's premise of formation of female groups, I have shown that male absence provides women with more opportunity and access to the valued natural resources and economic activities in the community. This analysis showed the ways and means by which women gain and maintain control over their informal networking and unique religious rituals. For example, certain magico–religious powers can be attributed to women which entitle them to control and which derive from a belief system where maternity and goddesshood is viewed as a sacred or magical function. Further, because fertility and reproductivity are valued so highly, even more highly in fundamentalist society than in mainstream LDS society, women's activities in these spheres are celebrated.

There are additional factors that contribute to the longevity and satisfaction that female's experience in the Harker Mormon Fundamentalist Branch. Among the most important are polygyny, the merits of which have already been discussed, and the additional factors of 1) females' separate unity, 2) matrifocality, and 3) hypergamy.

Females' Separate Unity

One of the maxims of patriarchal society is that men have power over women. Harker is no exception. Women are inferior, in the formal ideology of the patriarchal order. Females compensate for this imputed inferiority or "difference," by forming an opposing unity with other women. Because women are denied formal authority, they do not mix well with those—the men—who have that authority. Instead, they find others like themselves—co-wives, sisters, aunts, cousins, and sisters-in-the-gospel—who share reduced social status as well as economic and spiritual experiences. Through cooperation and discourse about home management, childbirth, menstruation, mother-hood, cleaning and cooking, Relief Society, testimonies, and husbands who are frequently away, they cement comforting bonds; despite personality differences or small jealousies and arguments. This valuable interaction occurs through an easy going, "open door" policy where women often enter each other's homes without knocking to discuss needs and issues. They also tend to meet at the mercantile, post office, or church/school complex to gossip and discuss problems.

As part of their uniting in opposition to male authority, women will often use affliction as protest. Definitions of femininity as frailty in society are turned to advantage by women who succumb readily to illness, prolonged post-partum recovery or menstruation.

Another way females manipulate their position in the community vis-à-vis males is in the exclusive part they play in propagating their kingdoms reproductively. Men may be able to influence their children's righteousness in a small measure, such as with a favorite son or daughter of a favorite wife, but it is women who bear and nurture these children, most often in the absence of their husbands. Hence, they have more direct control over whether the young will ultimately stay in the group; women have more religious influence over their children, through their testimonies, daily practice of prayer and scripture reading, and constant display of affection for the gospel, than do their husbands. In another study on conversion and integration rates, I found that out of 360 converts who had left the sect during the last 30 years, more than 75 percent were males (Cannon 1996).

Matrifocality and Hypergamy

Establishment of women as the residential core of the family is a positive factor in the formation of female groups in Harker. I have shown throughout the paper how women are permanent members of their households, whereas men are visitors without permanent singular residences. Women are in control of the family dwelling the majority of the time and make most of the decisions that affect the family. Women, further, are commonly married to men of high rank and status, which gives them an additional reason to stay in the community. It is quite common, for example, for convert women to be mar-

87

ried to established, upper-class men rather than converted or established (native) lower-class men.[13] This marrying up quality lends itself to permanence and a sense of belonging in the community.

CONCLUSION

As the data and analysis suggest, the question of female status and influence among contemporary Mormon fundamentalist women is not solved by simple association to any one feature, but is correlated to a number of factors—polygyny, the formation of female groups, matrifocality, hypergamy, and the prolonged absences of men. Also of great importance is the dominant feature of forced independence and self-reliance in economic, social, ritual, and spiritual activities.

In a separate study (Cannon 1993), based on a comparison of LDS monogamous women and fundamentalist polygynous women, I show how fundamentalist women have a relatively higher status than the LDS women based on their political, social, and religious influences in community decision-making, economic subsistence and ritual. It is my opinion that marginalized mainstream Mormon women will continue to find fundamentalism attractive because of these features.

In both societies females do not have access to the priesthood nor to formal political powers of any kind. I show that the fundamentalist women have more autonomy than mainstream Mormon women. Yet this raises additional questions about studies about Mormon women and Mormon society. What is the relative influence and powers enjoyed by these women? Do all women within the system enjoy freedom and empowerment or do some experience misery and bondage? What about women who do not accept male formal supremacy? Are they stigmatized, welcomed into the group, asked to leave? And finally, what is the cost the fundamentalist women pay for their relative power and influence within the context of an extremely rigid male-controlled society? This study of Mormon fundamentalist women provides a beginning point for further inquiries into the lives of women in American fundamentalist groups. More research is needed in the areas of conflict analysis, women's status, male and female relationships, and recruitment.

NOTES

1. These numbers are based on a census taken in the winter of 1989. At present, the community has increased substantially with a new wave of converts. The last census I took of total community population was in 1993, with the number closer to 1,000 individuals, including children.

2. Leaders of the Mormon Church formally abolished polygyny in 1890, yet did not completely discontinue performing plural marriages until around 1910 (Quinn 1985). For this reason, it wasn't until 1920 that the fundamentalists were seen as a separate group from the official church.

3. In order to reach the highest kingdom in the celestial glory, individuals must be

married. A man cannot, therefore, attain his full glory without a woman, nor can woman do so without a man.

4. Fundamentalist Mormons describe Adam as a polygynous being who, in addition to Eve, married Mary (Jesus' mother).

5. During this intensive period of fieldwork, I was in a constant state of pregnancy, lactation, and toddler chasing. I kept my hair long and braided and wore the appropriate long skirts and long-sleeved shirts. Near the end of my research, I cut my hair to a cosmopolitan bob, and noticed a palatable distance between myself and the members of the group.

6. Saturday work projects performed by males are also included in the united order; these male tasks are somewhat less thoroughly organized and effective than the school project run by the females.

7. Harker women are often arranged in clusters of houses where co-wives have direct daily contact with one another. In another study, I found that 45 percent of the women lived in the same structure as their co-wives, although most of the dwellings within this structure were partitioned off for privacy as in the case of a duplex, attic, or basement apartment.

8. Since 75 percent of the females of Harker are involved in non-domestic employment in and outside the home, that totals 113 out of the 150 women. All 50 men are employed, in addition to the religious callings. The ratio of working women to working men then comes to 113 to 50 or 2.25 to 1. What all this means is that women far outnumber men in the workforce in the community and in the marketplace. They are significantly adding to the family income because of this work, often strengthening their female solidarity and interdependence in the process.

9. Some local cures include yarrow tea for colds, plaintain as salve for diaper rash, "shepherd's purse" to make the blood clot in delivery, and corn silk, parsley and juniper for kidney problems. Tansey is used for menstrual cramps and as an insect repellent. Mullein is used for earache, diaper rash and general ailments. Comfrey is taken for diarrhea, dysentery, and general irregularity. Burdock root tea and sassafras are used for acne, and slippery elm for vomiting. A soothing potato and banana poultice is used for second degree burns: the skin is cooled with cold wet towels, then potatoes are applied, thinly sliced, followed by frozen bananas.

10. A typical Sunday is comprised of several meetings: an early morning male Priesthood conference, a Sunday school class in mid-morning where children and adults learn more about the gospel, an afternoon Sacrament meeting where all partake of the blood and body of Christ and bear their testimonies, and finally, an evening fireside of music and gospel stories.

11. According to Allred doctrine, it is believed that Adam, the Father of this world, chose Eve as his first wife to begin the creation of spiritual and temporal offspring. Mary, the mother of Christ, was another of Adam's wives, as Christ is the true biological and spiritual son of the Father.

12. In the field my access to sensitive information about childbirth and women's experiences was facilitated by the presence of my 18-month old daughter, Liza, and my pregnancy and the birth of my second child, Frances.

13. In order for polygyny to work in this community there needs to be an influx of women and an emigration of males. In Harker this is achieved through widespread female conversions and alienation of males.

REFERENCES

Cannon, J. 1990. *An Exploratory Study of Female Networking in a Mormon Fundamentalist Society.* Masters thesis, Portland, Oregon: Portland State University.

———. 1993. "A Comparison between LDS and Fundamentalist Women." In *Anthropology of Mormonism.* Engelwood Cliffs, New Jersey: Rutgers Press.

———. 1994. *Seeds of Discontent: An Analysis of Conversion, Commitment, and Integration in a Contemporary Mormon Fundamentalist Sect.* Unpublished manuscript.

———. *Kings, Queens and Covenants: An Analysis of Male and Female Conversion and Integration in a Morman Polygynous Community.* Ph.D. Dissertation, Anthropology, University of Utah.

Clignet, R. 1970. *Many Wives, Many Powers: Authority and Power in Polygamous Families.* Evanston: University of Illinois Press.

Leis, N. 1974. "Women in Groups." In *Women, Culture, and Society.* Eds. M. Rosaldo and L. Lamphere. pp. 223–242. Stanford, California: Stanford University Press.

Mernissi, F. 1978. "Women, Saints, and Sanctuaries." *Signs 3* (March) 101–112.

Quinn, M. 1985. "Mormon Polygynous Marriages from 1890 to 1905." *Dialogue of Mormon Thought.* 18:1:9–105. Salt Lake City, Utah: Dialogue Publishing.

Rogers, S. 1975. "Female Forms of Power and the Myth of Male Dominance." *American Ethnology* 2:741–54.

Sanday, P. 1973. "Toward a Theory of the Status of Women." *American Anthropologist* 75(5):1682–1690.

———. 1981. *Female Power and Male Dominance.* Cambridge, England: Cambridge University Press.

Schlegel, A. 1972. *Male Dominance and Female Autonomy: Domestic Authority in Matrilineal Societies.* New Haven: HRAF Press.

Wagner, J. 1976. "Male Supremacy: Its Role in a Contemporary Commune and its Structural Alternatives." In *International Review of Modern Sociology* 6:173–80.

———. 1982. *Sex Roles in Contemporary American Communes.* Bloomington, Indiana: Indiana University Press.

Widstoe, J. 1939. *Discourses of Brigham Young.* Salt Lake City, Utah: Deseret Press.

Mormon Literature References:

D&C, Doctrine and Covenants, 1835, a volume of revelations received by Joseph Smith used as scripture by Mormons, published by the Church of Jesus Christ of Latter-day Saints, Salt Lake City, Utah.

EMS, The Evening and Morning Star. 1832–1834. Vol. 1; no. 1 (June 1832), Kirtland, Ohio.

Moses, a volume of revelations received by Joseph Smith used as scripture by Mormons, found in the larger volume, Pearl of Great Price, 1981 (recent edition), Salt Lake City, Utah.

TPJS, The Teachings of the Prophet Joseph Smith, 1838–1854, Salt Lake City, Utah: Deseret Book.

A STRANGE ROAD HOME
Adult Female Converts to
Classical Pentacostalism

Nancy L. Eiesland

chapter 6

IN A SUNDAY school room off the main mint-colored gymnasium that
served as the sanctuary for Crossroads Assembly,[1] a classical Pentecostal congregation with 800 regular worshippers, 35 women stood in a circle holding
hands as they sang the worship chorus "Surely the Presence of the Lord is in
this Place." As the leader—a woman in her mid-60s dressed in tennis shoes
and a designer gold and aqua jogging suit—brought the singing to a close, she
asked the women to take both hands of the person next to her and to pray
together about needs. Finding private spaces in the crowded room was difficult but the women huddled near the walls, arms around one another to pray.
The soft murmur of prayer languages began emanating from each cluster.[2] As
the prayer time continued, weeping was intermixed with the prayer languages. After ten minutes, a hush fell over the room as the prayer partners
hugged and wiped away their tears. The chorus, "Jesus, Jesus, Jesus, There's Just
Something about that Name," wafted slowly through the room until it be-

came a harmonic strain. After several repetitions, the refrain again drifted away.

The leader asked the women to share what the Lord had done for them. During this time, each woman in turn shared a vignette from the past week or month that revealed how the Lord had been with her. Mostly the testimonies revealed in detail the women's detection of God's hand in the everyday routines of their lives, giving the patience needed for dealing with a repairman, helping them quit overeating, or finding peace in the midst of their busy suburban lives. This week Alda spoke about the difficulty of adjusting to the hubbub of having her daughter's two-year-old twins in the house after 20 years of "being mostly on my own." The girls' mother had been in treatment for drug and alcohol addiction for several months. The prayer group had prayed with Alda in the past as she sought guardianship of her grandchildren. Alda recalled their prayers, quipping, "But I've been asking the Lord's help to remember that this is what I asked for two years ago. (Laughing) I guess you have to be careful what you ask."

I had been to Alda's home two weeks earlier for an interview and could vouch for the clamorous wake of the twins—Hope and Joy—for whom Alda is currently the primary caretaker. The home was an attractive Tudor located in an upper-middle-class suburb outside of Atlanta's perimeter highway. When I pulled up, I was immediately struck by the steel gray Jaguar sitting in the driveway. When Alda came to the door, I commented on the car. With a mix of pride and embarrassment, she said she had won a three-year lease for being the salesperson of the year at the luxury car dealership where she had worked. Ending a successful career in her mid-50s to care for the twins and to engage in what she characterizes as "my first stab at homemaking," Alda said, was the result of a "sort of mid-life crisis." She chuckled, "I didn't need to go out and buy a sports car, I already had one."

The "crisis" coincided with Alda's arrival at the prayer group at Crossroads Assembly two years ago. In the succeeding years, Alda's life has taken a new direction. After taking early retirement from her job, Alda has become a full-time homemaker. Now instead of spending her days enticing the area's upper crust to purchase luxury cars, she fills her time with trips to the pediatrician, outings to the park, and religious meetings with other women. "I've done so many things in my life, but for the first time in a very long time, I feel at home with myself, my family and with the Lord," Alda shared. "I guess it's been a strange road to get to here—at least some people would say so."

Alda may have followed a strange road—from high-end retails sales to full-time motherhood in her 50s. Nonetheless, her biography has striking similarities with those of many of the adult converts in the women's prayer meeting at Crossroads Assembly. This essay depicts the experiences of women, like Alda, who converted to classical Pentecostalism as adults through their participation in a fundamentalist women's prayer meeting, addressing common characteristics of the adult converts and discussing the multiple factors attracting them to the group. The status of classical Pentecostalism within the fundamentalist Christian movement in the United States is described briefly in order to highlight the position of women within classical Pentecostalism and social theories related to it.

For the women who attend the prayer meetings at Crossroads Assembly, Pentecostalism is as much (or more) about emotional release and ritual practice as it is about ideas of God and the Bible. The expressiveness—characteristic of classical Pentecostalism—including intense experiences of belonging, testifying, and ritual touching, provides positive incentive for women's participation. In the case of the adult converts at Crossroads, the affective and reassuringly physical aspects of classical Pentecostalism contrasts with much of their day-to-day experience in economic and other social spheres.

Four factors were noted in looking at this sample of Pentecostal women:

(1) Of the women who were adult converts to classical Pentecostalism and currently attending this suburban Pentecostal church, all but one had been employed in typically masculine professions or worked in situations where their immediate colleagues were men. Like Alda, several other women worked in male-dominated retail sectors, such as construction and insurance; two women were in education—a typically female field—but had risen to positions of management where their colleagues were primarily male. These women had few if any close friends from their work settings.

(2) Most of the adult converts were either presently undergoing or had recently experienced significant changes in their kinship networks. Several had recently undergone marital separation and/or divorce (some more than once), while others had experienced the death of a spouse, parent or child. Two had recently remarried and were becoming acquainted with step-children and step-grandchildren.

(3) The majority of these women were Southerners but did not reside near their extended families.[3] In addition to having noticeable Southern accents, many of the women prized what they characterized as distinct Southern manners and style of dress, such as feminine appearance.

(4) All of the women were more than 40 years old at the time of conversion. Although the benefits of aging, such as more personal time and discretionary income, were not ignored, many of the women in the prayer group perceived this time of their lives as the beginning of relative physical decline and isolation. Noting the number of prayer group's members who had "female problems," such as hysterectomies and breast cancer, one member jested that the local hospital should give them a group rate.

These common characteristics not only provided incentives for many of the women to join the Bible study and prayer meeting, but they also fostered a culture of intense mutual identification and friendship within the group.

The women's prayer group at Crossroads Assembly provides these women with a setting in which they can compose and relate their life stories, both public and private aspects, among sympathetic listeners. Secondly, in contrast to their experience of workplace tokenism, the prayer group offers women with a "women's space" where physical touch and bodily freedom can be exercised within religious bounds. The group adds to ideals of the "traditional" family by supplying group members with additional support from other nearby families. Finally, within the social and cultural milieu of the suburban South, the group gives converts a sense of tradition and religious heritage.

Though these women's attractions to fundamentalism can be traced, in part, to their sociocultural experiences of the familial disruptions, social mobility, and female workforce participation of late modernity, this attraction can also be related to accounts of women's spaces and stories, physical engagement, and Southern gender identity. The women's prayer group at Crossroads provides them with powerful meaning-making and ordering ideologies and narrative practices. They, to some extent, nostalgically recall a more familiar, less chaotic past with which they can symbolically and ritually affiliate through fundamentalist practice. Yet they also gain support in coping with the modern challenges of everyday life as aging women in the South. At Crossroads they find and create an individually and communally relevant blend of Southern religious traditionalism and therapeutic personalism.

About half of the women who attend the Crossroads Assembly women's prayer group converted to classical Pentecostalism as adults. Of the approximately 40 women who attend the group at least occasionally, 19 are converts. Of the seven women who do most of the organizing and managing of the group's affairs, four are adult converts. The predecessor to this gathering was begun nearly a decade ago by women who had left their mainline Protestant congregations as a result of their participation in the Charismatic movement in the Presbyterian church. After leaving their denomination, the group met independently for 18 months. This group soon became a gathering place for women from many religious backgrounds, including marginal Catholics and Methodists, who were participants in home Bible studies begun under the auspices of the Charismatic movement. In part because of the intimacy of the meeting in homes and the efforts of then leader, Rosetta Lynn, a divorced mother of two who owned her own restaurant, the group became a magnet for women whose religious and social lives were "nontraditional" by standards of the suburban South.

The group's lack of a religious institutional home concerned some members, especially after several women, including Rosetta, began espousing a "health and wealth" doctrine, then common in Charismatic circles. Following the teachings of televangelists Kenneth Copeland and Kenneth Hagin, several members began advocating a theology of divine healing and financial well-being that consisted of positive confession and sensory denial (particularly as it relates to physical illness and financial worries). During the early months after the group became independent, one member claimed a healing for diabetes and refused to acknowledge ongoing symptoms of the disease until she was hospitalized. This tendency for what several members in the group perceived as heterodox theology, as well as the women's mix of theological and ritual heritage, prompted them to express a need for a religious institutional home that would keep them from "falling off the [theological] deep end," according to Ann, a founding member.

Members of the group who lived in the suburb where Crossroads Assembly is located had begun attending services at the congregation. The young energetic pastor who served the congregation had cultivated an upbeat, casual style of worship, that corresponded to the women's prayer group ethos. The congregation, then only 75 members, was beginning to establish programs to meet the needs of the area's growing suburban population. Several leaders from the Bible study group approached the pastor about continuing their meetings under the auspices of the congregation. The pastor heartily welcomed the group members, and the women joined the classical Pentecostal congregation *en masse*. Several members of the prayer group, however, left to attend a Word church that followed Copeland's theology.

The Crossroads' congregation, unlike their pastor, was not entirely enthusiastic about incorporating this group of unattached women with a hodgepodge of religious backgrounds. Commented Helen, a founding member of the prayer group, "We were kind of an odd group by their estimation I suppose. There weren't very many other women in the church who worked, and some of us were divorced. They were a bit stand-offish at first, but we were determined to make it our home and so we kept working at it." Their feeling of mild ostracism within the church further promoted close friendships among the women who developed prayer chains, i.e., pyramid lists of women to call when a member had a personal crisis or a prayer need. Although today only four of the original members of the prayer group remain, the character of the group has, in their estimation, changed very little. According to Helen, "We've kept it from being a little clique of us, but we have kept it our thing."

As adult converts to classical Pentecostalism are relatively rare, despite considerable evangelistic activity by Pentecostals, these women offered a particularly interesting case study of some women's attraction to fundamentalism.[4] In 1991 I conducted ten months of intensive field research at Crossroads Assembly. Though not a member of this congregation, I was acquainted with their ritual practices, theology, and denominational affiliation as a result of my childhood experiences in classical Pentecostalism. My entry into the group was facilitated by the sponsorship of a group leader who helped me to secure permission for my research from the pastor. During 1991, I conducted multi-

95

ple interviews with 15 adult female converts, several lifelong Pentecostal women who were group members, as well as interviewing key leaders in the congregation, including the senior minister and his wife and members of the pastoral staff and church board, and observing and participating in the full range of religious activities, including the women's Bible study and prayer meeting, coffee hours, prayer chains, regular Sunday morning, Sunday evening and Wednesday evening worship services. I was well accepted by the women in the group, invited to their homes for meals, accepted as a baby-sitter, and (since I am by their standards a Yankee) instructed on Southern protocol. Following the research, I have continued a friendship with several women in the group and have made occasional return visits.

While the members of the women's prayer group are relatively unique in that they are late-life converts, they share demographic similarities with other congregants at Crossroads. The membership of Crossroads is primarily white, upper-middle-class, college educated, and employed in professional or semi-professional jobs. Most families are now dual-income, although many women end employment outside of the home when a child is born. The congregation is a demographic mix of young families, middle aged couples, and an increasing number of singles.

The membership is very theologically, politically, and socially conservative. The pastor supports the goals if not the methods of Randall Terry, national leader of Operation Rescue, an antiabortion activist group which conducts "rescues" or protests at abortion clinics; and among the church leaders are several Atlanta spokespersons for Pat Robertson's political action committee, Christian Coalition. There are no women either on the six-person pastoral staff, or on the congregation's leadership board. While Crossroads' denomination does not formally prohibit women's leadership, jokes made from the pulpit and the absence of women in positions of decision-making in the congregation make it clear that women are not accepted as officially recognized religious leaders.

The cultural orientation of the congregation and senior pastor is self-consciously Southern. Despite numerous Northern transplants in the congregation, the pastor regularly includes Yankee jokes in his sermons or in the bulletin, and calls upon camp-meeting and revival traditions to distinguish Crossroads Assembly from other churches in the area. While the content of sermons generally includes a call to be different than the world and to search God's "inerrant" Word for all the answers to modern life's problems, the congregation and pastoral staff seem quite at home with many aspects of modernity. All the pastoral staff carry beepers and maintain contact with the church office using car phones; the sanctuary is equipped with state-of-the-art audiovisual equipment, including an electronically controlled curtain that parts on cue to reveal the 70-person, robed choir. This classical Pentecostal congregation is a model of suburban fundamentalism.[5] While its rhetoric maintains a high-tension stance toward modernity's perceived moral relativism and decay, it also employs the technological and therapeutic strategies of modernity.

CLASSICAL PENTECOSTALISM AND FUNDAMENTALISM IN THE UNITED STATES

An analysis of the relationship between classical Pentecostalism and fundamentalism will help situate Crossroads Assembly and, in particular, the women's prayer group and Bible study within scholarly conceptions of fundamentalism. However, identifying the status of classical Pentecostalism within the nexus of ideas, beliefs, and practices identified by historians, sociologists, and anthropologists as fundamentalism is somewhat problematic. Of course, neither is it a simple task to identify what is meant by fundamentalism. This essay follows the analytical framework set out by Martin E. Marty and R. Scott Appleby (1993), as a part of the Fundamentalism Project. Marty and Appleby have identified fundamentalism, as it has appeared in the twentieth century, as "a tendency, a habit of mind." They write:

> [Fundamentalism] manifests itself as a strategy or set of strategies, by which be-leaguered believers attempt to preserve their distinctive identity as a group. Feeling this identity to be at risk in the contemporary era, these believers fortify it by a selective retrieval of doctrines, beliefs, and practices from a sacred past. These retrieved "fundamentals" are refined, modified, and sanctioned in a spirit of pragmatism: they are to serve as a bulwark against the encroachment of outsiders who threaten to draw the believers into a syncretistic, areligious or irreligious cultural milieu. Moreover, fundamentalists present the retrieved fundamentals alongside unprecedented claims and doctrinal innovations. These innovations and supporting doctrines lend the retrieved and updated fundamentals an urgency and charismatic intensity reminiscent of the religious experiences that originally forged communal identity (1993: 3).

Appleby and Marty identify "family resemblances" among varieties of fundamentalism, thus making possible, in their view, cross-cultural comparison.[6] Classical Pentecostalism can be understood as having many of the family traits of fundamentalism, while it also has its unique characteristics. The unique characteristics of classical Pentecostalism include the practice of speaking in tongues or employing prayer languages, and belief in miraculous healing.

While contemporary classical Pentecostalism can be understood as part of the fundamentalist "family," historically feuding rather than mutual tolerance has characterized their relationship. In the early twentieth century, disagreement arose between classical Pentecostals and fundamentalists over the fundamentalist teaching of dispensationalism, i.e., that God dealt with the human race in successive dispensations, or periods of time during which people are tested in respect to obedience to some specific revelation of the will of God. Dispensationalist fundamentalists held that gifts such as speaking in tongues

97

EIESLAND

and gifts of miraculous healing were characteristic of a former dispensation but had ceased to be God's and, therefore, the church's work in the present day. Pentecostals, on the other hand, saw in the renewal of speaking in tongues and miraculous healing a sign of the end of the age and the imminent rapture, or eschatological removal, of the church. The break between classical Pentecostals and fundamentalists became firm in 1919 when the World's Christian Fundamentals Association resolved:

> Whereas the present wave of Modern Pentecostalism, often referred to as the "tongues movement," and the present wave of fanatical and unscriptural healing which is sweeping over the country today, has become a menace in many churches and a real injury to sane testimony of Fundamental Christians,

> Be it resolved, that this convention go on record as unreservedly opposed to Modern Pentecostalism, including the speaking in unknown tongues, and the fanatical healing known as general healing in the atonement, and the perpetuation of the miraculous sign-healing of Jesus and His apostles, wherein they claim the only reason the church cannot perform these miracles is because of unbelief (quoted in Synan 1988: 326).

Despite the internecine controversy with some fundamentalist groups, many classical Pentecostal denominations participated in the fundamentalist-inspired drive to identify religious "fundamentals." For example, almost all classical Pentecostal denominations, including the historic white Pentecostal denominations, such as the Assemblies of God, Church of God (Cleveland), and the historic black Pentecostal denominations, such as the Church of God in Christ, teach that the Bible is the inspired word of God and its content is infallible divine revelation. This approach to biblical interpretation has lead many Pentecostal denominations, as well as most fundamentalist groups, to discourage or prohibit the ordained ministry of women.[7] Thus though classical Pentecostals maintain distinctive beliefs, especially about speaking in tongues and miraculous healing, they nonetheless bear more than passing resemblance to other fundamentalist Protestant groups in the United States. Furthermore, many classical Pentecostal groups and individuals self-identify as fundamentalists. In fact, many of the women in this study identified as fundamentalists as often as they classified themselves as Pentecostals; when asked about what they intended by the fundamentalist label, most related their sympathy with pro-family, antiabortion stances of fundamentalist figures, such as Pat Robertson and Jerry Falwell. They also agreed with Robertson and Falwell that America was falling prey to moral decay, as exhibited, in part, by the increase in crime and open homosexuality.[8] They further noted that reversal of American moral decline is possible only if the entire nation turned to God.[9]

Finally, in order to understand the sociocultural milieu of classical Pentecostalism, one must also bear in mind the wide-ranging influence of the

Charismatic movement beginning in the 1960s that resulted in the diffusion of Pentecostal religious experience and beliefs, especially speaking in tongues and belief in miraculous healing, in numerous Protestant denominations and the Roman Catholic Church in the United States.[10] In addition to dispersing Pentecostal practices and tenets within non-Pentecostal denominations, the Charismatic movement also had a notable impact on classical Pentecostal denominations. Historically associated with impoverished populations, in rural and inner-city areas, ecstatic speaking in tongues and belief in miraculous healing was often interpreted by scholars and the general public to be a sign of physical or psychic deprivation (Pope 1973; Anderson 1979; Wacker 1988). Yet the acceptance by a largely middle-class, well-educated population of expressive worship styles, beliefs in miraculous healing, and speaking in tongues necessitated rethinking about scholarly and popular conceptions of Pentecostals, as well as the evangelistic strategies and ministries of many classical Pentecostal denominations.[11]

During the 1970s and 1980s, many of these denominations engaged in church planting projects in suburbs in an attempt to appeal to disaffected mainline Christians. As these classical Pentecostal denominations attracted a better educated and wealthier population, their public and self images changed. Modifying the traditional folksy style and toning down the hellfire-and-brimstone messages, many classical Pentecostals established a relaxed, leisurely, and informal style of worship and replaced indictments against sinners with more therapeutic messages emphasizing the emotional and spiritual bondage that prevents people from living fulfilled lives, reconciled to God. For many classical Pentecostal congregations, these changes in worship style and theology have resulted in phenomenal success in affluent suburbs (Thumma 1993; Vaughn 1993).

Whatever its setting—rural, inner-city, or suburban—Pentecostalism has had a unique appeal to women. Yet historically women have been prevented from public recognition of their religious leadership by male classical Pentecostal leaders; the religious experience of women in classical Pentecostalism has been undertreated in scholarly interpretations; and even in feminist analyses of women in fundamentalism these women's experience has been sometimes dismissed as false consciousness. Pentecostal women have been triply marginalized. In relation to their own religious traditions, classical Pentecostal women are often either formally or informally excluded from leadership. Despite the fact that women were instrumental in the founding and subsequent growth of early Pentecostal denominations, black as well as white, most of these groups began exhibiting marked declining percentages of professional women ministers within two decades of their inception (Blumhofer 1987/1988: 17). Even lay leadership options for Pentecostal women have historically been and are presently primarily sex-segregated (Gilkes 1985). Fundamentalist theological interpretations that disallow women exercising au-

99

EIESLAND

thority over men and married women assuming responsibilities outside the home thrive within Pentecostal ranks.

Secondly, Pentecostal women have been marginalized by social theories about classical Pentecostalism. These theories too frequently treat the experience of men as representative of the whole. For example, Robert Mapes Anderson's classic and widely influential deprivation and social stratification theory (1979), virtually ignored the status and place of women in early Pentecostalism (except for those early female founders and evangelists), despite the fact that women have consistently been significantly overrepresented in American Pentecostalism. Elaine Lawless (1988a; 1988b) notes that discussion of women's experience has until very recently been absent from most theoretical approaches to Pentecostalism. She studies the experience of women leaders and lay women in classical Pentecostal congregations in rural settings, maintaining that Pentecostalism provides a setting for women to develop "a forum for a traditional expressive verbal art within the Pentecostal religious service"(1988b: 109). Here women speak out, voicing their experience, thoughts, and beliefs in the authoritative voice of God for all to hear and consider. Yet, as Lawless also notes, the constraints on their expressions are considerable, including the efforts by male Pentecostal leaders to maintain exclusive authority to speak for God. Although Lawless's research is tremendously valuable for our understanding of women's experience within Pentecostalism, it also highlights the significant shortage of research related to non-rural, nonimpoverished classical Pentecostal women.

Lawless's research further reveals the inherent silencing of Pentecostal women that occurs in social theory when "official" religion, as revealed in the pronouncements of ministers and denominational documents, is taken as authoritative for the entire membership. Since women are under-represented in denominational power structures and in ministerial positions, social theory that relies inordinately on such sources de facto excludes women. Though these official structures and beliefs do have considerable influence over women's capacity to act and to construct meaningful religious narratives within classical Pentecostalism, they do not, as Lawless demonstrates, represent the multifaceted experience of women within these congregations and denominations (cf. Riesebrodt 1993).

Finally, Pentecostal women have too frequently been marginalized by feminist social theorists. To account for women's participation in the patriarchal settings of Pentecostalism, some feminists have relied on arguments that emphasize "false consciousness," or a powerlessness to change their contexts.[12] Others have lumped all fundamentalist, evangelical, and Pentecostal women together labeling them "antifeminist" or women of the "New Christian Right" (See Dworkin 1983; Faludi 1991). Further, the tension between advocacy for women's institutional empowerment and respect for women's actual experience can be seen in feminist analyses of conservative religious or fundamentalist women. Debra Kaufman (1991), in her study of returnees to Orthodox Judaism, identifies the tendency of some feminist scholars to generalize about the experience of conservative religious women and notes that theoretical categories cannot distinguish between an 'authentic' and an 'alienated' women's experience. Judith Stacey (1990) also maintains that we must avoid an analytical framework that reduces whole categories of women to 'robots,' 'fools,' or 'victims.'

As both Kaufman and Stacey indicate, a more adequate feminist approach to the study of conservative religious women identifies the importance of understanding the sociocultural matrix within which expressive practices and rituals occur, reconstructing with as much detail as possible both the constraints and freedoms of their experience. It involves attending to the complexity of women's lives even within religious groups that purport to give straightforward, uncomplicated answers. Finally, it necessitates the careful study—from women's point of view—of women's religious communities within fundamentalist movements. As we have come to see, fundamentalism is far from a "one-size-fits-all" phenomenon. Its attractions for women, its stance toward women, and its "women's spaces" vary dramatically. For the female adult converts of this study, Crossroads Assembly and the women's prayer group felt like "home." My efforts as a feminist social researcher were not directed toward identifying why they were misguided in that assessment, rather my task was to identify their sociocultural milieu and the experiences within that "home," exploring the reasons for and processes of their religious home-making within this fundamentalist Bible study.

101

TELLING STORIES AND MAKING SENSE

The homey quality of the women's prayer group at Crossroads Assembly was due in part to the emphasis these women, and the church at large, place on talking to one another about the intimate details of their lives and connecting those private matters with God's actions on their behalf. A ritual, known in the congregation as "telling what the Lord has done," encourages congregants to construct and share stories about the presence of God in their lives. The practice is a taken-for-granted component of nearly all interactions in the congregation. In formal settings, opportunities to share testimonies are built into the order of the service.

A common greeting among congregants, including the adult converts, is "What is God doing in you today?" The greeting is to be followed by personal sharing. The pastor regularly rails against the impersonal, "worldly" practice of asking people "How are you?" and then walking away. The practice demonstrates, he contends, that people in the world do not want anyone to know how they are because to tell someone honestly how you are doing requires that you become somewhat vulnerable. The pastor cajoles, "If you are going to say 'How are you?' and walk away, you might as well come up to someone and say, 'Keep your distance.'" Congregants of Crossroads Assembly are expected to stop everything and listen when they make such queries. They evidence Christ's work in their lives when they attend to the personal and spiritual stories of fellow congregants and nonbelievers. Further, this emphasis on personal sharing promotes a heightened vigilance among congregants as they watch for seeming mundane evidence of what the Lord is doing in their lives. They may find in the unexpected phone call or unanticipated check in the mail the attentiveness of God and the responsibility to tell what the Lord has done.

For the adult female converts, "telling what the Lord has done" has an additional meaning. For them, it also entails composing a life narrative. For many of the women in the prayer group, the "strange roads" of their lives have engendered incompatibilities and incongruous occurrences. Joyce, whose participation in the group began after she retired from education administration four years ago, explained, "There was just never a place where you could tell everything that had happened to you without someone's jaw dropping to the floor. I had about three different stories I told people depending on the situation. But I always felt a little crazy because I didn't tell anybody the whole story—including my ex." Joyce's story of divorce, job changes, and bankruptcy; of having her home robbed, winning a trip to San Francisco, and finding God in her 50s may not be so different from the tangled personal narratives of many individuals in her generation (Roof 1993). Yet Joyce experienced her life as without a meaningful coherent story until she constructed a narrative through her participation in the Crossroads prayer group. Telling what the Lord has done meant that Joyce ritually constructed a narrative that identified the Lord's hand throughout her life.

Eileen, a divorced real estate agent, spoke of the process of telling what the Lord had done as realizing "for the first time in a long time" that "God was making sense of things even when I couldn't do it." Eileen's spiritual journey had taken her from a rural Baptist background, to the Episcopal Church with her husband, to a ten year absence from the church, to faithful listening to Kenneth Copeland's "health and wealth" doctrine, and finally to Crossroads. In many ways, she considers her participation in the women's prayer group has brought her journey full circle. Although there is a considerable amount of nostalgia in her desire for the theological teachings of her childhood, so too is there a good deal of pragmatic religious guidance in helping her cope with the current challenge of growing older as a single woman in the South.

For both Eileen and Joyce, as well as many other women in the prayer group, finding the invisible hand of God in their lives has prompted them to construct meta-narratives that help them make sense of their public and private pains and joys. Telling what the Lord has done then becomes a practice of crafting a stylized, yet experientially "true" chronology that integrates the past, present, and future in relation to their experience of conversion. Orienting their lives from the point of conversion, rather than from a birth of a child, date of divorce or beginning of a new job, these women recast their lives as directed by God and permeated with the sacred.

Furthermore, these women's strategies to face their challenges are shaped in part by stories of other women. The stories are told as an "oral tradition" of the group to be recalled in appropriate situations. For many of the women in the Crossroads prayer group, their emotional and physical distance from their families of origin, as well as the lack of a community of women in their workplaces has meant that they have not participated in oral tradition passed from one woman to another in the daily events of tending to life. Confronted with new life experiences of late middle age they have a scant store of stories to help construct strategies of response. The "oral tradition" of the women at Crossroads is an often welcome source of practical advice and spiritual companionship. For example, when Leila returned to the group after her husband's death, there was a ritual "telling what the Lord had done" for past and present members who experienced the death of a spouse or child. Included in the stories were several testimonies of miraculous "inner healing" from grief and depression. In addition to the spiritual guidance that such stories provided, they also imparted practical wisdom, such as "change your breakfast food." Said Bonnie, who had lost her husband six years earlier, "We ate Raisin Bran for breakfast for as long as I can remember. So every morning when I got that box out, I started feeling down. Pretty soon, I decided that I was going to have to eat something else if I didn't want to start every day crying." For the adult women converts, this fundamentalist congregation created the opportunity and setting to compose and tell their life narratives and made available the practical and spiritual advice of a women-centered oral tradition. Through personal testimony and storytelling, the women's Bible study group at Crossroads created an all-women support group for what Raymond Studzinski has called "restorying" life so that the past is more fully understood and the future more fully realized (1985: 111).

The Crossroads Bible study group is also part of a larger socio-religious support group movement, chronicled by Robert Wuthnow (1994). According to his study 40 percent of American women are involved in a small group that meets regularly, provides caring and support for its members, and contributes to their spiritual development (55). These groups provide community in which common struggles are shared and collective visions for personal growth are bolstered. For the participants of the Crossroads Bible study, this group of like-minded women was an antidote to their familial, social, and work experiences.

WORKPLACE TOKENISM AND SEX-SEGREGATED WORSHIP

This all-women support and study group was particularly important to the majority of female adult converts at Crossroads who began their workforce participation before the feminist revolution and spent most of their working years in the company of men. Most experienced the workplace as a "man's world" to which they had been given day passes. Their personal interests, emotional concerns, and physical routines and preferences were often not expressed in the office, except in negative terms when a coworker overstepped the bounds of appropriate touch, or as was one woman's experience, when a colleague dismissed what she saw as justifiable anger at a professional slight as feminine raving. Alda recalls: "I felt real special because I was the only one [woman] that made it as top salesman. But the down side of being the only one was that you knew that there were more of them. Sometimes I felt that I was always making sure my butt was covered—excuse the language."

Rosabeth Kanter (1977) was among the first to study the situation of token women in the workplace. Using her fieldwork among women in an industrial sales force dominated numerically by men, Kanter developed a framework for understanding the social perceptions and dynamics of interactions that center on tokens. She identified that tokens tend to have greater performance pressures, which can detract from their feelings of enjoyment on the job. Further, tokens tend to be polarized within the group and either experience isolation within the workplace or become insiders by defining themselves as exceptions vis-à-vis other members of their social category. Finally, tokens can experience role entrapment, that is they may find it easier to accept stereotyped roles than to fight them. Although Kanter gave us some information on what happens to token women in the workplace, we still have little data on the effects of tokenism on other arenas of token women's lives. How have women who entered the workforce in the 1960s and 1970s coped with workplace tokenism?

As shown by my study, one way some women have coped is through sex-segregated religious involvement that reinforces traditional gender roles. These adult converts seem to have been drawn to classical Pentecostalism partially because of its sex-segregation and conservative gender roles. Said Jacque, "I love worshipping with just women in our prayer meetings. The voices are beautiful and when we pray together and they lay hands on you, you don't feel uncomfortable."[13] Although their evaluations of personal success in their careers varied among women in the prayer group, most said that they often did not feel completely at home in their work settings or among their colleagues. Though they enjoyed doing their jobs, many, as Kanter would predict, did not enjoy the circumstances in which they did their jobs. These newly Pentecostal women do, however, enjoy the familiar "women's space" at Crossroads. Here women run their own Bible studies and prayer luncheons, they have their own prayer chain, and they organize social activities for themselves.

Whether or not one characterizes these women's affirmation of traditional female roles and gender differences as "role entrapment," their experience as token women in the workplace has fostered a culture of brass-tacks femininity among the women. Their strategies for creating niches for themselves in their male-dominated workplace included adopting familiar feminine styles and roles, such as mother, kid sister, or sweetheart. These women were successful at manipulating these roles (and the men for whom they worked) in order to accomplish what they felt needed to be done. Thus on the one hand, classical Pentecostalism mirrors their workplace experience where the repertoire of female roles was severely limited. On the other hand, classical Pentecostalism's de facto sex-segregation, instead of replicating their experience in a male-defined workplace and the isolation of tokenism, nurtures the creation of women's spaces and female-centered support systems.

For group members, such connections with other women, are not taken for granted and provide an important link to a female culture. The group has grown for the most part through word of mouth, as the adult converts invite other women to join the support group. Alise, a 53 year-old former bank manager, describes her introduction to the group. She began each day with a prayer that "helped me face another day." "Of course, I would have just as soon die as let someone else know about it." But one day during a coffee break, for no apparent reason she related her ritual to a female teller. Immediately the teller invited Alise to attend a women's prayer luncheon that was held at the church. Alise, who was initially extremely embarrassed by the uncharacteristic self-revelation, credits that shared religious experience with her employee as "having made my office a little less lonely." Now despite the teller's disaffiliation with the church, Alise continues to be involved in the prayer meetings, and now is the weekend prayer chain coordinator.

The women's prayer group at Crossroads values and allows expression of some personal styles and practices, such as emotional expressivism and intuition, that are often suppressed or devalued in the rational, impersonal work world. Meredith McGuire (1982) in her study of Catholic Charismatics notes that charismatic and Pentecostal movements, in particular, counter two specific aspects of modernity as identified by Max Weber, i.e., the structure of institutions of the public sphere and the cognitive style of "functional rationality." A byproduct of the growth of large, seemingly immutable institutions is a sense of powerlessness to change the public sphere and the concomitant privatization of identity and religiosity. Among these classical Pentecostal women, the added strain of workplace tokenism seems to have contributed to a pervasive sense of isolation and persistent powerlessness in the public sphere and to an overriding concern with personal endurance and survival. Yet the women's prayer group at Crossroads has given them a tangible sense of their own capacity to promote change in a circumscribed public sphere—often separate from the world of work.

Many of the women in the church are actively involved in international mission work. Each year Alda makes at least one mission trip, usually to South or Central America, which is organized by the women of the church. "I feel like I am really making people's lives better. I see the power of this message to change the world." In contrast to their experience of frustration and constrained effectiveness and power in the workplace, they see themselves as powerful members of a life- and world-changing Pentecostal movement.

The other aspect of modernity that Pentecostal and Charismatic practice counters, according to McGuire, is functional rationality as a bureaucratic principle and cognitive style. In contrast to this dominant mode, Pentecostalism offers these women nonrational ways of knowing, which add to but do not replace workplace rationality. Several prayer group members report surreptitious prayer in tongues while at work. Bonnie, who returned as a stock broker after her husband's death, shares: "Sometimes I go into the ladies room and tune in to God. Sometimes I pray in my prayer language, and after I'm done I feel like I know what I should do about whatever I was worried over. I feel sorry for the brokers who don't have the gift." For several of these newly converted women, praying in tongues does not make them feel out-of-step with the work world, rather it provides them with a secret weapon in a setting that they experience as potentially or actually hostile. In the prayer group, women also pray for power and courage not only to tell what the Lord is doing in their lives, but also to oppose the unchristian actions of their colleagues, family members, and friends. Their requests for behavior or attitudinal changes among these individuals stem not solely from the personal desires and conveniences of the women, but also from the potent legitimation of God's plan for right personal relations and order.

Furthermore, these women's experiences in Pentecostalism contrast with the physical isolation promoted within the workplace. In addition to keeping one another on their rapid dial listing, many of the women make routine tasks an opportunity to spend time building each other up in the faith. Alda calls on other members of the prayer group when she cannot stand to be alone with the twins any longer. Eileen and Jacque regularly do their grocery shopping together, since Jacque's bad back makes carrying grocery bags difficult. Also the services of the women's prayer group, in particular, ritualize physical engagement. Prayer is an activity done while touching the one for whom you offer prayers, if possible. Group members regularly gather around individuals who are ill or emotionally down to lay hands on them, murmuring prayers in prayer languages and in English. Likewise during worship time, hand-holding is encouraged and generally practiced.

Through the women-centered prayer group, these converts are able to connect with other women. They perceive the women's group as genuine and unmediated, in comparison to their experience in the world of work in which they "put on masks" and communicated via technological means. It encourages supportive female bonds in contrast to their work experience of tokenism. It provides social situations in which they can express themselves in emotional and spiritual as well as rational terms. It sanctions appropriate physical touching and caressing as an integral part of the prayer and worship experience.

THE BROKEN HOME AND THE HOUSE OF GOD

Another commonality in these women's experiences is disruption in kinship systems. The women's prayer group at Crossroads Assembly provides strategies for constructing family units, support networks in times of family crisis, and, in some cases a de facto kinship network of close emotional relationship sustained through prayer chain and women's Bible studies. In her study of charismatic evangelical women in the Silicon Valley, Judith Stacey (1990) maintained that Pentecostalism can provide women with plausible religious strategies for the construction of stable family units, although not necessarily traditional families. Though these family units may be patriarchal in the last instance,[14] they may also incorporate many of the "feminized" affective attributes fostered by Pentecostal spirituality and teaching.

Although patriarchal families were not uncommon among the women in my study, neither were they the norm. A slight majority was single and had been divorced or widowed within the past eight years. The women in the prayer group seem particularly responsive in dealing with the stresses involved in such disruptions. The women's prayer chain not only facilitated spiritual solidarity, it also enabled quick mobilization of more tangible resources. For example, while Lucy, a single mother in her late-40s, was adjusting to her "boomerang" son, who had returned home after living independently for a half decade, members from the prayer group were regularly checking-in with her, offering prayer and moral support. Additionally several members of the prayer group combined households, including children, after the divorce of one woman. While the co-living experiment ended badly, both mothers involved noted that they received extensive support from other women in the group. Though a public rhetoric of "family values" is propounded by the congregation's pastoral staff, who fulfill the norm of the "traditional" family, and is generally accepted by women within the prayer group, the life experiences of these adult converts conform more closely to "postmodern" families, inclusive of step-children, grandchildren, second or third husbands, and other "loved ones."

For many of the adult converts, their involvement in the prayer group began or increased during or following kinship transitions, e.g., retirement, death of a spouse, or children leaving (or returning) home. This finding is similar to that reported by Lynn Davidman in her study among women returnees to orthodox Judaism. Davidman highlighted the role of conversion during "a transitional phase of adulthood" when young women are seeking to create and establish families (1991: 74). Although the women at Crossroads are much older, aged 40–60, they, too, are in a transitional phase of adult-

107

hood—one with even fewer cultural guideposts than early adulthood. With retirement from work and the absence of children and sometimes spouses, these women have an increased opportunity for self-evaluation and integration peculiar to older adulthood. For example, Sue, a retired science teacher, says, "When I turned 50 I knew my life was changing in just about every direction. I probably realized that I was no longer as young as I used to be." Said Kay, "It just seemed like the right time. I guess I had been running from the Spirit for a long time, but I always had to think of everybody else. Now the kids are grown and [her husband] is gone, and it's just me and God."

One finding that relates both to kinship system disruption and to aging is the consistency of reports of loneliness as a motivating factor for church involvement. The women's Bible studies and prayer meetings are particularly targeted to address that emotional need. In 1991 a divorced woman led a seven-week course entitled "Letting the Spirit Come In" that centered around inner healing for divorced and widowed women. Although the Bible study was well attended, and many women testified to the "spiritual healing" they had experienced, the senior minister of the church strongly disapproved of offering it again. He objected to a divorced woman leading the study, because it "sent the wrong message." Though several women expressed frustration with constraints imposed by their minister, the majority maintained that direct confrontation was not warranted. Instead one leader, over a year, convinced the pastor to permit the divorced woman to "co-teach" the seminar with a widowed woman, as long as the widowed woman's name was given first on the list of speakers. Thus while some groups, especially the women's prayer meetings, within Crossroads Assembly support alternative familial groups and provide systems of belonging for divorced individuals, this level of acceptance is not shared by the leadership staff.

SUBURBAN LIVING AND SOUTHERN HOMECOMING

The reserve regarding divorce and women's leadership is attributed by several women to the congregation's Southern conservative character. Although the well-to-do suburbs surrounding Crossroads are a far cry from the rural South once seen as especially fertile ground for classical Pentecostalism, these established subdivisions have proven to be fruitful terrain for a new generation of Pentecostals for a variety of reasons. In part, classical Pentecostalism provides a potent ally with conservative politics that thrive in Atlanta's suburbs. Additionally, classical Pentecostal and fundamentalist groups are well situated to foster close personal relations within emotionally responsive groups and to promote a degree of social embeddedness in the traditional religious rituals and beliefs of the South among mobile suburbanites craving tradition and community.[15]

Nancy Ammerman (1990), in her study of fundamentalists within the Southern Baptist Convention, found that fundamentalist beliefs were particularly salient among people who were transplants from rural to urban areas. These migration patterns between rural and urban areas were a significant factor in how likely an individual was to identify as fundamentalist. Her findings spotlight two groups that are likely to identify with fundamentalism. Ammerman writes, "among the people most disrupted by urbanization—those who moved from farm to city and those who fled big cities for smaller places—fundamentalism had its greatest appeal. If fundamentalism can be defined as a movement in organizing opposition to the disruption of previously accepted orthodoxy, then we would expect to find it thriving in just such areas" (148–149).

If we follow Ammerman's proposal that fundamentalism is likely to thrive where a once robust orthodoxy has been disrupted, we should not be at all surprised to find in these cul-de-sacs numerous new adherents to classical Pentecostalism. The suburbs, long reputed to be domains of modern conformism and homogeneity, are increasingly sites of fundamentalist innovation and religiously-based community building.[16] Though the newly converted women of Crossroads Assembly had resided in the suburbs for sometime, they, nonetheless, had a potent sense of dislocation and a palpable recollection of a past that was more coherent, stable, and secure. This past was not, however, generally their own experience—rather a received tradition of the troubled, yet connected extended kin and religious piety, usually carried on by significant matriarchs. During my interviews, individual women would speak with great feeling and expressiveness of their familial history, sometimes tracing it back to Civil War veterans. They would tell of early religious experiences in Southern congregations—none of which were classical Pentecostal, although several had attended Pentecostal meetings occasionally. These experiences of family and religion were partially constitutive of their experience as Southern women. To be Southern without extended family or religion was almost an oxymoron.

For the female adult converts at Crossroads, conversion to classical Pentecostalism was a homecoming of sorts, a retrieval of a religious and familial tradition associated not with their current suburban environs but with a rural or small town past that while it had never existed for them still had power as a cultural icon of Southernness. The women's prayer group and other meetings at Crossroads provided an incentive to engage in family-building around Southern traditions and beliefs. Here, too, age is a factor. As one convert stated: "It's impossible for a Southern woman to die without a Bible in her hand and her family at her side."

CONCLUSION

Clearly the women's prayer group is constrained by the male-dominated leadership of Crossroads Assembly who regulated the speakers in the prayer group and who kept a wary eye on the group's leaders for signs of heterodoxy. Yet as the workforce experience of many of these converts makes clear such constraint is not unique to fundamentalist religion. For these, as for many women, religious participation is not simply a matter of making the most egalitarian choice from a range of religious options. For them, conversion was a matter of God drawing them toward Himself until they had the capacity and willingness to respond. The "strange roads" that some of the women in the prayer group traveled had made them feel as though they were off God's map. But, in fact, they found that God could direct them home. As with most homes, this one is both inviting and from some perspectives fraught with dangers.

Although these women's attractions to fundamentalism can be traced, in part, to the unique sociocultural experiences of the familial disruptions, social mobility, and female workforce participation of late modernity, this attraction can also be related to accounts of women's spaces and stories, physical engagement, and Southern gender identity. Their experiences within the women's prayer group and other activities and rituals at Crossroads provide them with powerful meaning-making and ordering ideologies and narrative practices. Their experiences recall a more familiar, less chaotic past with which they can symbolically and ritually affiliate through fundamentalist practice. Yet they can also experience substantial support in coping more effectively with the modern challenges of everyday life as aging women in the South. They find at Crossroads an individually and communally relevant blend of Southern religious traditionalism and therapeutic personalism. Their experiences of conversion provide them with a new sacred center from which to reorient their lives and in relation to which they can compose a life narrative. Their paths do not reveal any particular calamity culture, in relation to which fundamentalism was uniquely attractive.[17] Rather their accounts suggest that "strange roads" may be the only routes open to us in late modernity.

NOTES

1. Crossroads Assembly is a pseudonym for a classical Pentecostal congregation in suburban Atlanta. Pseudonyms are also employed for the classical Pentecostal converts in this essay.

2. Prayer language is a term for glossolalia, i.e., the religious phenomenon of making sounds that constitute, or resemble, a language not known to the speaker. It is generally accompanied by an altered, either excited or meditative, psychological state, and in classical Pentecostal and Charismatic movements it is widely and distinctively viewed as the certifying evidence of the baptism of the Holy Spirit. The term prayer language has been popularized by Pentecostal and Charismatic televangelists and talk-show hosts.

3. According to Reed, "family loyalty" is the leading stereotypical trait held about Southerners by fellow Southerners (1993:73). Reed also notes that regional Southern norms, especially for women, accentuate familism

4. According to a study by Smidt, et al. (1994), the total percentage of Americans who belong to classical Pentecostal denominations is approximately 3.6 percent of the adult population. Two-thirds of these individuals belong to historically "white" Pentecostal denominations (9). Wagner (1988) estimates that approximately one-third of the additions made to the Pentecostal/Charismatic movement worldwide is purely demographic, e.g., births minus deaths; the remaining two-thirds are converts, according to his figures. In 1988, the growth in the number of classical Pentecostal adherents was approximately 5 percent annually. In recent years, however, the growth rate for several large classical Pentecostal denominations, e.g., the Assemblies of God and the Church of God, has declined.

5. For a discussion of fundamentalism's "fit" with American culture, see Marsden (1980; 1983).

6. Marty and Appleby identify the significant difficulties in making such cross-cultural comparisons. They write: "However diverse the expressions are, they present themselves as movements which demand comparison even as they deserve fair separate treatment so that their special integrities will appear in bold relief" (1991:vii).

7. Although women had been previously granted ordination in many fundamentalist and classical Pentecostal denominations, applications of biblical passages that restricted women's speech in religious gatherings and prohibited women from holding positions of authority over men became deeply entrenched in Pentecostal and fundamentalist circles, in part, as a result of reaction to modernist threat (Riss 1988). Furthermore, the Scofield Reference Bible provided legitimation for curtailing women's leadership roles within classical Pentecostal and fundamentalist congregations and denominations (Scanzone and Setta 1986:233).

8. Balmer sees in fundamentalist political action "a desperate attempt to reclaim the nineteenth-century ideal of femininity both for themselves and for a culture that has abandoned that idea" (1994:59). While this view may highlight the role of fundamentalist rhetoric within and among national and international special purpose groups, it fails to account for the multiple factors prompting of women's involvement in local fundamentalist groups, such as Crossroads Assembly.

9. Riesebrodt (1993) contends that fundamentalism is mobilization in defense not only of doctrine, but of a socio-moral milieu's ability to reproduce itself by educating its children and controlling other means for cultural and social reproduction. As such Riesebrodt characterizes fundamentalism, in particular in Iran and the United States, as a radical traditionalist movement which may have much in common with ethnically-based nationalist movements. Though I agree with Riesebrodt's general conceptual framework, his analysis over-emphasizes the elites' use of fundamentalism's ideological and political decision-making and rhetorical power and fails to account adequate-

ly for women's multiple uses of fundamentalist practice and community (cf. Kaufman 1991).

10. In addition to the Charismatic movement in mainline Protestant denominations and in the Roman Catholic Church, Pentecostal practices and beliefs have been propagated by what Wagner has designated, the "third wave" movement, e.g., the presence of the Charismatic movement in evangelical Protestant denominations and with nondenominational churches (Duin 1986). Although this movement has also influenced the contemporary style, theology, and growth of classical Pentecostal denominations, it is beyond the scope of this work to detail that relationship.

11. Berger (1970) asserted that supernaturalism was "likely to be restricted to smaller groups, typically those from social locations (in 'backward' regions, say, or in the lower classes)" (21). But Neitz (1990:91) less than a decade later reported that she had "met lawyers and business executives . . . speaking in tongues and practicing faith healing" at a large Roman Catholic charismatic prayer group in an affluent Chicago suburb (see Neitz 1987). Pentecostalism was no longer restricted (if it ever was) solely to the down-and-out: Gallup (1988:5) estimated that nine percent of all Americans, including 8 percent of all U.S. college graduates, took part in a charismatic group in 1986-1988.

12. Rosaldo (1980) addresses a similar phenomenon in cross-cultural feminist analysis.

13. Laying on of hands is a ritual practice of physical touching, usually on the head or shoulders, that accompanies prayers for healing, impartation of the Holy Spirit, or commissioning for a spiritual task.

14. This is Judith Stacey's term for family relations among many conservative Christians. "Patriarchy in the last instance" identifies the norm of employing the biblical concept of submission of wife to husband as the last resort if resolution of conflicts through discussion cannot be achieved (1990:133–139).

15. Wuthnow (1994) convincingly demonstrates religious organizations and leaders use small groups as a speedy means to incorporate and establish community among an increasingly privatized and mobile population. See also Eiesland 1995.

16. Ammerman (1987) notes that the neighborhood in which the fundamentalist congregation in her study is located "could be a suburban neighborhood anywhere" (25–26). Stacey's (1990) study of new Charismatics also takes place in suburban Silicon Valley.

17. This contrasts with Stacey's contention that women in her study were caught in a culture of calamity, e.g., hard-living, victimized by tragic events whose "circumstances and the lives they lived made them accidents waiting to happen" (1990: 244–245). Davidman's study of two groups of *ba'alot teshu-*

vah, i.e., women who adopt Orthodox Judaism as adults, identifies one group in Minneapolis/St. Paul whose participants' life experiences conform to a "culture of calamity." The members of a second group in New York City, on the other hand, lead stable lives, but joined the Orthodox Synagogue in response to a stressful experience in their family or career (1991). Although the converts and members of Crossroads Assembly women's prayer meeting and Bible certainly had their share of difficult life circumstances, they were no more calamity prone than I. Nevertheless, like the adult returnees from New York City in Davidman's study, these women sought support and religious guidance during a time of familial and career disruption.

REFERENCES

Ammerman, N. 1987. *Bible Believers.* New Brunswick: Rutgers University Press.

———. 1990. *Baptist Battles.* New Brunswick: Rutgers University Press.

Anderson, R. M. 1979. *Vision of the Disinherited: The Making of American Pentecostalism.* New York: Oxford University Press.

Balmer, R. 1994. "American Fundamentalism: The Ideal of Femininity." In *Fundamentalisms and Gender.* ed. J. S. Hawley, pp. 47–62. New York: Oxford.

Berger, P. 1970. *A Rumor of Angels: Modern Society and the Rediscovery of the Supernatural.* Garden City, NY: Anchor.

Blumhofer, E. 1987/88. "The Role of Women in the Assemblies of God: A New Look at an Old Problem: Women's Rights in the Gospel." *Assemblies of God Heritage* (Winter):13–17.

Davidman, L. 1991. *Tradition in a Rootless World: Women Turn to Orthodox Judaism.* Berkeley: University of California Press.

Duin, J. 1986. "What Does the Future Hold for Charismatic Renewal?" *Christianity Today 20* (May 16): 38–44.

Dworkin, A. 1983. *Right-Wing Women.* New York: McCann.

Eiesland, N. 1995. *A Particular Place: Exurbanization and Religious Response in a Southern Town.* Ann Arbor, MI: UMI Dissertation Service.

Faludi, S. 1991 *Backlash: The Undeclared War Against American Women.* New York: Crown.

Gallup 1988. *The Unchurched American—Ten Years Later.* Princeton: Princeton Religious Research Center.

Gilkes, C. 1985. "Together in the Harness: Women's Traditions in the Sanctified Church." *Signs* 10:678–699.

Kanter, R. 1977. "Some Effects of Proportions on Group Life: Skewed Sex Ratios and Responses to Token Women." *American Journal of Sociology* 82(5):965–990.

Kaufman, D. 1991. *Rachel's Daughters.* New Brunswick: Rutgers University Press.

Lawless, E. 1988a. *Handmaidens of the Lord: Women Preachers and Traditional Religion.* Philadelphia: University of Pennsylvania Press and the American Folklore Society.

———. 1988b. *God's Peculiar People: Women's Voices and Folk Tradition in a Pentecostal Church.* Lexington: University Press of Kentucky.

Marsden, G.M. 1980. *Fundamentalism and American Culture: The Shaping of Twentieth Century Evangelicalism.* New York: Oxford University Press.

———. 1983. "Preachers of Paradox: The Religious New Right in Historical Perspective." In *Religion and America: Spiritual Life in a Secular Age*. eds. M. Douglas and S. Tipton, pp. 150–168. Boston: Beacon Press.

Marty, M. E. and R. S. Appleby. 1991. "The Fundamentalism Project: A User's Guide." In *Fundamentalisms Observed*. eds. M.E. Marty and R.S. Appleby, pp. vii–xiii. Chicago: University of Chicago Press.

———. 1993. "Introduction: A Sacred Cosmos, Scandalous Code, Defiant Society." In *Fundamentalisms in Society*. eds. M.E. Marty and R.S. Appleby, pp. 1–19. Chicago: University of Chicago Press.

McGuire, M. 1982. *Pentecostal Catholics: Power, Charisma, and Order in a Religious Movement*. Philadelphia: Temple University Press.

Neitz, M.J. 1990. "Studying Religion in the Eighties." In *Symbolic Interaction and Cultural Studies*. eds. H. Becker and M. McCall, pp. 90–118. Chicago: University of Chicago Press.

———. 1987. *Charisma and Community: A Study of Religious Commitment within the Charismatic Renewal*. New Brunswick, NJ: Transaction.

Pope, L. 1973. *Millhands and Preachers: A Study of Gastonia*. New Haven: Yale University Press.

Reed, J.S. 1993. *Surveying the South: Studies in Regional Sociology*. Columbia: University of Missouri Press.

Riesebrodt, M. 1993. *Pious Passion: The Emergence of Modern Fundamentalism in the United States and Iran*. Trans. by Don Reneau. Berkeley: University of California Press.

Riss, R. M. 1988. "Role of Women." In *Dictionary of Pentecostal and Charismatic Movements*. eds. S. M. Burgess and G. B. McGee, pp. 893–899. Grand Rapids: Zondervan Publishing House.

Roof, W. C. 1993. *A Generation of Seekers: The Spiritual Journeys of the Baby Boom Generation*. San Francisco: HarperSanFrancisco.

Rosaldo, M. Z. 1980. "The Use and Abuse of Anthropology: Reflections on Feminism and Cross-Culture Understanding." *Signs* 5:389–417.

Scanzone, L. D. and S. Setta. 1986. "Women in Evangelical, Holiness, and Pentecostal Traditions." In *Women and Religion in America 3*, eds. R. R. Reuther and R. S. Keller, pp. 223–265. San Francisco: Harper and Row.

Smidt, C. E., L. A. Kelstedt, J. C. Green, and J. L. Guth 1994. *The Spirit-filled Movements in Contemporary America: A Survey Perspective*. Unpublished paper delivered at the Conference on Mainstream Protestantism and Pentecostal and Charismatic Movements, Fuller Seminary, Pasadena, California.

Stacey, J. 1990. *Brave New Families: Stories of Domestic Upheaval in late Twentieth-Century America*. New York: Basic Books.

Studzinski, R. 1985. *Spiritual Direction and Midlife Development*. Chicago: Loyola University Press.

Synan, V. 1988. "Fundamentalism." In *Dictionary of Pentecostal and Charismatic Movements*. eds. S. M. Burgess and G. B. McGee, pp. 324–327. Grand Rapids: Zondervan Publishing House.

Thumma, S. 1993. *Sketching a Mega Trend: The Phenomenal Proliferation of Very Large Churches in the United States*. Unpublished paper, delivered at the Association for the Sociology of Religion, Miami Beach, Florida.

Vaughn, J. N. 1993. *Megachurches and American Cities: How Churches Grow.* Grand Rapids, MI: Baker Books.

Wacker, G. 1988. "Playing for Keeps: The Primitive Impulse in Early Pentecostalism." In *The American Quest for the Primitive Church.* ed. R. Hushes, pp. 196–219. Urbana: The University of Illinois Press.

Wagner, C. P. 1988. "Church Growth." In *Dictionary of Pentecostal and Charismatic Movement.* eds. S. M. Burgess and G. B. McGee, pp. 223–265. Grand Rapids: Zondervan Publishing House.

Wuthnow, R. 1994. *Sharing the Journey: Support Groups and America's New Quest for Community.* New York: Free Press.

IDEOLOGY AND IDENTITY
Islamism, Gender, and the State in Sudan

Sondra Hale

chapter 7

INTRODUCTION

THIS RESEARCH is partially based on fieldwork in Khartoum, Sudan in 1988,[1] and is an attempt to integrate my interest in Sudanese women's studies with a theoretical examination of the relationship of the state to issues of gender, religion, and class. This essay is one component of my interest in the mechanisms the state employs for achieving both political and cultural hegemony. I am using Marxist concepts of the state and its hegemonic character to suggest the manipulation of culture (in this case, religion).[2]

Feminist theory, which proceeds deductively from a premise of gender asymmetry, offers a possible explanation in the demographic needs of the state to effect a gender realignment in the area of labor. Making "gender" central (however, always in its relationship to class and culture), is often seen as "Western" when, in reality, gender as a category is not exclusively a concept of Western feminist thought. For example, in relation to this research, "gender" is a central category of *sharia* (Islamic law).

Methodologically, I have observed two contradictory or antagonistic processes in juxtaposition. There are two Sudanese women's movements, or more accurately, two segments of activism—one among the "secular" left of the Sudanese Women's Union and the other among the cultural nationalists (and Islamists)—the women of the National Islamic Front (NIF). In reality, with regard to men's positioning of women to serve the culture, the two perspectives are not that far apart. Both lay claims to elevating the position and status of women, the former by placing the "woman question" and the emancipation of women at the forefront of the political struggle; the latter by also placing women and the family at the center of the culture.

In asking how we could account for women's participation in "patriarchal" religious movements and raising the question of whether or not women's own culture can hoodwink them, Marxists often use the concept of "false consciousness." Feminists, however, trained to make *women* central to their analyses, look to the personal experiences of women and to the real conditions of their lives, in the process, validating women's perceptions of their own situation and conducting interviews in which the investigator is not abstracted away and in which the woman interviewed becomes the subject of her own story.

This is the overarching theoretical construct of the research, in which I have generated hypotheses to account for (1) the Sudanese state's manipulation of religious ideology; and (2) the centrality of gender in this process, including the gender division of labor and gender arrangements. This has involved examining the Sudanese state to determine which apparatuses are being manipulated and why, how, and which segments of the population are experiencing the impact. Because these processes are dynamic, reflecting the changing interests of international capital and the collaborating bourgeoisie, I specify that I am interested in the contemporary Sudanese state, especially as it has interacted with its subordinate population from 1971[3] to the present, with special consideration for the impact on women and gender arrangements.[4]

The state—any state—seeks to control labor resources to balance the above processes, e.g., through the control of population (numbers, distribution, composition) and the control of human resources such as labor power resources. Various ideologies can be generated, resuscitated, or rejuvenated to control these processes, one of which is religious ideology.

Both in the historical context and in contemporary Sudan, focusing on religion means focusing, as well, on politics and state apparatuses. I am, in fact, investigating the *secular* processes which are set in motion as a result of the expression by the state of religious ideology. The ambiguous Sudanese boundary between politics and religion is not new. Islam has always been political; and

Sudan has historically exhibited sectarian politics. But I am examining how and why it is different today, and how that is affecting women and the gender ideology. I am asking what new elements, contradictions, and countervailing processes have entered Sudanese society and given rise to this "New Islamic Trend?" From 1971 to the present, Sudanese states have found it instrumental to mobilize support from "Islamists." I was recently drawn to this project by processes in Sudan which Western writers commonly refer to as "the rise of Islamic fundamentalism," a dubious term, and one for which I have substituted "Islamism."[5]

One of the most active and seemingly successful Islamic movements in the world is taking place in Sudan, headed by the National Islamic Front (NIF), the political manifestation and successor of the *Ikhwan* (Muslim Brotherhood) and the de facto single-party undergirding Sudan's military regime that took over the state in 1989. This essay looks at the role of and impact on women in that organization.

BACKGROUND: THE STATE, GENDER, AND RELIGION IN SUDAN

Sudan is one of the poorest countries in the world, some would say, made poorer, among other ways, by the influx of large numbers of international corporations and agencies, intent on developing the capitalist export segment of the economy. In a chapter on uneven development and class formation in Sudan, O'Neill and O'Brien critique "dependency" perspectives of progressive analysts, maintaining that these approaches have not dealt with the competition between fractions of Sudanese capital and the patterns of accumulation that have resulted (O'Neill and O'Brien, 1988: 9).[6]

Sudan has a mainly agricultural economy with a sparsely developed urban population except for the capital, Greater Khartoum (consisting of Khartoum, Omdurman, and Khartoum North), which dominates national and cultural life. For much of the forty years that the country has been independent from British rule, which lasted from 1899-1956, the military has been in power. For many of those years the country has also been split by a civil war between the North and South (intermittently since 1955). In 1985 a civilian coalition overthrew the Nimieri military regime which had been in power since 1969, and one that veered sharply away from its origins as a leftist coup d'etat. That civilian government, dominated by the Ansar brotherhood (followers of the Mahdi), and Saddig al-Mahdi, head of the Umma Party, established an "Islamic Trend" government.[7] In June, 1989, a "National Salvation Revolution," in another military coup d'etat, ousted the civilians, and in essence installed an NIF government, with philosopher and *Ikhwan* leader, Dr. Hasan al-Turabi, as its de facto ideological head.

Many observers of Sudanese politics have been surprised that northern Sudanese are attempting to develop an Islamic Republic. Until 1983, Sudanese had been relatively relaxed about Islam, the dominant religion (approximately

119

HALE

70 percent), displaying wide tolerance for religious and ethnic diversity. Although for some time there had been pressures for *sharia* to become the dominant legal/ethical code for the entire country, before 1983, civil and customary codes had remained dominant.

Like many Arab and Muslim women, northern Sudanese women have confounded Western observers. Although wearing a body "veil" called a *tobe* and practicing genital surgeries, they were considered by many to be among the more "emancipated" women of the Muslim world.[8] Women had been very active in the nationalist movements for independence, but their gains were especially marked in the 1950s and 1960s, the golden years of the Sudanese Women's Union (a Communist Party affiliate), after 1965, when women earned suffrage, and in 1973, when the Permanent Constitution assigned women and men a number of civil rights and freedoms, as well as singling out women for specific gender-related protections.

However, in 1983, President Nimieri imposed and attempted to enforce strict *sharia* and set mechanisms in motion for developing an "Islamic State," as well as inviting Islamists into his government, namely Turabi, then leader of the *Ikhwan*. Between 1983 and 1989 there was an intensified struggle between secular forces and cultural nationalist religious forces, who see an "authentic" Islam as Sudan's only defense and salvation against an invading West and the only answer to Sudan's dismal economic situation. This is not an unfamiliar pattern in the Muslim world.

The relationship of the contemporary Sudanese state to the Islamists, from 1971 to the present, has been complex. Until Prime Minister Saddig formed the "Government of Consensus" in the summer of 1988, in which he invited the NIF into the official ranks of government, some political leaders had already been courting the *Ikwan* and the NIF, while pretending to disavow "fundamentalism," or, at least, to distance themselves.[9] The Islamists have also made accommodations, giving themselves a "modern" look. Even the word "trend" that was used by Saddig in the mid-1980s suggests something forward-looking, a process which is keeping abreast of contemporary behavior. Again, dialectically, the NIF's attempt to look "modern" or *be* modern has meant reference to institutions we would generally consider secular, although used in an "Islamic way," e.g., Islamic banking, Islamic insurance companies, appeal to potential constituencies through the media (e.g., missionary work on T.V. and televised weddings), and the like.

Both the processes of "secularization" prevalent in the nationalist and post-independence period and the current Islamism have been manifested through the ideology of the gender division of labor, especially in the family. Islamism, or the recent "Islamic Trend," is as much about Sudan's changing class structure as it is about religion. The Islamists, mainly of the new middle class, are walking a precarious line between a regime that obliquely seeks to meet the

HALE

needs of international capital with its ideology of liberalism, at the same time that it is militantly avoiding cultural imperialism. The cultural positioning of women by men is relevant to the Sudan situation, i.e., women seen as the embodiment of the culture and being expected to serve the culture/society through particular forms of labor. Therefore, women and the family unit are integral to the state's response to the continuing crisis of Sudan's economy. Looking at women's domestic and wage labor and political participation is revealing.

In the years just after independence the state's expression of gender ideology usually took the form that a "developing" Sudan needed emancipated women. At that time, with the expressed need to build up the urban work-force, the term "emancipated" was thought of as synonymous with wage-earner in the bourgeois liberal parlance, as well as in the Marxist and some of the nationalist vocabularies of postcolonial Sudan. Government media and other state apparatuses (e.g., civil service recruitment, school curriculum) urged the necessity for gender comradeship in developing Sudan. Media images presented the new Sudanese woman as sophisticated consumer or respectable civil servant (earlier as nurse or teacher and later sometimes as doctors). By the 1960s the state could point proudly to the first women doctors.

However, in the decades following we have seen the growth of capital-intensive economic schemes, the appearance of multinational corporations and agencies, uneven regional development, radical changes in labor migration, ethnic power realignments, and Western cultural imperialism, which have all helped to precipitate sociopolitical/economic crises and which have had, as we might expect, a profound impact on gender arrangements. Some of the people I interviewed contended that the further development in the 1970s of the "Islamic Trend"—or more accurately, the "repoliticization of Islam"—resulted in a significant postcolonial "crisis" for many women. Women interviewees, in particular, pointed to ideological expressions in Islam that often promote an atavistic image of them (e.g., reintegrating their duties in the family, etc.). Furthermore, the romanticizing of reproduction could potentially manipulate women out of the labor force or manipulate them into "appropriate" jobs. If these processes develop further, they could set in motion a major contradiction for women, taking hold in less than three decades after an exuberant independent Sudanese society urged women's "equal participation." Yet, that contradiction is tempered by the fact that the NIF also uses the claim of "equal participation" for women.

No essay can present a full picture of the dynamics that produced some of these contradictions without analyzing the class structure of Sudan, describing the precolonial economic roles of women, outlining Sudan's religious history, and documenting the history of women's participation in the formal and informal urban workforce. What follows is only a summary.

121

HALE

CLASS, GENDER, AND ISLAM

A number of sources have compared the class structure of Sudan in relation to women with Egypt's (e.g., Gran, 1977; Tucker, 1985). Early in the century attitudes in Sudan towards women's "emancipation" took two forms, each associated with a particular social class and with a particular nationalist ideology. On the one hand, liberal and moderate nationalists of the upper and upper middle classes viewed social reform along liberal, Western lines as prerequisites for independence. The "emancipation" of women (e.g., reform in marriage and family structure, equal access to education and jobs) was viewed as essential. On the other hand, more "radical" nationalists of the lower middle-classes were demanding an end to British rule, and as a part of that nationalist struggle, tended to romanticize "indigenous" values, that is, fostered cultural nationalism. These cultural nationalists generally opposed women's emancipation in the Western sense, arguing that it was an imitation of the West and that it would weaken the nation's basic Islamic unit, the family. They also romanticized women's role in the domestic sphere.

What Sudanese are now experiencing, however, is a class shift. That is, it is now the newly educated urban middle-class which is espousing cultural nationalism and attaching profound importance to the family and romanticizing women's primary role in the abrogation of Western culture. This class shift, moreover, has been developing for a long time; it has its roots in the nineteenth century. Jay Spaulding tells us, for example, that commercial capitalism began to replace feudalism in the Nile Valley about 1800, a process which was accelerated after the Turco-Egyptian conquest of 1821. Aristocracy gave way to a new middle class which, consisting mainly of merchants, needed a more sophisticated legal and commercial code. Islam was the obvious choice (Spaulding, 1985). This relationship between Islam and the middle class and Islam and capitalist activity is on the rise today. That is, Islam, as an ideology, is often a reflection of these commercial class interests. Islamic "fundamentalism," at least in the form of the Muslim Brotherhood of Sudan (and Egypt), and now including Sudan's NIF, mainly recruits from the urban professional middle class.[10] Although the Brotherhoods of both Egypt and Sudan are interested in the commercial aspect of Islam, it is with Sudan's NIF that we see a highly sophisticated rationalization and articulation of Islam and commerce—especially banking.

THE GENDER DIVISION OF LABOR AND THE LAW

In a way, we can observe a progression from a postindependence period in Sudan in which, in reality, secularist men and women began to be in competition (e.g., for jobs), to the current Islamic period in which Islamist men and non-Islamist women often have conflicts of interest. The areas where Islamist men and non-Islamist women seem to have a pronounced conflict of interest are law and labor, as *sharia* carefully spells out women's economic roles, and non-Islamist women are often in violation.[11] Yet, there also emerge some surprising contradictions.

Sudanese women's participation in the formal workforce increased at a regular, if somewhat slow pace during the years following independence. Partially this was a result of the government propaganda mentioned above, but mainly in recent years as a result of Sudan's depressed economy. Many women now *have to* work for wages outside the home. That necessity, although allowed for in *sharia*, is not acknowledged by the state.

In the 1970s liberalism in the urban areas encouraged a view of wage-earning women as important elements in the society, and legal and constitutional apparatuses seemed to support that idea. But material and social conditions changed more rapidly in the 1980s, drastically calling into operation another strand of beliefs governing Sudanese society. These conflicting processes may be seen in the legal system and in the Constitution in the areas of human rights, labor law, and *sharia*.

A great deal has been written about Sudan's plural legal system (customary, civil, and *sharia*), but it is not the goal of this paper either to describe or analyze this pluralism. Rather, the focus here is on the evolution of Islamic precedence as it relates to women, and more particularly, to women and labor.

After the British "reconquest" (1899), two sets of courts were established: *sharia* courts were secondary to secular courts. However, in the postindependence period we began to see a growing movement toward the Islamicization of the legal system. Eventually the transitional Constitution was amended and the *Sharia* Courts Act of 1967 passed, ending the subordination of *sharia* courts (Osman, 1985: 125).

Although the military coup d'etat of 1969 was then seen as socialist, we all realize now that the ultimately prevailing ingredient was the influence of Pan-Arabism, or cultural nationalism. Therefore, throughout Nimieri's "left" period there was a growing tendency toward Islamicization, in general, but especially in the legal system.

After 1971, the Nimieri regime began to move further to the right; and this is reflected in the legal system. For example, the Judicial Authority Act of 1972 merged secular (civil) and *sharia* courts. With the adoption of the Permanent Constitution in 1973, Islamic law and custom were mandated as the main sources of legislation by Article 9. In 1983 Nimieri announced that major changes would be made to force the legal system to conform to *sharia*. The Judicial Decisions Sources Act of 1983 mandated that the court shall decide in accordance with the Quran and Sunna or principles of *Ijihad*. The Evidence Act of 1983 applies conservative laws of evidence to women and non-Muslims (e.g., the testimony of women in major crimes is inadmissible; two women are required to offset the testimony of one man). A process had been set in motion, therefore, for an Islamicized Civil Code in 1984 (Osman, 1985:

123

HALE

126), a process some saw in contradiction to extant ideologies about the status of women and in conflict with the Constitution.

The Uprising (*intifada*) of April, 1985, which overthrew Nimieri's military regime, left much of the Islamicization process in midstream. It soon became apparent, however, that the Islamicization trend would continue: a Mahdist (Saddig al-Mahdi) was elected—the Mahdists representing the land-owning and commercial ruling class as well as a special Sudanese combination of Sufism and fundamentalism.[12] The politicization of Islam continues as it has throughout this entire century and much of the last.

What are some of the contradictions for women? On the one hand, they achieved the vote in 1965; later were given equal pay for equal work; and in 1975 the right to pensions. Public Service Regulations awarded women special benefits such as paid maternity leaves. In addition, the same Permanent Constitution of 1973 that raised the spectrum of a more Islamicized Sudan, provided equality for women in a number of areas: Part Three, which dealt with human rights and duties, made no gender distinction, i.e., did not exclude women. In fact, Article 38 provided that " . . . The Sudanese have equal rights and duties irrespective of origin, race, locality, *sex,* language or religion" (Osman, 1985: 126).[13] Article 56 was a workforce antidiscrimination clause covering gender. Women were given equal education rights, the right to hold public office, freedom of association and unionization, and freedom of speech and *movement.* Women and children were even accorded *special* protection by the State in Article 55 (Osman, 1985: 126).

On the other hand, there is little doubt that the rules of civil and criminal law, procedure and evidence, discriminated against women. As for the freedom of movement guaranteed in the Constitution, a 1987 Women's Committee (consisting of one man) was formed in the Department of Passports, Immigration and Nationality for the purpose of assuring that any woman who is travelling alone abroad has the permission of a male relative—her father, husband, son, etc.—before she is issued an exit visa.[14]

These were significant messages being given women in the 1980s, even before the Permanent Constitution was suspended in 1989 and an Islamic Constitution developed. The needs of the new, young, recently urbanized middle class and threats to its hegemony created a greater need for this class, which had been moving into power in the government, to operationalize certain aspects of Islamic ideology in the family and in everyday life (including work).

There is a socioeconomic process we are seeing in much of the Islamic world: a competition between emerging men of the mostly newly urbanized middle- and lower-middle class backgrounds and quasi-emancipated women who are, by contrast, from predominantly middle-class, traditionally urban backgrounds. This conflict has a great deal to do with changing processes in the world economy and two material processes on a more local level: the exercise of political power and consumerism.[15] The use of Islam by the State, to nurture and appease these followers (and at the same time manipulate them) "makes sense because Islam speaks about power and self-empowerment" or "worldly self-enhancement" (Mernissi, 1988: 9). Such worldly benefits are attractive to a group of societies which has reluctantly had to confront "the inescapability of renegotiating new sexual, political, economic, and cultural boundaries, thresholds and limits. [They have seen] Invasion of physical territory . . . invasion of national television by 'Dallas' . . . invasion . . . by Coca-Cola . . . "[etc.] (Mernissi, 1988: 9). Not the least of these invasions and boundaries violations, to Muslim men, is the tilt in gender arrangements, which is a challenge to what Mernissi refers to as "authority thresholds" (Mernissi, 1988: 10).

Women, if only theoretically, have access to jobs, education, benefits, and political participation, and in many areas they are taking advantage of their opportunities and options. Women are becoming public people, which to some is a threat to social order.

In examining some of the contradictions in Sudan, we see that in the 1970s the unemployment rate rose, and salaries did not keep up with inflation. One of the results was an enormous increase in male labor out-migration. At first, the gender arrangements did not tilt because that out-migration was of working class or minor civil service personnel. But soon it was intellectuals and middle to senior level personnel, the "brain drain," especially to the Gulf States. This served the government, on the one hand, as there was pressure from lending agencies to prune the overburdened civil service. But, on the other hand, women began to move into some of these better jobs, ones seen as the preserve of men, i.e., the better paying and more prestigious jobs.

In the mid-1980s there was an active debate in Sudan that is an example of the above dynamic and one which also serves to underscore the NIF ideology and strategy. Segments of the authorities and the public were asking whether or not there are too many women being allowed to study medicine, especially at the main national university. For some years women had consistently been outscoring men in the high school certificate exams, and were, therefore, channeled into the more prestigious faculties such as Medicine. Many women taking part in the debate pointed out this fact in rather chauvinistic terms, e.g., "Should women suffer for being smarter than men?"[16]

This debate was occurring at a time when over 80 percent of the new male medical graduates were going abroad for more lucrative positions.[17] Conservatives, supported by *Ikhwan* and NIF ideas, mainly took the position that women doctors are needed, but that they should be directed into *appropriate* fields of medicine. Fields deemed inappropriate for women are surgery and obstetrics, seen as too physically strenuous for women. Obstetrics is inappropriate for women with families or women in general, as they may be called away from their family duties at any time of the day or night. Women

HALE

had begun to invade these fields, which are, revealingly, the most lucrative in Sudanese medicine. As one woman in obstetrics remarked to me:

> They expect us to believe their logic about why these particular fields were singled out as inappropriate for women when we know the underlying question is who will have economic power! They must think we are fools![18]

All of the women doctors that I interviewed maintained that it is no accident that women with impeccable credentials are deprived of senior positions in certain areas of medicine. There is an attempt by the Ministry of Health to channel women into Mother and Child Clinics, into Public Health positions, and more significantly, into general medicine, fields that may be seen as extensions of domestic labor.[19]

Secular and/or non-Islamist women were very active in the debates: writing in the newspapers, making public speeches, and generally speaking out. Also, women members of the Sudanese Communist Party and the Sudanese Women's Union actively campaigned against these attitudes. However, from 1985—89, such talk seemed harmless, and very little action was taken on the part of oppositional women. Islamist women doctors and others in professional positions tried to allay the fears of non-Islamist women, presenting themselves as active and successful women who were not suffering any loses as a result of the formation of the Islamic state. Besides, the replacing of women in these lucrative positions was handled in small, nearly imperceptible increments and was intended to extend over a long period of time.

126

Such is the "modern" and careful approach of the NIF. Women should only work if they do not have children and only if their income is needed by the family. This means, of course, that working-class women need to work. Islam and *sharia* make allowances for them. But there are limits. The jobs women have should not threaten the power structure and should be "appropriate," that is, when possible, should be extensions of their domestic labor. The process would be carried out by women themselves, once they realize their rights and duties in Islam, i.e., once they have a raised consciousness about the correct role of women in Islamic societies.

In a study of Iranian women in the post-revolutionary workforce, Val Moghadam examined the effectiveness of the initial state rhetoric discouraging women's employment and imposing an ideology of domesticity. She found that government employment for women is actually higher today than before the revolution (1988: 221), but that there is a class difference, i.e., the rates for working-class women has actually increased, but "Thus far, educated, Western-oriented, upper-middle-class women have borne the brunt of the regime's most retrograde policies. . . " (p. 239).

Similar to what Moghadam found in Iran, i.e., a "discrepancy between ideological prescriptions and economic imperatives" (p. 221), there are fascinating contradictions in the NIF's ideological prescriptions and the society's

HALE

economic imperatives. We have seen that this process is beginning to be borne out in Sudan in the fields of medicine and agriculture. Even when women are not directly fired from their posts, as I mentioned above, the ethos is changing. Women with lucrative jobs are no longer seen as making a major contribution to society, but are seen as competitors. One Islamist man explained it to me very carefully:

> It is not that we forbid women to work. If she must work, then perhaps it is to the husband or to other male members of her family where we should look for any criticism. We only blame her if she goes to work as a frivolous act and does not behave appropriately in the workplace. For example, she must dress according to the respect she wants. We *want* to respect her.[20]

Hasan al-Turabi himself claims that Islam is very democratic, including democratic toward women. Recently he made statements at a Round Table:

> The Islamic movement in Sudan chose not to allow women's liberation to be brought about by Westernized liberal elites or communists or whatever. It took the lead itself . . . it evoked religion against custom . . . With respect to the status of women generally in [Sudanese] society, we don't have any more problems . . . In the Islamic movement, I would say that women have played a more important role of late than men . . . Of course, I don't claim that women have achieved parity, for example, in business . . . There is a question whether women will ever be present in equal numbers in all domains of public life . . . but there is no bar to women anywhere, and there is no complex about women being present anywhere (Lowrie, 1993: 46–47).

But there is another set of contradictions so that the great divide between ideology and material conditions and requisites is not totally consistent. I am referring to those jobs in the informal sectors of the economy held by lower-class women, e.g., vendors of local brew, prostitutes, and some entertainers, that are under attack as affronts to Islam. Some of these women have been flogged in public, beaten by gangs of men, and jailed. Even working-class women in "respectable" jobs are made to feel the pressure in the workplace, as well as moving to and from work. Harassment by Islamic guardians is common.

Although individual acts of resistance are common, organized resistance is rare. The regime was very repressive from the start, banning the People's Assembly, trade unions, political parties and associations, women's organizations, all nongovernmental media, and the like. Opposition to the government is considered very dangerous.[21]

SOME WOMEN OF THE NATIONAL ISLAMIC FRONT AND OTHER MUSLIMS

For years debates on the woman question were dominated by the secularist Sudanese Women's Union (Communist Party affiliate). For complex reasons of politics and personnel, it had lost a great deal of influence during the "democratic" era of l985–89.[22] As is the case in Egypt and in a number of other societies, the debate on women's rights has been coopted by the activist voices of the Islamists and conservative wings of old sectarian parties—such organizations as *al-Jabha al-Nisa'iyya al-Wataniyya* (the National Women's Front or NWF), the women's wing of the *Ikhwan* and NIF, and the women's wing of the Umma Party (led by Sara al-Fadl, Saddig al-Mahdi's wife). The NWF used language such as: helping working women, fighting sex discrimination in employment, extending maternity leave, offering free transportation for women workers, organizing women in the informal sector, and the like, i.e., co-opting the left discourse. But the main goal was expressed in familiar essentialist language: to build an image of the "ideal Muslim woman" (El Bakri, 1988: 25–26).

The pattern for the "woman's voice" was set even earlier, however, in the waning years of Nimieri's regime. A l980s document issued by the SSU, the Sudan Socialist Union (for some years the only legal party), Union of Sudanese Women, outlined various "fields" for women's activism, e.g., family and legal affairs, education, thought and training, media, and health.

Organizing by these Muslim women was clearly directed toward designing the ideal Islamic woman and family. Goals were to educate women about Islam, "make women aware of their rights according to the Quran and Sunni and to tell them about the values of religion . . . to educate her with the values and beliefs of the religion." With the establishment of kindergartens, the "children should be brought up in an Islamic way" (Sudan Socialist Union, c. 1980).

In the 1980s Islamic welfare work was certainly a dominant function of the women's organizations registered under the Ministry of Social Welfare and virtually all the twenty-some organizations aimed to create nurseries; work on childrearing, health and nutrition; build awareness; and "eradicate bad customs" (e.g., the *zaar*).[23] The Association of Sudanese Women Believers stated as its objectives that they want "the whole of Sudan together in one group as God wishes; [to] teach correct childrearing, Islamic Studies, and patriotism . . . [and to] make people aware of Islam . . ." (Ministry of Social Welfare, n.d.: 5). The Charity Union of Worshippers of God aimed "to give importance to Muslim women . . . [and] encourage Islamic instructions" (Ministry of Social Welfare, n.d.: 5). The Charity Association of Imam al-Mahdi for Women (Ansar sect) aimed "To encourage a modern Islamic society and make a link between individual behavior and the behavior of a person in Islam and to encourage Mahdist culture under Islamic culture" (Ministry of Social Welfare, n.d.: 4).

One of the more active moral welfare groups was the Association of Leading Reformers that militated against illicit unions by performing free mass wedding ceremonies for the poor in the football stadium, *zowag el-kora* (reference to putting all the people in a bowl and marrying them). Because marriage and wedding expenses had become prohibitive for most of the poor, this *Jumaya Raidat el-Nahda* was an effective organizing strategy and spread to other Islamist political parties such as Umma.[24]

Even Islamic economic institutions have been active in creating the ideal Islamic woman and her family. A Development Cooperative Islamic Bank was established in 1983 "to enable women who have training in home economics to purchase their work requirements; the bank strives to establish family production societies" (*Sudanow*, 1985: 14).

During the end of Nimieri's regime, proper social conduct was being monitored, not only in the streets by the moral guardians, but in various government institutions. The Chair of the SSU Women's Union, Nafissa Ahmed al-Amin, was barred from chairing a session in Khartoum on "Women's Rights under Islam" at the First International Islamic Conference on the Implementation of *sharia*. A protest had been filed by the Saudi delegation that it was not Islamic to permit a woman to chair a meeting where men were present (*Sudanow*, 1984: 12).

As I indicated above, there was considerable individual resistance to these attempts to remold Sudanese women to fit an ideal image of the Muslim woman. Although many women of the middle class with whom I spoke expressed doubt that anything would change in their everyday lives if *sharia* were implemented, there were outcries in 1988 from very religious working-class women. Nurses and workers from Abu Anja Hospital in Omdurman expressed defiance against attempts to shape their lives through *sharia*. One very old Arab Muslim said she would "take to the streets again" if *sharia* were reimplemented. Another, a Muslim woman from the Nuba Mountains, said:

> I am just a Muslim. I pray, but I am not as fanatic as the Muslim Brothers. I greet men with my bare hands [Islamist men and women do not shake hands]. I'm not fanatic, but I am religious . . . I'm religious because I pray and that's all . . . What they say about the equality of men and women in *sharia* is false. They [women] are not equal in the eyes of *sharia*—even if they do the same job their wages are not equal; the way they are viewed is not equal. There is discrimination . . . I want absolute equality with men . . . I'm doing the same job, so why not? I am doing my job better than any man and I think that, in general, in Sudan women do their jobs better than men.[25]

Secular intellectuals such as lawyer Taha Ibrahim, a leading voice in opposition to the implementation of *sharia* before the 1989 *coup*, took grave exception to the notion that nothing would change. His interpretation of the cynicism of Nimieri, Saddig, and Turabi's motivations was that all of the religious manipulation was to save the Islamic banks, a common thread throughout my interviews.

Batoul Mukhtar Mohamed Taha, noted legal analyst and Republican ac-

129

HALE

tivist, wrote a series of provocative newspaper articles in the 1980s, one of them challenging the right of the two NIF women representatives in the People's Assembly to represent all women. Claiming that society needs to value women as human beings, "not as a mere type, the 'Female'," she argued that the two NIF women accept traditionalist assumptions that men are the custodians of women, agree with the marriage of four women to one man, the woman's "house of obedience," with the beating of women, and concede the exclusive and unilateral right of divorce to men (Taha, 1988: 8).[26]

Among liberal, middle-class professional women, I found a great deal of self-reassessment in relation to society. Some expressed uncertainties and were clearly affected by the activism of the Islamist women. One told me:

> There are elements in society—mainly women—who are creating a revolution—and because it is coming from women considered conservative or "traditional," it is very confusing to women like me—educated, liberal women.[27]

By the mid 1980s, NIF ideology about the nature of woman and the ideal role of women had permeated middle-class urban society. Five students I interviewed at the University of Khartoum, none of whom were NIF, but were members or sympathizers of the Democratic Unionist Party (the DUP's base is the Khatmiyya sect), Umma, and the "secularist" Baathist party, expressed views of women amazingly close to those of the NIF. One hejab-wearing[28] woman, whose family is DUP, exclaimed:

> I still do believe that woman's place is in the home. She has something more important to do at home—looking after the children, teaching them properly—their norms, their values.[29]

A woman from an Umma Party family, wearing what we would refer to as "Western dress," reminded me that women get equal pay in Sudan, but that there is a problem with women being hired, mainly because women themselves have a poor work record. A male student, who is a self-described Sufist from a DUP family, valorized the traditional role of women:

> She has babies and she deals with the three stages of the human being. She has a wide experience. This job cannot be done by a man. It is the most important job, more so than engineers or architects.

All of the students agreed that it was the man's *responsibility* to work outside the home, but the woman's *duty* to be at home.

In the mid-1980s the most visible Islamist woman activist was Suad al-Fatih al-Badawi, one of only two women representatives in the People's Assembly, both of whom were NIF members. In her statements to the press, she took great effort to be forward-looking and open, stating, for example, that,

HALE

"We [NIF] are not opposed to corrections and changes [in the current *sharia* laws] so long as . . . [they do not] take us back to the English laws." Moreover,

I do not believe in separatist roles [for men and women]in the construction of the nation. Men and women complete and perfect each other . . . It was an obligation for women [to make] the representation of women *authentic* and *real* . . . Those women who have attained a high level of consciousness which is *progressive* and *untainted* by blind imitation of both the East and the West must not be stingy with their intellectual effort . . . This era is marked by issues of development which the *enlightened vanguard* must struggle to solve in a fundamental way (*Al-Badawi*, 1986: 10).

Hikmat SidAhmed, the second woman Assembly representative, echoed Suad al-Fatih's statements and also presented women as responsible for the education of the new generations. In an *Al-Sahaafa* article and in my interview with her, she presented a "correct model" for teaching that is the same for home, school, and work. She expressed concern for women who are gainfully employed as "partners" in the construction of the nation. She made a plea for good Islamic childcare institutions, but also for technical training in the use of local raw materials to substitute for foreign imports (*Al-Badawi*, 1986: 10).

For Hikmat SidAhmed,[30] only women who have to work should work, and only if they have "appropriate" childcare (preferably a close relative). When I pressed the issue, it became apparent that Islamic nurseries were to be constructed for working-class women whose abilities to raise their children in an "Islamic way" are seen by the NIF as limited. The state, then, would substitute its Islamic teachings. In the interim, intense missionary work was being carried out by NIF women in existing nurseries.

Three of the Islamist women I interviewed—well-educated, professional, and upper middle-to-upper-class—gave me the fullest explanation of the *ideal Muslim woman*. Nagwa Kamal Farid, my ex-student and someone I have known for thirty-four years, was Sudan's first woman *sharia* judge, but dissociates herself from public politics; Wisel al-Mahdi is a lawyer, wife of Hasan al-Turabi, sister of Saddig al-Mahdi, and an NIF activist; and Hikmat SidAhmed, mentioned above, at the time I interviewed her, was an NIF representative in the government and is an Arabic teacher.

Judge Nagwa explained women's many rights in *sharia* and what she described as the "differences in small detail" in the everyday life of men and women. Concerning going to the mosque, she said:

Men get 27 percent more benefit from praying at the mosque. Going in a group gives more benefit than if you pray alone . . . it is better for women to pray at home and not go to the mosque at all. She has duties at home. But if she prays at home, she has the same benefits as men. Men are compelled to go [i.e., for women it is voluntary].

131

HALE

With regard to the rationale for polygamy, she commented:

> The reason for this [men being allowed to have four wives] is that for some men
> one wife is not enough. Instead of playing around with other women, he should
> get married. He should be a good Muslim. This acts as discipline . . . some men
> have a wife at home, but they run around and play with other women. Our cul-
> ture, Islamic, hates that. If the first wife does not have kids, this gives him a better
> excuse. But even if there is no excuse, he has the right for another wife—just be-
> cause we want him to be a good Muslim . . . Maybe the first wife was not one
> he wanted . . . maybe his first wife got old, and men do not get old as quickly as
> women, so he thinks of having another wife. Why not? It is better than having
> him look around outside of marriage.

If there are inequities in inheritance, there is a strong rationale, claimed Judge
Nagwa. She insisted that *sharia* protects women so that they never have to
support themselves:

> If *sharia* were implemented here in Sudan, life would be very different and peo-
> ple would be much happier. No woman would be needing anything . . . People
> keep asking why in *sharia* women get less [inheritance] than men. But the situa-
> tion is that she is not supposed to support herself; that burden falls on men, so
> they need more inheritance.

Judge Nagwa was even more forceful about women's equality under *sharia*, a
woman's responsibility to be "respectable" at all times, and the compelling
reasons for remaining at home with family duties, unless there are more compelling reasons (e.g., financial need) to enter the workforce.

All of the Islamist women agreed that *sharia* permits a woman to work, but
Nagwa added:

> There is one condition in Islam [in allowing a woman to go out to work] . . . It
> says that the first . . . message for the woman . . . is to raise her children and take
> care of her house. So, if she wants to go to work she should be well-dressed,
> not too much perfume so as not to attract attention. . . She has to go out re-
> spectably . . . to cover her hair, all of her face and hands should be inside, not too
> colorful. . . When a man stands beside her, he should remember work and noth-
> ing else.

Some women workers set very bad examples, claimed Judge Nagwa: lack of
punctuality, too many sick days, and the like: "She's there; her effect is there
[distraction], but she's not there working."

Wisel al-Mahdi claimed on the subject of work that, "there is no program
as such of the NIF to take women out of the workforce." And Hikmat added
that they need women to work. But they all agreed that conditions must be

HALE

appropriate and that women need to raise their children first, and should not leave them in the care of "servants."

The three narrators of these interviews also commented on the *nature of woman* and the inherent differences between men and women, especially related to the dictate in *sharia* that during criminal proceedings, two women witnesses are required to offset the testimony of one man. Hikmat explained:

> We know that women are different from men . . . women, by their *nature*, sometimes forget. Sometimes they sympathize with somebody. Perhaps he may be a criminal . . . when one of them [woman witness] forgets, the other will remind her, and if one of them sympathized with the criminal, the other could correct her . . . I don't think it is a problem for women to find themselves treated differently in the court . . . because it is *natural* . . . the entire principle [in *sharia*] is in accord with the way women are *created*, since women are *naturally empathetic* (italics mine).

Wisel gave an example of a murder trial:

> . . . in a situation of somebody taking a . . . knife and stabbing another, a woman would be so much *excited* that she would not recognize exactly what happened, because afterall, a *woman is weaker than a man* and all her *nervous system* is made different [from a man's] . . . so she may say something that she believes . . . happened, not what she saw happen . . . women are more *sentimental*, because they are the mothers who breed children . . . That is why, in *sharia* law we guard against the sentimentality ['*aatifiyya*, 'empathy,' 'compassion,' 'sympathy'] of *womankind* (italics mine).

She added:

> This does not mean that a woman is less than a man, or that her *mental capacity* is less than a man. It means that her *disposition* is different than [a man's]. We are equal in all rights in Islam (italics mine).

Wisel al-Mahdi maintained that women have a broad range of options under Islam and *sharia* and that, if there are differences spelled out in the law, it is because women are different by nature—and that they should want it that way: "We are *women* afterall . . . I am *not* like a man." But she went on to say that a woman can be anything or do anything.

In all three interviews Islamist women agreed that men oppress women, that Arabs have a low opinion of women, and that Arab men try to give a false idea to women about their rights under *sharia*. Judge Nagwa commented, "Sudan is still a man's society . . . the man is the boss." Wisel, in commenting on a very conservative group, *Ansar al-Sunna*, which opposes any public activity by women, said, "They are against women . . . They think a woman's

133

voice is like women's breasts showing." She repeated it in Arabic, "*Sawt al-mar'a 'awra,* a woman's voice is a private part that must be concealed."

Wisel al-Mahdi was the main feminist commentator in her defiant statements against the male oppression of women:

> They [Arab men] are against women, and that is why *we are much against them.* We know our rights; we have learned the Quran and *sharia;* we know what *sharia* gives us . . . we think that *women are better human beings* than they think . . . And . . . *we are standing up for our sex.* We are working in the NIF *to praise women* and to make women have a better status and to tell the world that we are as equal as men and are as efficient as men and we are as educated as men and we are as good as men and as great as men (italics mine).

Wisel attempted to speak for all women when she stated that women "in all the other parties feel the same." She asserted that, "We are Muslims *by nature,*" and that the NIF is not doing anything different except to give more emphasis to the Islamic nature of society. To her, there is no distinction between politics and religion, nor between public and private life. Women are active in the NIF because of equal rights in *sharia,* but also because,

> We want Islam to judge our cases; we want Islam to judge our economical activities; we want Islam to judge our foreign relations ["judge"=*yahkum,* "rule"?] We want Islam to be practiced in everyday life, not just inside the house . . . we don't want it to be only in a corner of the life of the family. We want it to be the *core* of life . . . [for] the whole society and the whole Sudan and the whole Muslim world. That is the only difference between the NIF and the [rest of] Sudanese society as it has existed since independence.

The militancy and defiance of the NIF women was striking, differing from the Islamist men I talked with mainly in their insistence that Arab customs and patriarchy have oppressed them. However, even Hasan al-Turabi has tried to distance himself from the Arab past with regard to women and other issues (Lowrie, 1993).

CONCLUSION

As one might expect in a developing Islamic state, there are a number of inconsistencies and paradoxes when one contrasts state requirements for maintaining the gender ideology and labor needs. We can see the same contradictions within the NIF between the availability of human resources and the imperatives of the organizational strategies of such a small group. That is, despite some ideological prohibitions, in a number of ways, women are truly the nexus of the NIF. They are among the active organizers in the schools where women constitute the majority of teachers, in neighborhood medical clinics, in NIF nursery schools in the mosques, as consumer/producers, etc. The NIF has strong appeal to women— especially at the universities, where at the time of my fieldwork in 1988, some 70 percent of the students were wearing the *hejab* (modest Islamic dress)[31] Women are relied on to socialize the young with Islamic values and receive a great deal of praise and attention for this work. The NIF can point to the public activity of NIF women in answering the clichéd charge that the NIF will send women back into the homes. As I indicated above, the only two women elected to the People's Assembly before the current regime banned it, were NIF representatives, Suad al-Fathi and Hikmat Sid Ahmed. They both had high public visibility and were community leaders.

We should also not underestimate the powerful partners of NIF politicians, women known to be active behind the scenes and in public. Wisel al-Mahdi, university-educated and well-travelled, may be seen as living some of the contradictions of the Islamic regime. For example, although her house is segregated into "women's quarters" and "men's quarters," and although she wears the *hejab* and adheres to other strict Islamic dictates about the roles of men and women, she considers herself a powerful force "behind" her husband and an activist in her own right.[32] In my interview with Wisel, I found a confident, proud, and politically informed and committed activist—clearly someone exerting a great deal of influence on the women around her.[33] The views she expressed to me were "feminist" in the sense of her belief in working on behalf of other women, respecting women, and wanting women to get the most from *sharia* law. She did not oppose women in the workforce, but believed women should behave modestly in that environment. She was confident at the time that the Islamists would come to power, that they would ban the Permanent Constitution, that *sharia* would be enforced, and that the plight of women would improve immensely[34] For one thing, according to Wisel, it was the Arab customs and traditions, not Islam, that had been oppressing women, which is the last potentially transformative process I would like to discuss in reference to the attempt by the state to impose a totalizing Islamic culture on Sudanese.

There are a number of potentially transformative processes currently taking place in Sudan, some of the most significant of which are related to gender dynamics and manifested in some of the diatribes (as above) against Arab men. This is part of the disaggregating of "Arab" and "Muslim," two categories which are now being treated as discrete that have historically been conflated. This strategy simultaneously includes the invention of the "New Muslim Woman" and the reinvention of "Muslim," as it is disaggregated from "Arab."[35] The guiding ideas behind the centrifugal/centripetal strategy related to Arab identity and the forms of identity manipulation the current regime is using are that (1) foregrounding Arab identity hinders north-south integration under Islam (e.g., it is easier to "become" a Muslim than an Arab, and southerners' memories of Arab slaving in the south can be minimized);

HALE

and (2) women are more willing to see themselves as potentially liberated from certain patriarchal Arab customs upon a return to "pure" Islam. Also, being accepted by the outside world, especially the Arab/Middle Eastern world, as integral to the "Middle East" is facilitated by Sudanese becoming participants, even leaders, in the region's *Islamic* movements; whereas, being embraced as "authentically Arab" had always been problematic. The Muslim woman is presented as modern, forward-looking, dutiful, and enlightened— yet moral and authentic.

But there remained the flip side of the coin, the dark side of the image of devout and dutiful Muslims, the fact of men oppressing women through various patriarchal customs. A strategy had to be worked out whereby Islam could be the *deus ex machina*, a method for rescuing women from oppression. To do that, it would be more effective to demonize some aspect of the population, not necessarily men, but a *category* of men, i.e., Arab men.

The Islamist women with whom I talked all agreed that men oppress women, and then at some point in the statement, shifted to conflating *men* and *Arabs*. Arabs (meaning "Arab men") have a low opinion of women, these Islamist women maintained, and cannot be trusted in that they try to give a false idea to women about their rights under *sharia*. As Judge Nagwa reminded us, "Sudan is still a man's society...the man is the boss." Women I interviewed had engaged in a chorus of abuse toward Sudanese Arab men, reminding me that any man could be a woman's boss and that Arab men do not have respect for women. The "bad ideas" that Sudanese men have were presented as being "like the ideas of *the Arabs before Islam*." Hikmat even referred to Sudanese Arab men as *jaahiliin* (ignorant, pagan). In response to the word *jaahiliin*, Wisel added:

> Yes. Because they are *Arabs*, actually. And these instincts have come to them for these last 15,000 years and still it's there. In North Africa, in Saudi Arabia, in *any Arab country*. They have the same things against women. And that is why we are much against them . . . we are against them [Arabs] and we think they are presenting a *false idea about Islam* (emphases mine).

Appealing to women, appeasing Muslim feminist critics, and distancing himself from the (Arab) past, Hasan Turabi stated that "Segregation is definitely not part of Islam . . . the *hareem* quarters, this is a development which was totally unknown in the model of Islam, or in the text of Islam; it is unjustified" (Lowrie, 1993: 36).

Turabi combined the above with such statements about Sudan and Arab culture as: " . . . the North is not Arab. . . They speak Arabic, but they are not Arabs; they are part of East African people . . . "(Lowrie, 1993: 66–67).

Other Islamist women expressed similar views, all of them convinced that women would have a higher status and be more respected under *sharia*. Their convictions were contagious, and they managed to influence some liberals and fence-walkers to soften their views of the NIF or to have at least a "wait-and-see" attitude. Those, like the *sharia* judge, who know the law well, were quietly informing women of their rights under *sharia*, and trying to convince them to self-educate.[36]

Perhaps the legal and personal/family rights of women are now spelled out more clearly. But it remains to be seen what will happen to the economic conditions of women's lives. It seems unlikely that any Islamist group would greatly diminish the numbers of women in working-class or traditional occupations. But that does not preclude tight control over women's access to power and privilege—both private and public. So far it is difficult to know the exact impact on middle-class women. Since this Islamist movement is a movement of the middle class, one can expect significant changes there.

As of the writing of this essay, the most dynamic component of the state is the NIF. One of its important tasks is the control of human resources by reconstructing the gender ideology. Now economic crises and their solutions can be articulated in religious terms, and women have been positioned to respond appropriately. The prescriptive nature of Islam (and most religions) regarding sexuality, reproduction, the gender division of labor, and the family, are useful in protecting class interests.

NOTES

1. This project, the fieldwork for which was carried out in the summer of 1988, was partially funded by a grant from the UCLA Center for the Study of Women and the Gustave E. von Grunebaum Center for Near Eastern Studies. I would like to thank various Research Assistants: Amal Abdel Rahman, Sunita Pitamber, William Young, and Sherifa Zuhur. This component of the study focuses on *northern* Sudan.

2. I am referring to Antonio Gramsci's work on state hegemony (1971; 1977; and 1978). It may be useful here to describe a concept of the "state," which I interpret as a cluster of interrelated institutions organized by the ruling class (whether this is ruling class by election as in bourgeois democracies or by self-appointment) for the purpose of controlling the subordinate population and disseminating the ideology of that class. State apparatuses of control are, of course, the military, police, militia, intelligence units, the courts, immigration and citizenship laws, and the like. Often less obvious, but just as relevant to this research, are some of the apparatuses for the dissemination of the dominant group's ideology, e.g., the media, the arts, the educational system, social welfare departments, religious institutions, and the like. Liberals or bourgeois democrats forward the concept that the state is an institution to which the *people have access,* perhaps through the apparatuses I have just mentioned. But I try to turn this concept on its head in the same way, perhaps, that some have turned the model of patron/client on its head (in reference to Michael Gilsenan, 1977), and present the state as functioning to give itself (ergo, the ruling class) *access to the people* and their resources.

It is not the purpose here to enter into the debates on the nature of the state, e.g., whether or not the precapitalist state was an autonomous entity separate from its class base or is an extension of the ruling class. It should be clear that I am using a revision-

HALE

ist approach to the latter, one which derives from the ideas of Gramsci (e.g., 1971; 1977; and 1978), but borrows from others, e.g., Nicos Polantzas (1969); Perry Anderson (1974a; 1974b). I have also consulted Bob Jessop (1977: 354–357), in which he lists six different approaches to the theory of the state in the classical Marxist literature: the state as a parasitic institution, epiphenomena, a factor of cohesion, an instrument of class rule, a set of institutions, and a system of political domination, as well as his analysis of Polantzas' debt to Gramsci (Jessop, 1982). Useful also is David Held, et al. (1983), in which the authors discuss different conceptions of the state. As for state apparatuses, I have used ideas from Clark and Dear, especially a section on "State Apparatus and Everyday Life" (1984: 60–82).

3. In l971 a leftist coalition carried out an abortive coup d'etat; partially in reaction, military dictator, President Jaffar Nimieri (who had come to power as a leftist), began to move to the right.

4. I am using "gender arrangements" to refer most particularly to the gender division of labor, but also to domestic arrangements in general, e.g., how the family is structured, family ideology (including reproduction), and, specifically, to the relationship of men and women in terms of status and power. The term also refers to production, reproduction, and social reproduction. In this essay I focus on one example of the gender division of labor.

5. Especially since the Iranian revolution in l978 there have been popular and scholarly debates over the use of the term "fundamentalist," more often a misnomer. There is a tendency to mistake the rise in Islamic "sentiment" (i.e., people feeling more religious and being willing to express this religiosity in public) and "fundamentalism," often an atavistic tendency. To suggest a movement which uses Islam as a guiding principle, many are using the term "Islamism," or in some cases, "political Islam." It is difficult to escape the totalizing effect of any of these terms.

6. Instead, the authors seek to develop an analysis of the contention between "an agrarian fraction of the emergent bourgeoisie and a commercial (and increasingly bureaucratic) fraction [that] has dominated Sudanese politics" (O'Neill and O'Brien, 1988: 10). Proceeding from the expansion of capitalist food production (in the 80 percent agrarian society where as late as the 1950s cotton accounted for 80–90 percent of the GNP,) the impact on the rural population, foreign capital intervention and the restoration of export dependency, they outline the shifting patterns of capital accumulation, class formation, and concomitant economic crisis. Sudan's indigenous industrial capitalist class was very small and dependent on foreign capital. "The primary source of domestic capital accumulation for other nascent capitalists was in agriculture . . . [e.g.,] private pump schemes along the Nile" (p. 18). The result has been the increasing impoverishment of the peasants, making them susceptible to drought and starvation (pp. 18–22).

7. This term, however, is recent (l988), used by the NIF and others in the government to denote the new Islamic tendency in Sudanese politics. Here I am using it in a general sense to mean the rise of interest in Islam and an Islamic State.

8. Although I do not regard veiling and genital surgeries in and of themselves as indices of lack of "emancipation," many observers do—especially feminists in the West. I use them here almost metaphorically, to suggest that notions about "emancipation" are

very complex and that, according to the indices of some Western frameworks, Sudanese women would be both emancipated and nonemancipated.

9. The NIF, led by Hasan al-Turabi, is a group that broke off from the *Ikhwan* as a result of political and personality differences centered on Islamic banking. It is now the most powerful "fundamentalist" group in Sudan, concentrating more on secular politics than religious on ideology.

10. Including medicine, law, university faculty, and women professionals in various fields.

11. Unless one acknowledges patriarchal economic systems that give Islamist and non-Islamist men interests in common, this statement by itself tends to lay women's economic subordination at the feet of Islam.

12. Sufism is often referred to as a mystical form of Islam in contrast to "orthodoxy." A basic difference is the way knowledge and truth are thought to be obtained. "For the *sufi, marifa* (divine knowledge) can only be achieved through spiritual experience and its final goal is absolute truth; for the *ulama* [orthodox clergy], *ilm* (learning) is what is gained through study of scripture, tradition . . . and the like . . . by means of formal education" (El-Hassan, 1980: 72–73).

13. Italics hers.

14. See El Bakri (1987: 3).

15. The phrases, "exercise of political power" and "consumerism," I have taken from Mernissi (1988: 9), as well as some of the ideas for this section of the paper. But Mernissi leans toward psychological interpretations, or at least individualistic or nationalist ones. I look to the international economic forces which create these.

16. Interviews in Khartoum, Sudan, 1988.

17. Interview in the summer of 1988 with an ex-member of the Council of Surgeons.

18. Interview with a woman doctor, Khartoum, 1988.

19. The same debate arose around the increased numbers of women being admitted to the Faculty of Agriculture, University of Khartoum. Through Sudan's unique and complicated "boxing" system for placing students in faculties based on the high school certificate exams, women are often admitted to Agriculture whether or not they request it. Since Sudan is basically an agricultural society, the agricultural establishment is very powerful. Agricultural policy-making is probably the most significant in Sudan's economy. Allowing women into the field means gender power-sharing in an agricultural society. Part of the debate was captured in Letters to the Editor in *Sudanow* (October, 1979 and January, 1980). For example, in the October issue, Omer el Farouk Hassan Heiba called for the "banning of girls from agricultural education."

20. Interview with a male member of the NIF, Khartoum, 1988.

21. With women at the center, Ellen Gruenbaum gives us a taste of the fear and intimidation that have pervaded Sudan since 1989 (1992).

22. In Hale (1991), I analyze my interview with Women's Union Head, Fatma Ahmed Ibrahim; in Hale (1993 and 1996a), I critique the relationship of the Sudanese Women's Union and the Sudanese Communist Party.

23. I obtained this typed registry in July, 1988, from the Ministry of Social Welfare in Khartoum (n.d., probably 1985–1988).

HALE

24. Some of this information was supplied by my research assistants, Amal Abdel Rahman and Sunita Pitamber, who had watched a football stadium mass wedding on television.

25. A series of interviews with doctors, nurses, and workers at Abu Anja Hospital were carried out, June 20, 1988. Because of the repressiveness of the current regime, I have not named anyone in this essay who is still in the country, whose views were not already written or well-known, or who said anything self-incriminating against *sharia,* Islam, the Islamization process, or particular political parties.

26. Taha also informed me that the Republicans [formerly Republican Brothers] had spent years in court trying to prove the unconstitutionality of *sharia.* Written interview response, August 3, 1988.

27. Interview in Khartoum, July 14, 1988, with a professional woman with a Ph.D. in Public Administration.

28. Sudanese use the term *hejab* to refer to a range of modest Islamic dress for women, from a long dress with long sleeves and a scarf to a full covering, sometimes including veiling the face.

29. The quotes from the University of Khartoum students are all from a June 30, 1988 group interview.

30. The following statements by Hikmat SidAhmed or Wisel al-Mahdi are from an interview at the home of the latter and her husband, Hasan al-Turabi, July 12, 1988. Judge Nagwa Kamal Farid participated in that interview, but was also interviewed alone July 4, 1988, in Khartoum. Her statements are taken from both interviews.

31. Interview with Mohamed Osman who was carrying out thesis research on Islamic dress, Anthropology Department, University of Khartoum, summer, 1988. I was informed in 1994 that there is now a reaction to the *hejab* and that the numbers have declined. I have been unable to verify the information.

32. Interview with Wisel al-Mahdi, Hikmat Sid Ahmed, and Nagwa Kamal Farid, Khartoum, July 12, 1988.

33. When I mentioned her name to other Islamist and even non-Islamist women, they were immediately respectful. And even though she was not then, nor now, a "first lady," many people told me the usual "first-lady" jokes that one hears in the United States about Hilary Clinton, i.e., jokes that imply that she is really the power behind the two powerful men in her life.

34. The Permanent Constitution was banned as soon as the Islamists came to power in 1989; an Islamic Constitution is still being developed.

35. For a fuller discussion of this topic see Hale (1996a and 1996b).

36. Much of the organizing of Islamist women before 1988 was done in social environments, e.g., visiting, funerals, weddings, and the like. Nagwa Kamal Farid, for example, a widow living quietly with her children, is not a "public person," and, in fact, as a *sharia* judge has never sat on the bench. But she is an important figure, not only because she is the first woman *sharia* judge, but also because she is a member of a large and influential family. Her uncle was once a minister in one of the military regimes. Her opinions on women and *sharia,* therefore, matter and are influential on other women.

REFERENCES

Al-Badawi, S .F. 1986. *Al-Sahaafa* [Khartoum] (May 3): 10.

Anderson, P. 1974a. *Lineages of the Absolutist State.* London: New Left Books.

————. 1974b *Passages from Antiquity to Feudalism*. London: New Left Books.

Clark, G. and M. Dear 1984. *State Apparatuses: Structures and Language of Legitimacy*. Boston: Allen and Unwin.

El Bakri, Z. B. 1987. "Will the Minister Be Vetted by the "Women's Committee?" *The Sudan Times* [Khartoum]: 3.

————. 1988 Unpublished Manuscript.

El-Hassan, I. S. 1980. *On Ideology: The Case of Religion in Northern Sudan*. Unpublished Ph.D. Thesis, Anthropology Department, University of Connecticut.

Gilsenan, M. 1977. "Against Patron-Client Relations." In *Patrons and Clients in Mediterranean Societies*. eds. E. Gellner and J. Waterbury, pp. 167–183. London: Duckworth.

Gramsci, A. 1971. *Selections from the Prison Notebooks*. London: Lawrence and Wishart.

————. 1977 *Selections from Political Writings, 1910-1920*. London: Lawrence and Wishart.

————.1978 *Selections from Political Writings, 1921-1926*. London: Lawrence and Wishart.

Gran, J. 1977. "Impact of the World Market on Egyptian Women." *MERIP Middle East Reports* 58: 3-7.

Gruenbaum, E. 1992. "The Islamic State and Sudanese Women." *MERIP Middle East Report* 179:29–32.

Hale, S, 1991. "Feminist Method, Process, and Self-Criticism: Interviewing Sudanese Women." In *Women's Words: The Feminist Practice of Oral History*, eds, S. Gluck and D. Patai, pp. 121–136. New York: Routledge.

————. 1993. "Transforming Culture or Fostering Second-Hand Consciousness?" Women's Front Organizations and Revolutionary Parties— the Sudan Case. In *Arab Women*. ed. Judith Tucker, pp. 149–174. Bloomington: Indiana University.

————. 1996a. *Gender Politics in Sudan: Islamism, Socialism, and the State*. Boulder: Westview.

————. 1996b. "The New Muslim Woman: Sudan's National Islamic Front and the Invention of Identity." *The Muslim World* 86 (2): 177–200.

Held, David, et al, eds. 1983. *States and Societies*. New York: New York University Press.

Jessop, B. 1977. "Recent Theories of the Capitalist State." *Cambridge Journal of Economics I*: 353–373.

————. 1982. *The Capitalist State: Marxist Theories and Methods*. New York: New York University Press

Lowrie, A, L., ed. 1993. *Islam, Democracy, the State and the West: A Round Table with Dr. Hasan Turabi*. Tampa: The World and Islam Studies Enterprise, Monograph No. 1.

Mernissi, F. 1988. "Muslim Women and Fundamentalism." *MERIP Middle East Report* 153: 8–11.

Moghadam, V. 1988. "Women, Work, and Ideology in the Islamic Republic." *International Journal of Middle East Studies* 20 (3): 221–243.

O'Neill, N. and J. O'Brien, eds. 1988. *Economy and Class in Sudan*. London: Gower Press.

Osman, D. S. 1985. "The Legal Status of Muslim Women in Sudan." *Journal of Eastern African Research and Development* 15: 124–142.

Polantzas, N. 1969. "The Problem of the Capitalist State." *New Left Review* 58: 119–133.

Spaulding, J. 1985. *The Heroic Age in Sinnar*. East Lansing, Michigan: Michigan University Press.

Sudan, Ministry of Social Welfare n.d. *Women's Organizations Registered under the Ministry of Social Welfare*. Khartoum: Ministry of Social Welfare (probably 1985–1988).

Sudan Socialist Union n.d. *Summary of Working Plans for the Offices of the Executive Office of the Union of Sudanese Women*. Khartoum: Sudan Socialist Union, Section for Political and Organization Affairs (1980?).

Sudanow (Khartoum) 1979 (October): 10

———. 1980 (January): 11

———. 1984 (November): 12.

———. 1985 (September): 14.

Taha, B. M. M. 1987. "Today, No Guardian." *Sudanow* 13 (January-February).

———. 1988 *Sudan now* (May 16): 8.

Tucker, J. 1985. *Women in Nineteenth Century Egypt*. Cambridge: Cambridge University Press.

IDEAL WOMANHOOD IN POSTREVOLUTIONARY IRAN[1]

Erika Friedl

THIS DISCUSSION of Iranian Ideal Womanhood is based on almost two years of anthropological fieldwork in Iran since the revolution, carried out in 1981, 1983, 1985, 1989, 1992, and 1994.[2] I spent most of this time in a rural–tribal area in Southwest Iran but have also stayed in Tehran, Isfahan, and Shiraz, talking to as many people as possible from all walks of life. My conclusions are based almost exclusively on verbal communications and on observations of behavior rather than on the analysis of printed matter,[3] and are drawn on everyday life experiences of ordinary women rather than of especially rich or very highly educated ones. This needs to be said because as the rift between rich and poor in Iran is widening, cultural rifts between members of the urban, educated, relatively wealthy middle classes and all other people is widening too, and representations of life in Iran for Western audiences are dominated by members of Iranian old and new urban elites who tend to have a literate, "Tehran-centric" bias when talking about social conditions in their country.

ASSUMPTIONS

By way of introduction I will briefly clarify those of my major assumptions that are relevant for this paper to avoid distracting explanations later.

1. Presently in Iran various postulates of "true" Muslim femininity influence all aspects of women's lives, from access to health care, food and education[4] to conditions of employment and the workings of the courts. These we label "fundamentalist," suggesting thereby that they are more or less restrictive for women.

2. The constituting features, the basic concepts of the models of ideal womanhood are functions, i.e., consequences, of local gender paradigms. Although today these are said to be supported by Islamic teachings, for the most part they are deeply rooted in Iranian popular culture. They transcend religion. The gender paradigms in turn are understood to be collages of concepts taken from different traditions, from different "scripts," as it were, and are more or less well integrated logically.

3. Gender paradigms are located within sociopolitical programs and may be used to support and validate ideologies of a hierarchical system of power—in this case, one that places women below men legally and culturally. Thus they are closely connected to the Iranian class structure and reflective of class-cultures and inter-class relationships in urban and rural-tribal regional settings. Class factors in women's identity and in models for ideal behavior and world view are not paid much attention to in scholarly work on women in Iran, but this does not mean that they are unimportant.

4. Fundamentalist ideals of womanhood and their underlying gender paradigms are articulated directly and metaphorically in various ways, including in sermons, school texts, television and radio programs, newspaper articles, laws and their applications, and generally in popular culture as monitored by governmental agencies. Especially radio, television and schools reach people even in the most remote hinterlands in Iran today, disseminating to all Iranians centrally formulated messages.

MODELS OF IDEAL WOMANHOOD

The term "Ideal Womanhood" here is used as a gloss for overt and covert ideological constructs that define and validate demands on women and provide models for women's self-understanding as members of the Community of the Faithful in the Islamic Republic. It is thus understood as formulated on top, in the religio-political elite, and propagandized downward. However, ideals of womanhood, or, better, definitions of what being a "good woman" *(zan-e khub)* is all about, are also formulated in political space on the ground by ordinary women. There, defining criteria for feminine "goodness" are located within the parameters of everyday life, and pertain to ethics expressed in mastering life's problems and in managing social affairs, and to personal styles in enduring hardships. These formulations often run counter to the spirit of official ideals expressed in sermons, in religious teachings, textbooks and laws, sidestepping or even subverting them. They pertain more likely to qualities deemed desireable for harmonious co-existence, such as honesty, kindness, generosity, truthfulness, reliability, supportiveness, than to religio-legal factors like meticulous accounting of good deeds and sins, eye-for-an-eye justice, ritual punctuality, and many outward signs of mainstream piety. Women construct models for good, proper behavior in life crises such as widowhood, divorce, sickness that may win them approval, influence and help in their community. Meaning of life thus is derived from other, or many more, sources than strictly Qoranic and theologically supported ones.

Women's philosophies and ethics, and the everyday life experiences they reflect and inform are little documented in Iran (or elsewhere, for that matter)[5]. Talking about "Ideal Womanhood" in a fundamentalist context thus is a rather one-sided, limited way of looking at the issue of ideal models women employ in identifying themselves vis-a-vis other women and vis-a-vis men.

Contradictions between ideological constructs and behavior requisites in practical life account for hardships for women who try to be both pious and successful in this world and other-worldly oriented at the same time. The contradictions, however, also open opportunities for manipulation: a whole plethora of different behaviors and personality traits can be justified in reference to "goodness" by shifting among different options. For example, a meek, quiet woman who does not amount to much in her social community and is not successful by criteria of looks, her children's achievements, or status among other women, may still be called, and see herself, as a model of a morally good woman on account of her very docility and subservience, qualities that are regarded highly on one fundamentalist scale of Muslim womanhood. Yet a woman who is neither docile nor subservient but resolutely furthering her husband's and sons' interests may still be seen by others, and certainly may see herself, as a "good" woman because of her drive and social success within her family (provided that she does not overstep local boundaries of propriety) which rank high on another "fundamentalist" scale. And a young woman physician working in public in a hospital day and night, alongside men, outspokenly making life-and-death decisions, may earn many religious merits in the eyes of even very strict fundamentalists because she competently does indispensable good work for others.

With this model of different options that women can manipulate, seemingly contradictory reports of the idealized strength of fundamentalist women (or women in a fundamentalist society) vs. their idealized weak, subordinated social position can be contextualized, if not reconciled: there is plenty of room to accomodate widely different aspirations and lifestyles under the umbrella of Muslim femininity, at least in Iran today.

This needs to be emphasized the more emphatically wherever "Ideal Womanhood" is taken to be an ideological-fundamentalist construct, i.e., as formulated and propagandized in the politico/religious elite. I will focus on the contradictions the elite concepts create internally, but also mention those that appear when compared to constructs from below, to those women formulate themselves. I suggest that the contradictions and ambiguities allow for room to maneuver in social and moral space, and for a variety of lifestyles for women within the matrix of "ideal" feminine traits. As even a casual visitor to Iran today can notice, neither is life for most women there nearly as uniform, bleak, and restricted as, ironically, both advocates as well as critics of so-called fundamentalist ideals for Muslim women alike paint it to be, nor is it as liberating for most women as so many of the optimistic-idealist thinkers are willing it to be. (The last group includes, as an extreme, those who claim that Iranian women have formulated a "Muslim Feminism" that answers modernists' challenges to allegedly androcentric, misogynist fundamentalist practices, and liberates or protects women from oppressive Western demands on women.)[6] Rather, by using contradictory rationalizations for demands on women's behavior and for restrictive standards of propriety, women can accomodate both of these trends as well as others, too.

SOURCES FOR BASIC CONCEPTS IN FUNDAMENTALIST GENDER PARADIGMS

Muslim Religious Scriptures

Religious texts—the Qoran, Hadith, *rizala* (i.e., exegetical texts by high ranking theologians)—are claimed to provide the most logical, just, and comprehensive definitions of womanhood, including psychological, social, and political dimensions. Theoretically these texts are beyond negotiation because they are claimed to emanate from divine or divinely inspired authority. Practically, however, Holy Writ has to be translated, taught, made understandable to the faithful, especially to illiterate and semiliterate people who cannot read original Arabic texts, i.e., most Iranians, and especially most women in Iran. This means it has to be interpreted. Interpretation is a political process: the selection of texts from among a great many that potentially give widely divergent messages, and their exegesis are unavoidably influenced, if not outrightly motivated, by the political programs and the interests of those who control the formulation and dissemination of ideologies. Exegesis by different people and at different times may lead to contradictory formulations of "true" Muslim femininity. For example, one and the same mullah before the revolution told us that only the crown of a woman's head had to be covered according to the Qoran; after the revolution he said that according to the Qoran a woman's

146

FRIEDL

hair has to be covered completely, including eyebrows. His earlier opinion, he said, had been "erroneous," formulated under pressure from the Shah's regime. In 1994 the new factor of "local custom" was introduced in the national debate on hair: now the same mullah said that local women who traditionally had shown some hair under their tribal scarfs could continue to do so because it did not upset local sensibilities. Over the past twenty years we have heard similar arguments, always supported by learned reasoning, about schooling for women, about the propriety of certain fields of study for women, about contraception and abortion. Even in fundamentalist interpretations of texts there is room for variation.

Although currently in Iran there seems to be a certain consensus on some fundamental feminine qualities and on some indisputable postulates for women which are said to be divinely ordained, these qualities and postulates do not amount to a fixed, well circumscribed body of knowledge. Universally demanded are modesty in self-presentation (*hejab*) and circumspect, understanding cooperation with father/husband/state, together with pious and knowledgable observation of religious rules and routines such as prayer, fasting, and giving alms. However, obviously on a different matrix, assertion, striving for excellence (e.g., in school), and intelligent input by women into attempts to solve the Islamic Republic's many problems and to build a nation strong in science and services to its citizens are equally demanded of women who are capable of providing it. For example, each year a certain percentage of the highly competitive and highly coveted openings in the universities is reserved for women students, and pressure to perform well is as great for them as it is for their male colleagues, even if not all fields of study are open to them. Obviously, on the practical level, a woman has much room to maneuver, to define herself in different ways, as long as at least outward signs of compliance with requirements of propriety and piety are given.

Indeed, over the past ten years in Iran there has developed a code of dressing, of behavior, of comportment for women in public (for men too, to a lesser degree), a politically correct way of presenting oneself, which stands in public as testimony to the acceptance of fundamentalist ideals of the feminine. This comportment also serves as a camouflage for those women who resolutely pursue their own goals and ideals, such as careers, for example, that might not fit a limiting ideal of womanhood otherwise: the dark coats, headscarfs, downcast eyes, hurried steps serve as a cover under which "a woman can do and think whatever she wants," as a middle-aged woman teacher in Isfahan told me. This woman speaks for many others. Their "ideal womanhood" includes skillful manipulation of signs, successful dissimulation, and cultivation of a circle of influential people who may further their aspirations. This "ideal" may be seen as a reaction to the official, fundamentalist one, but it is real enough in Iran today nevertheless.

Outward signs of compliance with government readings of religious texts

147

FRIEDL

on Muslim women's propriety thus may be manipulated cleverly to one's advantage. But religious scriptures also are used by people to support and validate ethics that are based on positive interpersonal relationships in small groups such as family and neighborhood. These are marked by mutual help, generosity, wisdom, patience, and dignity that spring from the depth of a woman's character rather than from explicit piety and ostentatious observation of rules, and are linked by people to the legendary qualities of members of the Prophet's family. They are taken as signs of high moral excellence. They amount to "goodness," to images of "good" women, to homemade ideals that render the fulfillment of ritual and other official demands of demonstrations of piety secondary. For example, to help a poor relative quietly the year 'round counts more before God, people say, than to finance a spectacular commemorative mourning session for Imam Husein[7] (*rowze*) once a year; to visit the sick diligently is more meritorious than to spend money on a visit to the shrine of Imam Reza[8] in Mashhad; God very likely will forgive a good, hardworking mother of many children her laxity in praying than forgive a meticulously praying bad mother the neglect of her children.[9] In the ethics of everyday life women of all walks of life and in most socioeconomic circumstances find qualities that define them as "good" and give them assurance of moral superiority no matter how far away they might be from prerequisites for other ideals of womanhood, those based on fundamentalist interpretations of scriptures.

Hagiographies.

The allegedly faultless personalities and attractive qualities of a few Muslim women "saints"[10] are used widely to manipulate public sentiment. An illustration of the ideological manipulation of a legendary woman (in this case into a negative figure) is the case of Aisha, the Prophet Muhammad's last wife. By all scriptural accounts Aisha was a spirited, beautiful young woman, one of the most colorful women around the Prophet Muhammad, a model of a loving and well-loved wife.[11] As such she is acknowledged and promoted as an exemplar in Turkey, for example, where her name also is a popular first name for women. But in Iran her good looks and high spirits are interpreted as insolence, and an alleged link to treachery against her husband is used to paint her as a bad, disloyal, dishonest woman whose name is used as an insult.

Women are exhorted from the pulpit, in school, on television, to take as role models exalted exemplars such as Muhammad's daughter Fatima. Fatima is presented as a model of a virtuous woman who bears her womanhood with humility, understanding, and endurance.[12] Popular stories of unquestioned obedience to her father and her husband are told by women in a spirit of awe, accompanied by a strong undercurrent of " . . . this is how women should be, BUT. . . !". In one such legend, for example, Fatima is ordered by her father to serve tea to a blind beggar. She does so only after having covered herself completely with a veil. Told that this was superfluous because the man was blind, she answered, "I know, but I am not blind, and I might be tempted by the sight of this man." Such self-effacement, although undeniably of high moral quality, is not within the self control of most women of the ordinary kind.

On the ideological level of rationalizations of demands on women such a "good" woman is spared unpleasant dealings with the harsh world in return for her propriety. She is taken care of under the triangular protective roof of father-husband-son, free to accomplish her feminine tasks, and given exclusively feminine properties to be proud of: virginity and motherhood. This model seemingly is internally consistent: a blameless character and faultless behavior are linked to the promise of a busy, fulfilling, sheltered life as a daughter, sister, wife, mother. As such it is a frequent theme in sermons. However, Fatima herself did not enjoy the good life that ought to be linked to high morality: rather, she had to endure more suffering and hardships than most other women. Here lies an obvious contradiction, but it is not addressed by questioning the model. Rather, Fatima's modesty, self-effacement and obedience are held up as ideal feminine qualities whenever women are exhorted to behave like her vis-a-vis father or husband, for example, an ideal created at the politico-ideological top, while her incongruent suffering is linked to another realm, that of practical life experiences. Fatima the ideal, and idealized, woman is removed from ordinary women's everyday experiences: no woman in the shuffle of life has the moral strength to be obedient and quiet always, women say. In addition, unlike ordinary women, Fatima was of exalted descent, the only daughter of the Prophet Muhammad. To be like her thus is to be unlike any other woman, and this is an unrealistic, an unattainable goal. Indeed, Fatima as a Muslim superwoman looks like an image created by men, perfect for rationalizing demands for quiet and unquestioned cooperation from women. The most famous formulation of this image of Fatima as a being that transcends the ordinary realm of a woman's social and emotional ties is Shariati's "Fatima is Fatima," a text widely read and quoted in Iran:

149

FRIEDL

"I wished to say, Fatima is the daughter of the great Khadijeh." I sensed it is not Fatima. I wished to say, "Fatima is the daughter of Mohammad." I sensed it is not Fatima. I wished to say, "Fatima is the wife of Ali." I sensed it is not Fatima. I wished to say, "Fatima is the mother of Hasan and Hosein." I sensed it is not Fatima. I wished to say, "Fatima is the mother of Zainab." I still sensed it is not Fatima. No, these are all true and none of them are Fatima. "Fatima is Fatima."[13]

In the iconography of Fatima (such as, for example, in posters and murals) her contradictory, liminal status is expressed in her lack of a face: she is depicted as a black-clad figure, fully enveloped, faceless, yet obviously in the thick of violent political happenings, not seeing, not seen, yet fully, actively present. By contrast, real-life women who want to be active participants in their society are visible, even seen marching in the streets on television by the whole nation, and want to see where they are going, as a woman student said in Shiraz.

While Fatima the superwoman is somewhat beyond emotional reach, Fatima the suffering wife and mother is easily appropriated by women, not so much as an ideal of femininity, though, than as a source of empathy for the women's own hardships. Fatima is remembered and invoked when a mother mourns for her son, when she cries for her family's troubles, for her own sorrows, because Fatima knows what a woman's suffering is all about.

Ideal Fatima-femininity marked by docility, submission and great moral strength and courage can be accepted easily by women as meritorious in a religious sense. However, on the level of everyday life, women who are discharging their obligations the most successfully are said to be sharp, assertive, daring, and quick to use their powers to their own and their families' advantage. Meek and unassuming women, no matter how pious they might be are pitied as "dumb, poor, quiet" (*biharf, faqir, suqut*) and are admired only within the framework of lip-service to "goodness" in a moralistic sense. They might be "ideal" in some sense but are not realistic role models.

Zeynab, Fatima's daughter, serves as embodiment of another, quite different, femininity: according to legends of Zeynab, she stood up to oppression more visibly and with much less ambiguity than her mother; she fought for the good cause of her grandfather, father, brothers, and brother's son resourcefully and courageously; she knew about the burning political issues of the community of the faithful, was aware of the larger political situation, spoke up assertively; she was not dependent for opinion and action on husband or father, but counseled the leaders of the Shi'a community. Legends and descriptions of her role in her nephew's political struggle provide an image of the ideal Muslim woman as an assertive, tough, daring, knowledgable, brave revolutionary fighter—the woman guerilla who readily sacrifices herself for the good cause. During the Iran/Iraq War, Zeynab was invoked by government functionaries whenever Iranian women were exhorted to be brave, to advise their sons to volunteer for the front, and to take arms themselves.

Since then the most obvious political use of the example of Zeynab is in the "Sisters of Zeynab," a fundamentalist women's organization in the Islamic Republic that models its goals and purposes as well as the conduct of its members on Zeynab's militant virtues. Although Zeynab is not presented as a *mater dolorosa*, a grieving mother, a homemaker, women can identify with many aspects of Zeynab's personality: Zeynab was outspoken, so are many women; she resisted oppression, so do they; she gave advice to her male relatives, so do they; she defied force and challenged authority, and so do they, even if all of these actions often are criticized when they are taken by ordinary women, and women are chastized for them by those who are being challenged, counseled or defied.

Yet, this powerful Zeynab-image contains a contradiction too: according to Muslim law and theology, at no stage in life is a woman a completely free agent. She can become a freedom fighter or engage in political matters only with the permission of the man responsible for her (her father, her husband). Such activities will not likely be condoned and supported if she has other obligations to fulfill that are considered more pressing in everyday life and more fitting for a woman according to popular ethics, such as taking care of her husband's house and children. On the level of everyday life no respectable and self respecting woman simply can leave home, hearth, husband, children to take up a public cause, let alone fight a war, without having to do a lot of explaining. For by far most women the two lifestyles are mutually exclusive. Indeed, Zeynab herself performed as a defender of her menfolk's causes, on their permission or sufferance. She did not perform as a mother but as a sister and aunt. There are very few adult women who stand in this peculiar and un- usual kinship position, and thus, as an exemplar, Zeynab fails most women. An unmarried, childless adult woman is an anomaly, not an ideal. The career of a woman freedom fighter can, if at all, at best be realized while the woman is in a transitory stage between childhood and marriage, as a young, as yet relative- ly unencumbered adult. The two ideals personified in Fatima and Zeynab can be realized only in sequence: first Zeynab, then Fatima.

But even then a difficulty arises: the personalities and conducts required or fostered by these two ideals are psychologically incompatible: a politically as- tute, assertive, aggressive, combat-oriented, physically active young woman must, upon marriage, transform herself into an obedient, quiet, caring, house- bound homemaker, a feat few women are optimistic about being able to per- form.

Fatima and Zeynab are constructed from above and from below. From above they are infused with idealized qualities most useful for the state's and men's interests—the ideal woman backs her husband and male relatives, fights for them, if necessary, takes care of her husband's children in the spirit of self- effacement. From below, Fatima and Zeynab are constructed as compassion- ate and powerful saints familiar with the plights and problems of women. The shrine over Zeynab's grave in Syria is a popular place of pilgrimage for Iran- ian women. Women today can draw on the memory of Fatima and Zeynab's sufferings and strength as sources of comfort. In this respect the two saints are ideal women, but not so much to be emulated as to be supplicated. The names of Fatima and Zeynab are invoked in difficult situations, in pleas for help, as expressions of sympathy, as reassurance of a sisterly bond. They also are among the most popular names for women in Iran today.

"Scientific" Facts of Nature

Differences between the sexes are taken to be rooted in God's natural order and revealed not only in scriptures but also by science. They set men and women apart in such a way that women, although equal to men before God, are unequal on many consequential counts to men in society. The differences make it reasonable, if not unavoidable, to place women under men's responsibility, i.e., under men's authority and protection. The ideal woman accepts the characteristics of her sex without misgivings, lives up to the special abilities of her sex, and bears the consequences of her sexed being with understanding and humility. Briefly sketched, the most consequential characteristics of womanhood taken to be supported by scientific findings, and their logical consequences, are:

1. Women have smaller brains than men and therefore have less reason, less intelligence even, because reason and intelligence are located in the brain. This means they have less mental endurance, are easier to tire in taxing mental activity, and are prone to have their judgment clouded by emotions, by persuasion, and by seduction. Thus they are vulnerable emotionally, intellectually, and morally, and need guidance, protection, and supervision.

2. Women's bodies are smaller and weaker than men's: thus, women are said to need less food[14] and should not be expected or asked to work as hard as men. Men should take care of women's needs. Women should not try to be like men, e.g., in career- work- or sport-aspirations, because they might hurt themselves by being overly ambitious.

3. Women have less control over their emotions than men, which means that they have stronger emotions, especially empathy (*delsuz*). This makes them better equipped to be nurturant, less well equipped to be impartial and cool-headed, (a quality needed in judges, one of the jobs women are excluded from); they are more easily upset and excited, especially during pregnancy; they are prone to cry, bitch and spar. Thus, mothering comes naturally while dealing with harsh realities and quick, hard decisions does not. The ideal woman will stress the positive side of her innate nature and will make good use of it by elaborating nurturance, mothering, care for children and the men she is dependent on and who are dependent on her for services.

4. Women's sexuality is "known," proven, as it were, to be qualitatively different from men's: it is at a constant level, more or less, while men's sexual urges rise and fall; women have no urgent physical need for sexual gratification, unlike men, whose health and emotional well-being are at stake if gratification is delayed or denied. For this reason, a wife who refuses sex to her husband is a bad wife, while a husband who refuses his wife commits no sin. And a sexually very demanding wife is considered to be dangerous for her husband's health, while a sexually demanding husband has to be accomodated by his wife for the sake of his health. Female sexuality is taken to be potentially dangerous for the

social order because it may excite men to the point of scandalous behavior; it is up to women to prevent this by observing modesty if contact with men other than close relatives is unavoidable.

The ideal woman acknowledges the physical, mental, and emotional short-
comings of her sex by accepting men's guidance and counsel and by avoiding
situations where her natural inclinations will pose a danger to herself or others: she will stay with other women, avoid strange men, dress modestly, and
not aspire to careers that are unsuitable to her temperament as a woman.
However, there is also acknowledged a great variation in individual women's
actual personalities, talents and abilities, and inclinations. This allows some to
achieve in fields which we, in the United States, for example, practically consider men's, such as mathematics. The sex-segregated schooling in Iran allows
women to learn without having to play submission games with men, which
lead, in the West, to high underachievement for women students in so-called
"male" fields of study.[15] In Iran, women with special talents may be given
credit as exceptional women. For example, in July 1992 the case of a young
married woman pilot was discussed in the daily Iranian newspaper KAY-
HAN. She was said to be the only woman in her class, and exceptionally
good in her studies as well as in the cockpit. In the interview with her, her
achievements were lauded but it was stressed over and over again how exceptional her career was. She was quoted as saying that she did not think that another woman could do what she was doing. Presenting such cases as exceptions proves to all women who read about them that women with such talents are extraordinary but can be accomodated within a fundamentalist frame
of womanhood.

To my knowledge very little, if any, research has been done on how women
themselves, in the course of living their lives, work their notions and experiences of intelligence, emotions, strength and weaknesses, of their bodies'
physical processes, of sexuality into models of "good" womanhood. Currently,
the dominant, so-called fundamentalist pronouncements on female nature
furnish the most powerful rationalizations for restrictions placed on movements of women in physical, intellectual, and social space. Yet the number of
unmarried women with careers, of women students and of female adolescents
who say they want to study, and of young adults who question the inevitabil-
ity of marriage and children or say that they do not want large families seem
to be rising rather rapidly in Iran.[16] Intense governmental propaganda since
1991 for birth control and small families is taking away the earlier stigma associated with having few, or no, children. Organized recreation activities like
hiking, martial arts, ball games are now offered—and attended by unmarried
young women—even in villages. All this indicates that women reconsider issues of moral dimensions of femininity and limitiations without necessarily
having to leave the frame of their fundamentalist society's norms and expec-

153

FRIEDL

tations. They find it possible to "modernize" without overtly challenging dominant doctrines. For young women with such aspirations the main hurdle is their families' and communities' traditional gender expectations and standards of propriety rather than religion. A mother or brother concerned with public appearances more likely will forbid a teenage daughter/sister to go hiking in the mountains than will the local mullah.

Anti-West Rhetoric

In Iran the ideal Muslim-Iranian woman is described as the opposite of so-called "Western" women, especially those living in the United States. These are variously characterized by (and accused of): refusing to have children; frequent divorce; flaunting their sexuality; promiscuity and adultery; frivolity; being luxury and money oriented and materialistic; working very hard at their careers so that no strength is left for husband and family. All this is said to render women in the West not only misguided and evil but also easy targets for exploitation, from overwork to prostitution. Western feminism is taken to be the ideology promoting this type of woman, fit for the evil, inhumane U.S. capitalist-exploitative society. Islamic women are in danger of being seduced by the glitter of Western women's appearances and by false promises of feminists, and thus ought to be kept sheltered from Western influences. For example, during a parliamentary debate the widely held opinion was voiced that Iranian women students might want to go overseas to study in order to have access to men, and therefore only married women students ought to be permitted to study abroad.[17] A so-called "Muslim feminism" containing Zeynab-Fatima features is offered to channel attention away from Western ideas.

Anti-West rhetoric profilizes ideal Muslim womanhood in contrast to a negative, foreign womanhood that is expressively constructed for this purpose. "Western" ways of being a woman thus are discussed and circulated, and enter the script for Iranian women unintentionally together with white-dress weddings, Hollywood movies (on smuggled videocassettes) and other items of popular culture. For example, although cosmetics are banned officially in public, sales are soaring; hairdoes of the fashion conscious strata of the new middle class are modeled after American movie stars; brand name foreign shoes and clothes are known, admired, and, if at all possible, bought. At least in the monied, urban elite the admired woman looks very much like a "Western" one, and "goodness" is measured with different criteria. However, in the anti-Western rhetoric Iranian women appear as morally superior to Western women no matter what they look like or watch or wear as long as their actions, unlike their Western sisters', do not undermine the androcentric, "patriarchal" power structure—as long as they are Muslim and Iranian women.

EXISTENTIAL EXPERIENCES

Glaringly absent in the list of sources for qualities of fundamentalist ideals of womanhood are features that pertain to women's existential situations. These include: the joys and sorrows, victories and defeats of everyday life experiences; women's resourcefulness in solving everyday problems, especially under the steadily worsening economic conditions in Iran; their ambitions, even if acted upon and cultivated not for themselves but for the success of a son; their hard work under restrictive circumstances such as sex segregation, cumbersome clothes, being pronounced ritually unclean from menstruation and from handling babies' excrements, very limited access to resources outside the home; women's spirituality, which receives hardly any attention from anybody, including social scientists; women's skills and knowledge that account for feelings of self-worth and are instrumental for being counted as successful as well as "good." Many of the qualities women say they need to be successful in everyday life are belittled, even condemned as gossip, pushyness, immodesty. These issues are not topics of sermons and fundamentalist discussions of womanhood, but they surface in discussions among women, in newspaper and magazine articles, in debates among intellectuals. I submit that with these factors alternative ideals of womanhood are constructed from below, subverting the androcentric one presented by Islamicist ideologues, men as well as women. We know little about them. Yet, concentrating on the "official," spectacular, media-friendly one, the one that presents Iranian women as voiceless, as black shapes on our television screens and in so many reports and analyses from the Islamic Republic, leads us to neglect the women's own efforts in shaping their religious and cultural lives. Such stereotyping means either that we tacitly accept the politico-ideological structure in Iran (which disadvantages women) as uniform, immutable, all-powerful, which I tried to show it isn't, or else that we define women in contrast to extreme fundamentalist models. In this case, we must assume that women have to reject or question Islam if they want to "deviate" from the fundamentalist models, no matter how relevant or irrelevant these actually are in women's daily lives, and this is not the case either.

The different models of ideal womanhood available to women in Iran today are applied to support demands on women and in judgments of women's behaviors within various relationships of power.[18] Fundamentalist models likely will be activated to support demands (by men and women) on women in subordinate positions, such as, for example, demands by a husband of quiet surrender of his wife's salary; demands by a brother of unquestioned acceptance of a particular suitor by his sister; demands by a mother-in-law of obedience by her daughters-in-law; demands by a woman school principal of observation of the strictest possible dress code by women students. The very same women will position themselves and others in quite different "ideals of

155

FRIEDL

womanhood" when they in turn are in a subordinate position: the bossy mother-in-law will dismiss as unimportant her own insubordination to her husband, which is a sin by fundamentalist standards, and instead will stress her success as mother, her generosity, her skills as a teacher or weaver or peacemaker as important attributes of morality. The various ideals amount to a roster of possibilities that allow women to position themselves, and others, close to one or the other ideal at various times and in various situations. Not only is the social field in which women in Iran operate a dynamic one, but the ethical-philosophical one is just as dynamic. While fundamentalist rhetoric dominates public discourses on women, women themselves have created many choices that allow them to justify a wide range of thoughts, values, and behaviors.

NOTES

1. I am grateful to Western Michigan University, the National Endowment for the Humanities and the Social Science Research Council for financial support for various stages of the research in Iran on which this paper is based.

2. My thanks and appreciation also go to Reinhold Loeffler, my collaborator in the field and at home, whose insights and critiques contributed essentially to the shape of my work.

3. For a recent discussion of ideals of femininity in the Iranian press and in books, see Najmabadi, 1994.

4. See Aghajanian, 1994.

5. A new Journal, *Frauen in Der Einen Welt*, carries the subtitle: Journal for intercultural research on women's everyday-lives (Zeitschrift für interkulturelle Frauenalltagsforschung) to fill this particular gap in social science literature on women.

6. See other contributions in this volume.

7. Imam Husein (i.e., "Leader Husein"), a grandson of the Prophet Muhammad, together with many followers was killed in the battle of Kerbela, the site of decisive defeat in the struggle for political power over all Muslims. His suffering and death are commemorated by Shi'a Muslims in the month of his mourning, Muharram, every year.

8. Reza, a direct descendant of the Prophet Muhammad is venerated as the eighth leader (Imam) by Shi'a Muslims. A pilgrimage to his shrine in Mashhad in Northeast Iran bestows the honorific title "Mashhadi" on the pilgrim.

9. For an elaboration of this world view see Loeffler, 1988.

10. There are no saints in the Christian sense, which is the one that gives the term its essential meaning. Rather, in Islam, exalted, efficacious personalities are descendants of the Prophet Muhammad through the line of Imams, leaders of the faithful in Shi'a Islam, and derive their super-human powers from their descent. They are supplicated or thanked for help during visits to their tombs and burial places.

11. See Abbott, 1942; Knappert, 1985

12. For a discussion of Fatima as ideal Muslim woman, see Combs-Schilling, 1989.

13. Shariati, 1980: 226.

14. See Aghajanian, op.cit.p.52ff.

15. See, for example, Mahony, 1985. In Iran, teaching materials in academic subjects are the same for male and female students, although school attendance, the quality of instruction, courses offered and accessibility of high school education are not equal for both. For a discussion of education in the Islamic Republic see Higgins and Shoar-Ghaffari, 1994.

16. This suggestion is based on observations and discussions I had with women in Iran in 1994, and cannot yet be backed up with statistics. Women report—and I felt—that a shift in these attitudes is occurring in Iran since about 1990.

17. See Esfandiari, 1994: 75f.

18. For a discussion of issues of power for women in Iran see Friedl, 1994. For a historical-sociological overview see Tohidi, 1994. Hegland, 1983, describes the circumstances under which village women participated in the revolution of 1979.

REFERENCES

Abbott, N. 1942. *Aisha the Beloved of Mohammed*. Chicago: University of Chicago Press.

Aghajanian, A. 1994. "The Status of Women and Female Children in Iran: an update from the 1986 census." In *In the Eye of the Storm: Women in Post-Revolutionary Iran*. eds. M. Afkhami and E. Friedl, pp. 44–60. London: I.B. Tauris.

Combs-Schilling, M.E. 1989. *Sacred Performances*. New York: Columbia University Press.

Esfandiari, H. 1994. "The Majles and Women's Issues in the Islamic Republic of Iran" In *In the Eye of the Storm: Women in Post-Revolutionary Iran*, eds. M. Afkhami and E. Friedl, pp. 61–79. London: I.B. Tauris.

Frauen in der Einen Welt: *Zeitschrift für Interkulturelle Frauenalltagsforschung*. Nürnberg: Verlag für Interkulturelle Kommunikation.

Friedl, E. 1994. "Sources of Female Power in Iran." In *In the Eye of the Storm: Women in Post-Revolutionary Iran*, eds. M. Afkhami and E. Friedl, pp. 151–167. London: I.B. Tauris.

Hegland, M. 1983. "Aliabad Women: Revolution as Religious Activity." In *Women and Revolution*, ed. G. Nashat, pp. 171–194. Boulder: Westview Press.

Higgins, P., and P. Shoar-Ghaffari 1994. "Women's Education in the Islamic Republic of Iran." In *In the Eye of the Storm: Women in Post-Revolutionary Iran*, eds. M. Afkhami and E. Friedl,. pp. 19–43. London: I.B. Tauris.

Knappert, J. 1985. *Islamic Legends: Histories of the Heroes, Saints, and Prophets of Islam*. Leiden: E.J. Brill.

Loeffler, R. 1988. *Islam in Practice*. Albany: State University of New York Press.

Mahony, P. 1985. *Schools for the Boys: Co-education Reassessed*. London: Hutchinson.

Najmabadi, A. 1994. "Power, Morality, and the New Muslim Womanhood." In *The Politics of Social Transformation in Iran, Afghanistan and Pakistan*, eds. M. Weiner and A. Banuazizi, pp. 366–389. Syracuse: Syracuse University Press.

Shariati, A. 1980. *Fatima is Fatima*. L. Bakhtiar, transl. Tehran: The Shariati Foundation.

Tohidi, N. 1994. "Modernity, Islamization, and Women in Iran." In *Gender and National Identity*, ed. V.M. Moghadam, pp. 110–147. London & New Jersey, and Karachi: ZED Books and Oxford University Press.

157

FRIEDL

GIVING BIRTH TO A SETTLEMENT
Maternal Thinking and Political Action of Jewish Women on the West Bank

Tamar El-Or, Gideon Aran

ON OCTOBER 27, 1991, busloads of Jewish settlers from the West Bank, members of the right-wing political movement Gush Emunim,[1] made their way to a mass demonstration in Tel Aviv to protest the beginning of peace negotiations in Madrid. Their banner read "You don't sell out your mother," and it reflected their fear that the meetings would lead to the withdrawal of Israel from the West Bank. A Palestinian attack on one of the buses left two dead: the driver, a Jew from West Jerusalem, and Rachel Drouk, a settler from Shilo and mother of seven. After Rachel's funeral, 25 women from settlements all over the West Bank made their way to the site of the killing—a barren, rocky hillside in Samaria—set up tents, and stayed the night. The night stretched

AUTHORS' NOTE: *We wish to thank Judith Lorber, Daphna Izraeli, Nitza Yanai, and Sarit Hellman for their helpful comments on this article. A previous version of this article was presented at the annual meeting of the Israeli Anthropological Association. February 1993.* Reprinted with permission from *Gender and Society.* Vol. 9, no. 1, February 1995. pp. 60–78. Sage Publications.

into a week (the traditional mourning period), then a month, and finally culminated in the founding of a new settlement. The women called it Rachelim[2] in memory of Rachel Drouk, Rachel Weiss, who burned to death with her three children in a Palestinian attack on a bus near Jericho on October 30, 1988, and Rachel, one of the four matriarchs of the Jewish people.

The act of founding Rachelim was highly exceptional. Right-wing women—most of them orthodox, all married, all mothers—established a protest settlement in the West Bank. Most of these 35-to-45-year-old college-educated women worked, and some held political positions in their community. Orthodox women are accustomed to operating separately from men, because of the traditional seclusion of the sexes. This separation created a vital society of women capable of carrying out spontaneous acts on a community level, as well as organizing in large leagues. Emuna is the largest such league of religious women (Sasson-Levy 1993).

Religious-Jewish fundamentalism as meta narrative contains numerous and varied references to women's roles, status, motherhood, and femininity. Since it constitutes a holistic religious world view based on mainstream orthodoxy, while tending toward a radical interpretation, these references are in dispute with Western feminist ideologies (Davidman 1991; Heschel 1983; Kaufman 1991; Koltun 1976; Weidman-Schneider 1984).

The expansion of traditional women's performances beyond founding day crèches and girls' schools and beyond performing acts of charity is indicative of essential changes in the status of these women. These changes stem from the open cultural market and the democratic state within which the women live. They bring the women to reinterpret the feminist messages embedded in Jewish culture. The Rachelim event is a prime example of the extension of Orthodox women's performance. It was an attempt to operate as women and mothers within the political arena—not as supporters of the men and not as claimants for a fair share, but as initiators of a novel strategy based on novel arguments.

It is tempting to analyze the event according to feminist theories of motherhood, peace, and political action. Evaluating fundamentalist women's actions in terms of Western feminist theory, however, produces unsound results. In Western feminist theory, religious women, especially those who are not part of the West, are seen as a homogeneously powerless group, as victims of their culture (Mohanty 1988). We suggest that it is more appropriate to listen to the narrative presented by the women involved in the Rachelim event. We attribute significance to their experience of motherhood and its political potential in the local cultural context, and we reread the narrative through the theory of maternal thinking (Ruddick 1989). The insights gained from the local event also serve as a critique of Ruddick's essentialist and universalistic theory. Examining the feminist value of the act of founding Rachelim reveals the significance of the event for the women and their society, at the same

EL-OR, ARAN

time unveiling basic social structures underlying the gender category (Strathern 1988).

THE CHAIN OF EVENTS

Immediately following the funeral in the settlement of Shilo, 25 women made their way to the site of the murder. Inside the tent erected at Rachelim, Naomi Sapir recounted the following to one of us (El-Or):[3]

> It could have been me, just the opposite of the sentence we use so often in Israel, "It can't happen to me." I, like each woman there, felt that it could easily have happened to me. Orphaned children were sitting now in some house, and that was what was so acutely distressing. Rachel was the first woman from the settlements who was killed, and for us that was the shock. We understood the price we might have to pay, we grasped the enormity of the risk, the responsibility we have towards our children who travel the roads every day, and mainly the helplessness. We made the decision—we were staying. It was a form of protest, a kind of cry to the world. We are still here, going on with life, still founding settlements. In a place of death, lights will begin to twinkle at night. There will be life. We decided to name the spot Rachelim in honor of Rachel Drouk, Rachel Weiss, who was burned to death with her three babies in a bus attack near Jericho, and, of course, after our Biblical matriarch, Rachel.

The husbands of these women were not partners in their decision or the act. Their role was limited to the technical matters of preparing the equipment needed for staying the night at the bare, hostile location. Both the Israeli military and civil administrations in the area opposed the women's move and raised logistic and legal obstacles to persuade them to go home. Finally, both authorities agreed to allow the women to hold a vigil at the site until the end of the traditional week of mourning. Through parliamentary and extraparliamentary actions and negotiations with the military, the seven-day period was extended to one month, then two months, with the women still in place.

The army erected a large tent for the women and a smaller tent opposite it to house soldiers guarding them. The original 25 Rachelim women took turns sitting in the tent, accompanied by another 200 women, who came in shifts from all settlements in the territories. Girls of all ages from all over the country made pilgrimages to the site, and organized groups of girls arrived from diverse public and religious schools to study in the tent. Rabbis and male and female teachers gave lessons in Judaism. The Rachelim women related their story to visitors—the chronology of events leading up to the founding of the settlement—over and over again. During the first week, the women remained day and night; later, they began going home in the evening, leaving their husbands, sons, and brothers to stand guard.

Three weeks later, the women of Rachelim issued a call to other women in the territories and Israel. It was published in *Nekuda*, the settlers' monthly

EL-OR, ARAN

periodical, distributed in leaflets, and hung on a large poster in the tent. It read:

> We the women of Judea, Samaria and Gaza have established a memorial vigil. We demand we be allowed to found the settlement of Rachelim at this spot, on this hill, where the murderers lay in ambush. There are sufficient government lands for the establishment of a permanent settlement. We remain at this site demanding to found a settlement, for this is the only Zionist response to this criminal murder. We hold vigil at this place, and we will persevere in the hope that the Government of Israel will decide to found a civilian settlement at the spot from which the shots were fired. This will be the way to prove to those who would uproot us that they will never achieve their goal. Not only will we not be uprooted, our roots will only grow deeper. We call upon every woman and mother in the settlements and every woman and mother in Israel to stand up and be counted with us at this memorial vigil. And, of course, men too, husbands and sons, are invited. Let us find comfort in the building of the land. Haim (1991: 13)

The women called it "The Feminist Manifesto." The gender used throughout the document was feminine plural—a powerful statement in Hebrew, which is a gender-sensitive language and in which the generic plural is masculine. The ending explicitly includes men and brings the feminine formalization to a climax.

The choice to unite spontaneously and act on a separatist basis is formalized here. The call is addressed to Jewish residents of the territories and Israel, as well as the government, and is completely by and for women. It concludes with the call to all women and mothers in Israel to express their support for the vigil. The call to men begins with "And, of course . . .," but the opposite is implied: men are addressed only as an afterthought. There may or may not have been a brief ideological debate at this point, but the upshot was that the ladies of the manor had decided to invite the lords as well.

One could say that the tent guards had been invited to step in. Once the seven-day mourning period was over, the women no longer stayed at the tent during the night. Their men, while not part of the protest settlement, stayed to guard at night—perhaps out of concern or worry. Some came to visit during the day, bringing the children to see their mothers, but they were always visitors. The invitation "to step in" seems more like a plea for consent and support rather than for joining in.

"The Feminist Manifesto" and extensive media coverage brought a massive response throughout the West Bank. Following vigorous public lobbying by the women, the government approved Rachelim as a permanent settlement and study center for women. Within three months of the Rachelim incident, two more Jews from the territories were murdered, and other settlers adopted the women's model and established memorial settlements at the sites. The women of Rachelim had revived an act from Zionist history in which a settlement was founded at a site where Jews were killed and the site was named after them. Unlike Rachelim, the two subsequent memorial settlements did not last. Following the change of government in June 1992 from Right to Labor, all projects in the West Bank, including the development of Rachelim, were frozen.

DOINT IT THEIR WAY—THE APPROPRIATION OF THE POLITICAL ACT

The women passed the time at Rachelim debating their case with the military and the civil administration, attempting to regulate and contain the storm they had created. They prayed, kept the dietary laws with respect to food delivered to the tent, and studied. Traditionally a male endeavor in Judaism, religious study has for some time been undergoing female appropriation (El-Or 1993, 1994; Weissman 1976).[4] Local rabbis came to teach the women at Rachelim; it was reminiscent of how women used to come to mostly men's settlements to cook and launder for them.

In the November 1991 issue of *Nekuda*, journalist Emuna Elon wrote about the reaction of nonorthodox Jews to the phenomenon:

> Anyone passing by would probably have been surprised to see a group of tired, eccentric women dressed in long, full skirts and head scarves, sitting around a rabbi and listening to a lesson. The soldiers who came to guard there had never seen such a sight. These poor men had to stand there in the biting cold. But the women went up to them and offered them homemade cakes sent by their families. They invited them to warm themselves by the small heater. (p. 44)

The Rachelim women told guests from outside their political group about soldiers guarding the site who wrote words of admiration in the guest book. Some of these were kibbutz-born men who are identified with the left-most sectors of Israeli society. The women told of officials and senior army officers who expressed admiration for their courage and resolve. The women took every opportunity to thank these people; they referred to them by first names to not disclose their identity and to show their familiarity with them and their gratitude for the personal connections. While visiting the tent, we watched the women receiving reporters and visitors in traditionally feminine ways: they smiled, played the role of gracious hostess, and offered food and drink and warmth by the stove. Numerous children ran underfoot, and the women's arms were full of the babies they had not left at home.

Conversations in the test were "women's room "ones; the tone and content were set by the women. Visitors, including us, were obliged to acknowledge that the primary actors were mothers and women and that the topics of discussion were children and motherly concerns. One way or another, it led to talking about their men and to listening to criticism and a rereading of masculine politics. The women also wished to speak about their appearance. With

163

a reflexivity typical of women and minorities, they repeatedly and somewhat sarcastically alluded to how the press was not accustomed to their "garb," their long full skirts and dresses, in the bitterly cold, barren landscape. Their head coverings were wrapped in the manner of religious women. They objected to the description of them in the media as "sloppy orthodoxesses" and to the detailed account by a Tel Aviv female reporter of the mud around the tent and the filth in their makeshift toilet.[5] As Geula Tzroia told one of us(El-Or), "It's important to us to look pretty and feminine. We have no need to come across as Amazons on the mount. Our strength is quiet, beautiful, and positive."

At a political rally at the Jerusalem Theater (described below), the women of Rachelim were elaborately dressed, wearing fashionable hats, earrings, and the 1,000 women present that evening, the women of Rachelim stood out for the elegance of their clothing.

The act in question was neither perceived nor depicted by the women in violent heroic terms. No alienation was created between those disobeying the law and those upholding it. The women were tired, the soldiers were cold. The women were not afraid to couch their political action in terms of the interaction between the players. These terms were not abstract; rather, they referred to the people behind the action. They chose to diminish the political struggle and to emphasize instead the possible dialogue between the rival Jewish sides. Thus, the traditional rivalry between those who believe in the Greater Land of Israel and those willing to give it all back for peace became mere appearance and the shared human values were underscored—the hunger and cold, the presence of both parties in the occupied territories—soldiers, government officials, and citizen-residents.

THE SENSIBILITY OF WOMEN'S IRRATIONALITY

Women are often described as acting instinctively and emotionally. Rationality and sensible thought are preserved for masculine action (Harding 1986; Ortner 1974). The women of Rachelim employed this convention for the expressed purpose of deconstructing it. They were proud to describe their action as motivated by a bundle of feminine (motherly) emotions, free of the institutionalized and abstract thought of the dominant male group. They described their action, however, as spontaneous, as the only possible path of rational action, and therefore blurred the accepted distinction between the rational(masculine) and the irrational (feminine).

In the November 1991 issue of *Nekuda*, Emuna Elon's article stressed the spontaneity of the act of founding Rachelim by referring to a tale from the Midrash (a major corpus of Biblical explication) known to every orthodox girl and boy. The tale attributes the Hebrew people's delivery from bondage in Egypt to the initiative of the Hebrew women, who were pious and righteous. Pharaoh, King of Egypt, sentenced all the newborn Hebrew males to death—a decree, the Midrash intimates, that caused celibacy among the men. The Hebrew women, nevertheless, went out to the fields, seduced the men working there, and became pregnant. They hid from the Egyptians, bore their infants alone like the beasts of the field, and hid their babies. God helped the women's initiative with miracles that provided them with the food and shelter necessary to raise their children. These "madwomen" were the progenitors of the next generation that was responsible for Israel's salvation and exodus from Egypt. These "madwomen" combined their powers of seduction and drive for pregnancy and childbearing with the feminine optimism that sees raising children as feasible under any circumstances. The men, on the other hand, were fearful, obeyed authority, and tried to act rationally.

Elon compared the settlers' wives to these Hebrew women in Egypt. Today's men, she claimed, were once radicals under the Labor Government in the mid-seventies but became part of the establishment when the Likud party, which favors annexation of the territories to Israel, came to power in 1977. Today, the men fill official positions and work to further their objectives through accepted conventional channels, while the women do not feel constrained by the establishment and are free to act as "madwomen." This is no time for "rational" conduct, said Elon. "It is an emergency—a time for 'mad' action" (Elon 1991: 44) to continue the previous policy of Jewish settlement of the West Bank despite the political changes and the Intifada. The women realize this and will be the ones to jar the system, carrying both men and women in their wake. A seemingly irrational act, according to Elon, has become a necessary and logical strategy: women can bring off what the dominant but immobilized men cannot permit themselves. The article described the motherly practice itself as madness:

> One hand stirs the soup, the other bandages a scraped knee, the third holds the telephone and the fourth turns up the volume on the radio to catch the news. (Elon 1991: 45)

According to Elon, women with four hands can do anything.

In the past, these women were in no hurry to free themselves from the group's policy. They progressed in step with the men, following their vision and distinguishing themselves at the tasks the men vacated for them (Aran 1991). This active involvement did not prevent Elon from saying, "We've been wasting our time. Giving birth and making homes isn't enough. The feminine voice (in Hebrew, *Hakol Hanashi*) should have been heard in the political system too" (1991: 44). The women's voice had not been silenced previously, but its tones had been in harmony with the men's. For several years, a woman named Daniella Weiss held the position of secretary general of Gush Emunim, and women established Eli—Mothers for Israel—an organization that mobilized support based on concern for the well-being of the children in the West Bank. Now, however, as women reflected on the past, they were intensely critical of their previous efforts.

> We attended parlor meetings after the children were fed and put to bed, after we had hung the laundry and washed the dishes. We held a large assembly at a Jerusalem hall, everyone applauded the beautiful speeches and drove home. But we stayed on the dangerous roads, went on having more babies, carefully monitoring high-risk pregnancies and tending husbands with flu. (Elon 1991: 44)

Politics custom-tailored for men and the masculine fantasy of transcendence were not suited to the women's lives. In the act of founding Rachelim, their point of departure was the practical reality—acts not words, the concrete concern for their children, which men customarily translate into ideology. They were not afraid of the kitsch or sentimentality that is attributed to motherhood in any case. They accomplished a political appropriation with unique features, features that derive first and foremost from their experience, from the basic commonality that unites orthodox Jewish women—motherhood. Together with the practical concerns, they drew the suitable images of women from the Midrash about the women in Egypt. This configuration, when given historical-cultural legitimization, allowed them to come close to Western feminist experience.

The appropriation of political action by the women of Rachelim comprises two central moves: adoption and feminization.

Adoption. The women chose to lay a claim to a symbolic tract of land. It is accepted strategy in Zionist history to settle sites identified as ancient Jewish settlements and disputed lands that represent a risk to the reemerging Jewish entity. In this sense, Gush Emunim sees itself as following the pioneering Zionist line formerly dominated by the local labor movement. By the mid-seventies, Gush Emunim was appropriating Zionist politics, in both ideological and practical terms (Aran 1991). While Gush Emunim represents itself as the authentic interpreter and implementor of pioneering Zionism, the women now wished to single themselves out as bearers of a flag the men had tired of carrying. The women of Gush Emunim were doing to their men exactly what the movement as a whole had done to the Zionist pioneers before them.

Feminization. Feminist action or research may be defined as having the following characteristics: an organization based only on women; the determination of a feminine-maternal motive as the motive for acting; the description of the aim of action as treating a problem with special ramifications for children and mothers; the aspiration to create widespread identification with women and children outside the acting group; criticism of male politics; and construction of fields of feminine creativity and response (Duffy 1985; Rein-

166

harz 1992). The Rachelim event shows such features. It also includes references to Israeli women outside the territories, a certain reflexivity relating to
Palestinian women and left-wing Jewish women, a reinterpretation of the
history of Gush Emunim, an on-site designing of feminine discourse about
women and mothers, feminine media coverage, attempts to change the image
of the female settler, and amplification of the feminine (Jewish and orthodox)
voice in the local and national political discourse.

WE ARE HERE BECAUSE WE HAVE WE HAVE CHILDREN—THE
MATERNAL MOTIVE

Inside the army tent on a cold rainy day, a group of women sat around a
makeshift table as a small gas stove struggled to warm the area. Miri Mass, a
woman of about 36 years, a textile artist and handicraft teacher, told us the
following:

> First of all I have an obligation to my children, as all of us mothers do. I'm a moth-
> er of seven children, God be blessed, and I'm responsible for their safety. The chil-
> dren travel to school every day by bus, and to after-school activities every after-
> noon. They come home and ask, "Why is nothing done? Why aren't they shot?
> Why doesn't someone finish off those Arabs?" These are natural questions for a
> child to ask when he is attacked. His bus is escorted by the Israeli army and what
> does he see? He sees that when stones are thrown at him the soldiers either flee or
> do nothing. We, of course, raise him to revere the soldiers and our sons enlist in the
> elite army units, so what can I tell him? How should I raise him? I should also raise
> him not to hate Arabs, shouldn't I? And not to want to kill them, I should convey
> that to him too. What can I tell him? So this is my answer! I'm building a settle-
> ment. This is how to live in peace. Not by killing and war. By creating.

"Yes, but this settlement is dangerous," one of us offered. "It just increases the
risks." Miri replied,

> Childbirth is also dangerous, isn't it? Have you considered that? When a woman
> becomes pregnant she is taking a risk. So? Do women stop having children?
> There are still places in the world with a 40 percent risk of infant death during
> labor. Do women stop having babies there? Giving birth is a huge beginning,
> with some amount of risk. We are the ones who know how to do that. And I'll
> have you know that our settlement here has given the children a lot of strength
> and a lot of meaning. Someone is doing something, not just sitting and waiting
> for the Arabs to throw stones. I can tell you stories that would set your teeth on
> edge about what we have gone through here in five years of Intifada. How my
> husband and myself with nine children(two of them friends' children) happened
> into a village by mistake and how the women closed in on us. Yes, yes, the
> women blocked the way and I could already glimpse my approaching death. I
> radioed the army and got no answer. Finally, there was no choice. My husband
> got out of the car and fired a few shots in the air. The women moved aside, the

army arrived and we were saved. And the children have come home many times through a hail of stones and I've never heard them say, "Mother, I don't want to go, I'm scared." I must think of my children and that's that.

Naomi, also one of the founders of Rachelim, was standing on the side and interrupted Miri at this point:

And have you ever thought of the Arab children? Of a child who is awakened by soldiers in the middle of the night, in the cold, so they can search his house? Have you thought of him?

Miri replied,

I think of him at the humane level, of course I do. But his parents are the ones who aren't thinking of him. They should have made sure that there would be no reason to search their house. Just like they take him to demonstrations and then they're surprised when he's wounded.

Naomi went on to express what we the researchers refrained from saying:

They have no tanks or rifles to bring to demonstrations, so they bring women and children. I really respect the Palestinian woman. Her perseverance. She knows that the one who is stronger will be the one who will stay here. I have a lot of respect and admiration for her—she acts.

"And 'Women in Black'?"[7] one of us asked. Geula answered,

Those women? They're barren. They do nothing but stand and talk. I respect their persistence but not the practical application or the attitude. They know very well how to count the Palestinian children killed in the territories but not the Jews who are killed. Why didn't they express their sorrow about the murder here? When they went to kiss Hanan Ashrawi [spokeswoman for the Palestinian delegation to the peace talks]before she left for Madrid, they could have stopped at Mrs. Rofeh's [the wife of the Jerusalemite driver killed in the incident] and offered condolences, without going out of their way. But no, that didn't occur to them.

Naomi said,

I have no problem with the Palestinian women. As a mother, I totally understand them. The problem is that their leaders and our leaders aren't doing what has to be done. So they're on the roads and we're here.

Miri responded,

That's really the point. It's not the problem of feelings that I don't have for those children and those women, it's the political dispute I have with them over who should be the landlord here.

This emotional identification appears to be fed by the steadfastness attributed to women, especially mothers. The Palestinian women are perceived by the women of Rachelim as their counterparts: bearers of life, caregivers, and victims of male politics. The practice of motherhood that they share includes three basic tasks: works of preservative love, nurturing for personal growth, and training for social acceptability (Ruddick 1989). These are expressed overtly by the women of Rachelim.

WORKS OF PRESERVATIVE LOVE

As Ruddick has written, "Preserving the lives of children is the central constitutive invariant aim of maternal practice; the commitment to achieving that aim is the constitutive maternal act" (1989: 19). The primary importance of the physical safety of children was stressed by the women of Rachelim, the Jewish women who came to visit and offer support, and newspaper articles written by women. In a lucid voice, uncamouflaged and unafraid of being accused of melodramatics, they pointed out the direct danger to the children and the indirect danger to them should one of their parents be injured or killed. The women described in detail incident after incident where their own lives and those of their children were nearly lost. After five years of Intifada, there was no lack of such incidents: stones thrown at the windows of the yellow school busses carrying the settlers' children, roadblocks, and, lately, attacks with firearms.

As Hanna Dotan asked during our conversation in the test,

> What good is the lovely house I built with my own hands if I can't go outside? True, the children aren't scared, but I am very worried. Things can't go on like this.

169

None of them raised the elementary question, "Why are we here in the first place?" Their presence in the territories required no explanation, especially in view of Israel's possible full or partial withdrawal from these territories. Holding fast to the demand for a Greater Israel, the women refrained from ideological discussions and focused on the practical matter of the children's safety. By working the maternal issue, they shelved the unbridgeable political debate between themselves and other schools of thought in Israeli society. They felt that on that issue they could garner a broad base of support. Speaking about the safety of children, they urged listeners to accept a fait accompli in which the children were there (with the government's support, of course), and their safety somehow had to be ensured.

When forced to address the ideological issue, the women of Rachelim tried to bring it into line with the questions hurled at the settlers by their opponents, and the doubts and dissent sometimes voiced among the settlers. Their answers were part of their firm belief that Israelis are duty bound to occupy and hold all parts of the historical land of Israel, that living in the territories was a risk to be taken today in the interest of securing complete safety in the future.

At this point, it is tempting to analyze the women's structured discourse with their surroundings as a play between maternal *practice* and maternal *rhetoric*. Direct concern for the children's safety requires immediate departure from the area, while the rhetoric exploits the danger surrounding the children's lives. Did the event emerge as a maternal reaction to the reality? Or was it a counterfeit maternal discourse plucked from an altogether different discourse? A discourse of nationalism and the legitimate ownership of lands, of a messianic dream of the Greater Land of Israel—in short, the macro narrative of Gush Emunim? To discern which interpretation is appropriate to the event, the maternal narrative must be heard before it can be critiqued.

A novel element in the act of founding Rachelim was the women's lack of shame in verbalizing their fears for the safety of their children and the settlers in general. Their action, they claim, had originated in a mortal fear for the lives of their children. They introduced fear into the discourse of the settlers' community, a subject absent from the male ideological discourse and thus denied. The women's admission of fear was a source of empathy and identification. True, they did not seek the legitimization of this fear, as did the "Women in Black." They intended to eradicate it by harnessing its reverberations to the drive for increasing security.

DEVLOPING A FEMINIST STAND POINT(?)

The fact that the women of Rachelim were not alienated from the value system in which family and maternity are central accounts for their ability to draw strength from the maternal practice. Using their maternal power, they strove to better their position in the social arena, or even control it for a while. In doing so, they somewhat paradoxically reformed (or redefined) maternal practice. The same traditional maternal motif that mobilized them was in partial contradiction to the task they had undertaken. In this sense, they may have been giving precedence to their responsibility to the new baby—the settlement. They had left their homes, gone off and left their children, husbands, jobs, kitchens, and households. It was not a total absence. The distances are short and they could and did travel home from Rachelim in no more than one hour; yet, the act of founding Rachelim, at least in its initial spontaneous stages, separated the women from their homes and routine roles.

Through these transitions between home and the camp, the women were rediscovering their practical status, by no means novel, but partially obscured by their traditional roles. They were discovering the motherhood that lies outside the glorifying discourse of family in Gush Emunim (Aran 1987; Burgansky 1977). They were experiencing the beginnings of acknowledgment of their status as fighting women capable of overcoming the guilt feelings cast at them from every direction. They enjoyed putting aside their sense of duty to husbands and children and carrying on with the task they had set themselves. As Avigail Haim of *Nekuda* reported from one of the women, "The kids are okay, the women next door are helping out, there isn't much in the fridge, but so what; it's no catastrophe" (1991: 12).

The women's settlement increasingly resembled a consciousness-raising workshop for women. With their husbands back home, at work, at the house, or at their studies and teaching, the women of Rachelim remained in the tent and came to reflect on their femininity. Through dialogue—among themselves; between themselves and the rest of the Jewish population of the territories; with the authorities, the army, the government, the media—negotiations on the subjects of their femininity, religiosity, and radical womanhood developed. Reckoning a whole rereading of the history of Gush Emunim was taking place, singling out and underlining the women's role in the success of the settling of the territories, even to the point of reducing the entire saga of the Greater Land of Israel to the women's unswerving, radical belief and devotion. In the interviews granted to journalists during the first few days, women avoided the term "feminism."[8] They replaced it, when offered, with terms including "motherhood" or "daughters of Israel." In time, however, new formulations began to appear. After hours of discussion and thought, and encouraged by the relative success they were gradually able to claim by staying put and becoming a role model for other groups, they dared to change their terminology. The following are selected quotations from Shelomo Dror's article entitled "Women Settlers on the Frontier Line," in the newspaper *Hadashot* on February 2, 1992:

171

[Naomi Sapir:] We didn't come here out of boredom or to rebel against conventions. We were the ones who created them in the first place. It was we who built this society.

The men need to undergo a process to make them understand that we are equal partners. Fifty percent of the settlers are women. How can anyone come and tell me to stay at home. That's absurd. The women can go out and make their own livings and ensure their own security. We came out of the kitchen long ago.

[Miri Mass:] They ask us how our action is viewed by the religious society around us, which wishes to see woman as "a helpmate" (Genesis 2:18). I answer that for me coming to Rachelim didn't mean going beyond the pale. It wasn't the act of a woman who wanted to show the men that she too can do things like this. That much is clear by now. The distance between me and my grandmother is as vast as the Middle Ages. Once, women used to walk behind the men and even hide themselves. Today it's different.

[Naomi to Miri:] I'm not crazy about all the violent action that's been taken by men recently. It lets a genie out of the bottle and who's to guarantee that extremist elements won't jump on the band wagon and hurl it downhill? We women don't believe in the use of force but rather in quiet protest and persuasion.

EL-OR, ARAN

Naomi summed up the feminine thesis that motivated the act of founding Rachelim and served as a kind of ideology:

> By remaining here we express the idea that life for us in Judea and Samaria[9] is not a political demonstration, but a simple and day-to-day wish to live. We state that life goes on and that our answer to death is—life! We organized on a feminine basis because the women provide the emotional and organic justification for the entire idea of settling. As to the political authorities, some of us are of the opinion that we should make do with exerting influence on the decision-makers, while others think that we should actually be in there [in parliament]. Either way, we've wasted a lot of time and there's a lot to do.

In February 1992, the women of Rachelim, with a large number of supporters (one thousand of whom were present at the Founding Conference), founded a women's lobby. They called it the Zionist Women's Lobby, since a nonpartisan women's lobby already existed. They claimed the existing lobby worked exclusively for the advancement of women's personal status and avoided confronting social and political issues. Their lobby did not deal with women's personal status, since they maintained they were satisfied with the status assigned to them within traditional Judaism. The new organization was founded to rejuvenate the nationalist–Zionist ethos as they understood it, on a foundation of women's solidarity.

At this point, the initially spontaneous activity began to take on organized aspects. The original act of the women was being formulated and distributed in pamphlets. The former government had promised the establishment of a permanent settlement at Rachelim, but the women continued their vigil in the tent for two years. Major political changes in the region prevented the site from becoming a settlement; today fewer and fewer groups of female students go there to study.

Ruddick has defined a standpoint as an "engaged vision of the world opposed and superior to dominant ways of thinking" (1989: 128). The women of Rachelim were attempting to form precisely such a vision. Again, Ruddick's definition of feminist standpoint is "to generalize the potentiality made available to the activity of women, i.e., caring labour—to society as a whole" (1989: 132). This was what the women of Rachelim were speaking about. Still missing is an examination of how these actions and experiences, and the feminist consciousness they created, relate to political conclusions and the pursuit of peace. It remains to be seen just why all the women of Rachelim agree that there is no rightful place for Palestinian children and their mothers on the political level.

GIVING BIRTH TO A SETTLEMENT: FROM A CASE STUDY TO A TEST CASE

The Rachelim event can serve as a test case for two major theoretical concerns in feminist research:

1. The discourse about the practice of care. The essentialistic attributions rendered to this practice such as the pursuit of peace, and the impact of an expressed maternal discourse on alternative ones (Chodorow 1974; Gilligan 1982; Kruse and Sowerwine 1986; Rosaldo and Lamphere 1974; Ruddick 1989; to cite a few).

2. The discourse about feminism and fundamentalism. There appears to be something attractive about the connection between fundamentalist radicalism and women's activism. Much has been written on this topic, especially on Middle Eastern Muslim women (El-Guindi 1981; Kandioti 1991; Macleod 1992; Moghadam 1993a, 1993b; Williams 1979; to cite a few).

The Practice of Care

Gush Emunim, of which the women of Rachelim form an essential part, is doing its utmost to sound a voice that has been growing progressively weaker in Israeli discourse. This voice conceives of the relations between Israel and its neighbors as a state of either war or surrender. Within this voice, the women of Rachelim were attempting to improvise a feminine chord. They sat in the tent and studied the Bible while their husbands were uprooting olive trees in Palestinian olive groves, obstructing highways, and demonstrating outside the homes of Intifada leaders with firearms in hand. The women preferred to describe their political action in a terminology of creating, giving birth, continuity, and education, which supplanted the usual vocabulary of seizing, struggling, constructing, and resisting. They claimed to have chosen a nonviolent way of remaining in the territories. The fact that they wished to depict their activities in these terms while dissociating themselves from the male choices should not be underestimated. These choices were important, even if the women were not actually changing the objectives toward which the men were striving.

173

There is no doubt that their variation on the theme bears a close affinity to the model of "maternal thinking" and contains many of the elements identified by Ruddick. From their point of view, the women were responding to the violent acts of the Palestinians. Had they discussed Ruddick's theory, they might have wished to employ her sentence that at times it was necessary to "refuse to judge from a distance the violent response of others to violent assault on them" (1989: 138). The women of Rachelim were contending that until now they had stood behind and beside the men. Now, in this hour of urgency, they could no longer settle for this: the time had come to stand in the place of the men, or in front of them. Disappointment in the men's spirit led them to propose a feminine alternative. Although graceful and pleasant in tone, this alternative, however, was actually a form of feminine radicalism.

The women of Rachelim accepted as given the nationalist religious Zionist interpretation formulated in radical Jewish groups since the early seventies. The roots of this interpretation, which is shared not only by radicals, originate far from maternal practice in totally different layers of Israeli social reality. The essence of motherhood as expressed by the women of Rachelim—of responsibility for their children's well-being, of concern for their nurturing and social training—can only be understood within the context of that interpretation. The practice and experience of care indeed form a unique discipline bearing both emotional and mental power. This is a power immanent to the practice itself, a practice that at the moment is carried out mainly by women. The hermeneutics of this practice do not take place within a domestic void. It exists within a rich and complicated cultural structure.

The full realization of the experience of motherhood would mean evacuation of the territories, or at least an acknowledgment of the contradiction between the wish to ensure the safety of one's children and the national conflict. Other women in Israel face a similar problem. A mother in Tel Aviv can also be said to be undertaking unnecessary risks in the interest of realizing a given social goal—life in an independent Jewish state. If this mother does not believe in a totally national narrative, she may experience the contradiction between her two tasks and acknowledge the fact that her life in Israel poses a continuous threat to herself and her children, as well as a threat to the Palestinians. This is a difficult and demanding but real possibility. The women of Rachelim cannot live this incessant tension, which would endanger the messianic dream of Gush Emunim. Instead of combating the danger, they cultivate a metaphor in which the risk becomes an opportunity; thus, they desired the impossible: to realize the totality of a messianic, religious, radical dream through feminist practice. Since the feminine practice triggering the event in question bears only an artificial tie to peacemaking, the very nature of this maternal practice is undermined. The sentimental peace of the women of Rachelim—which they represented as a kind of metaphor, a dream that will come true only with the coming of the Messiah—in turn presents motherhood under the same metaphor. By so doing, they are able to dodge their human/maternal responsibility for the safety of their children, or the safety of Palestinian mothers and children, and supplant it with the rival strugglers' duty to endure and win. They described Palestinian mothers and children as respected rivals with motives identical to theirs and their children's. The entire conflict between Jews and Arabs was recast by the women of Rachelim as a struggle between the mothers and children on either side. The grounds for identification become the grounds for the struggle.

The reports they stimulated in Israel's critical press took a skeptical, cynical view of their femininity, their motherhood, and their feminism. The practice itself, which drew all its strength from an authentic feminine and maternal experience, could not be expressed, because it was held captive by a fundamentalist religious world view in which peace is part of a utopian messianic discourse.

174

Feminism and Fundamentalism

The combination of feminism and fundamentalism carries major dilemmas. At the beginning of this article, we noted the gap between the metanarrative of Western feminism and the Middle Eastern context. After several years of political-cultural efforts to detach the Jewish Israelis from the Orient, it is time to draw more on local experiences and decode them within their own context. Rather than going into cross-cultural comparisons, we suggest another dialogue: one between the local feminism/fundamentalism experience and the self-awareness of the group being examined. One would study a practice carried out and experienced by women in terms of whether there is a growth of reflexivity, of self-awareness, of observing other groups and thinking, talking about them (sometimes criticizing them). A growing self-awareness, a consciousness, can indicate empowerment. This parameter of self-awareness can serve as a tool for cross-cultural comparisons.

EPILOGUE

Feminist research drawing on the ideas of "maternal thinking" must examine the local context of each group of women. It must examine the cultural richness and diversity, the perceptions of history, and the overt and hidden social levels on which the maternal experience takes place. It is only within this context that the unique local meaning of the universal experience of care may be understood. There is no doubt that in making an effort to design a feminine solution of their own to a problem shared by the entire public, the women of Rachelim were involved in innovation and in improving their status as women; however, from the standpoint of peacemaking, there is no automatic or even evolutionary connection. This kind of connection will be possible only when women and men together create a society within which the pacifying attributes of the practice of care are freed from their particularistic, nationalistic, and glorifying meanings.

175

NOTES

1. Gush Emunim is a radical offshoot of religious Zionism associated with the teachings of Rabbi Abraham Isaac Kook the senior (died 1935), as interpreted and taught by his son, Rabbi Yehuda Tzvi Kook (died 1982) (Don-Yehiya 1987). This religious-political movement embodies ultra-rightist hawkish politics that focus on the "Greater Land of Israel" view that resists all efforts to dismember present-day Israel. Behind this ultra-Zionist ideology lies an original, mystical, messianic theology. The combination of mystical religion and political activism puts Gush Emunim under the canopy of fundamentalism (Aran 1991).

2. Rachelim is Hebrew for Rachels. Interestingly, Rachelim is the masculine form of the plural. Rachelot is the feminine form.

3. We obtained this quotation and others in this article through interviews conducted between November 1991 and June 1992. El-Or interviewed the women and Aran interviewed some of their husbands.

4. Even today, most of the orthodox women do not study Talmud, the major Jewish corpus that informs and determines the substance of religious Jewish life. They do, however, study the Bible, biblical exegesis, Mishna, and works of Jewish philosophy and moral philosophy.

5. Women's appearances become a major issue when they become visible as political actors. The women of Greenham Common, for example, received fairly extensive coverage in the British press. But Ruth Walesgrove (1984: 21) points out that all the papers related to the women's looks. They mocked their vulgar, sloppy, and dirty appearance, described the mud around their tents and caravans, and doubted their feminine sexuality. Gabriel's (1992) work on "Women in Black" relates to the same issue (see note 7).

6. Both men and women in Gush Emunim show a warm, hospitable attitude toward the soldiers because of their positive attitude toward the army, which they see as "the army of God." It carries a different meaning when done by women in the traditional context of domesticity.

7. "Women in Black" are Israeli women who maintain a peace vigil every Friday afternoon on several major intersections throughout Israel. Initiated as a result of the Intifada in 1988 by former activists in other peace movements, they wear black and carry placards reading "Stop the Occupation." Some of the women base their motivation for peace on their maternity. When passersby mock and curse them and tell them to go home and prepare the Sabbath and take care of their kids, one of them answered, "I am here taking care of my child" (Gabriel 1992: 320). Gabriel points out that these women stand quietly, passively, while the counter demonstrations and onlookers are noisy. The women of Rachelim hold this against them and claim, "They do nothing, they are barren."

8. Israeli-born women hesitate to refer to themselves as feminists. Because of the Socialist-Zionist ideology that offered equality and because of their reluctance to associate themselves with the Anglo-Saxon aura attached to the feminist movement, they tend (or perhaps tended) to overlook the discrimination against women and deny its political aspects (Izraeli 1991; Swirski and Safir 1991).

9. The settlers insist on calling the West Bank Judea and Samaria to stress its Jewish past and present. Other Israelis use designations like "the bank" (*hagada*) or "the territories" (*hashtachin*). People on the political left refer to it as the "occupied territories."

REFERENCES

Abu Odeh, Lama. 1993. "Post-colonial Feminism and the Veil: Thinking the Difference." *Feminist Review* 43:27–37.

Appadurai, Arjun. 1986. "Theory in Anthropology: Center and Periphery." *Comparative Studies in Society and History*. 28:356–361.

Aran, Gideon. 1987. *From Religious Zionism to Zionist Religion, the Origins and Culture of Gush Emunim*. Ph.D. diss., Hebrew University, Jerusalem.

———.1991. "Jewish Zionist Fundamentalism." In *Fundamentalisms Observed*, edited by M. E. Marty and R. S. Appelby. Chicago: University of Chicago Press.

Burgansky, Michal. 1977. *The Kalel in Israeli Society: The Case of Marcaz Harav*. Master's thesis, Bar-Ilan University, Ramat Gan, Israel.

Chodorow, Nancy. 1974. "Family Structure and Feminine Personality". In *Women, Cul-*

176

EL-OR, ARAN

ture and Society, edited by Michelle Zimbalist-Rosaldo and Louise Lamphere. Stanford, CA: Stanford University Press.

Davidman, Lynn. 1991. *Tradition in a Rootless World*. Berkeley: University of California Press.

Don-Yehiya, Eleizer. 1987. "Jewish Messianism, Religious Zionism and Israeli Politics: Gush Emunim." *Middle Eastern Studies* 23:215–234.

Duffy, M. A. 1985. "A Critique of Research: A Feminist Perspective." *HealthCare Women International* 6:341–52.

El-Guindi, Fadwa. 1981. "Veiling Infitah with Muslim Ethic: Egypt's Contemporary Islamic Movement." *Social Problems* 28:465–485.

Elon, Emuna. 1991. "You do not kill Mammy." *Nekuda*, November, 44–45.

El-Or, Tamar. 1993. "Are They Like Their Grandmothers—Literacy and Modernity Among Ultraorthodox Women in the Hassidic Sect of Gur." *Anthropology and Education Quarterly* 24:63–82.

———. 1994. *Educated and Ignorant: On Ultraorthodox Women and Their World*. Boulder, CO: Lynne Rienner.

Gabriel, Ayala. 1992. "Grief and Rage: Collective Emotions in the Politics of Peace and the Politics of Gender in Israel." *Culture, Medicine and Psychiatry* 16:311–35.

Gilligan, Carol. 1982. *In a Different Voice: Psychological Theory and Women's Development*. Cambridge: Cambridge University Press.

Haim, Avigail. 1991. "Rachelim." *Nekuda*, November, 12–14.

Harding, Sandra. 1986. *The Science Question in Feminism*. Milton Keynes: Open University Press.

Heschel, Susan. 1983. *On Being a Jewish Feminist*. New York: Schocken Books.

Izraeli, Daphna N. 1991. "Culture, Policy and Women in Dual-earner Families in Israel." In *Dual-Earner Families: International Perspective*, edited by S. Lewis, D. N. Izraeli, and H.M. Hootsmans. New York: Russell Sage.

Kandioti, Deniz. 1991. *Women, Islam and the State*. Philadelphia, PA: Temple University Press.

Kaufman, D. 1991. *Rachels Daughters: Newly Orthodox Jewish Women*. New Brunswick: Rutgers University Press.

Koltun, Elizabeth. 1976. *The Jewish Woman*. New York: Schocken Books.

Kruse, D., and Charles Sowerwine. 1986. "Feminism and Pacifism: Women's Sphere in Peace and War." In *Australian Women: New Feminism Perspectives*, edited by N. Grieve and A. Burns. Melbourne: Oxford University Press.

Macleod, Arlene E. 1992. "Hegemonic Relation and Gender Resistance: The New Veiling as Accommodating Protest in Cairo." *Signs: Journal of Women in Culture and Society* 17:533–57.

Moghadam, Valentine. 1993a. *Gender and National Identity: The Women Question in Algeria, Iran, Afghanistan and Palestine*. London: Zed Books.

———. 1993b. *Modernizing Women: Gender and Social Change in the Middle East*. Boulder, CO: Lynne Rienner.

Mohanty, Chandra. 1988. "Under Western Eyes: Feminist Scholarship and Colonial Discourses." *Feminist Review* 30:61–88.

Ortner, Sherry. 1974. "Is Female to Male as Nature is to Culture?" In *Woman, Culture, and Society*, edited by Michelle Zimbalist-Rosaldo and Louise Lamphere. Stanford, CA: Stanford University Press.

Reinharz, Shulamit. 1992. *Feminist Methods in Social Research*. New York: Oxford University Press.

Rosaldo, Michelle and Louise Lamphere. 1974. *Woman, Culture, and Society*. Stanford, CA: Stanford University Press.

Ruddick, Sara. 1989. *Maternal Thinking*. New York: Ballantine Books.

Sasson-Levy, Orna. 1993. "A Case Study of Religious Women's Political Representation in Israel." Paper presented at the annual meeting of the Association for Israel Studies, Atlanta, GA.

Strathern, Marilyn. 1988. *The Gender of the Gift*. Berkeley: University of California Press.

Swirski, Barbara and Marilyn F. Safir. 1991. *Calling the Equality Bluff: Women in Israel*. New York: Pergamon.

Walesgrove, Ruth. 1984. "Press Coverage." *Space Rib* (May):21.

Weidman-Schneider, Susan. 1984. *Jewish and Female*. New York: Simon & Schuster.

Weissman, Deborah. 1976. "Bais Yaakov—A Historical Model for Jewish Feminists." In *The Jewish Woman*, edited by Elizabeth Koltun. New York: Schocken Books.

Williams, John A. 1979. "A Return to the Veil in Egypt." *Middle East Review* 3:49–54.

A MIXED BLESSING
The *Majales*—Shi'a Women's Rituals of Mourning in Northwest Pakistan

Mary Elaine Hegland

FOR SHI'A[1] Muslim women in Peshawar, Pakistan, expanding participation in *majales* (mourning rituals for their leading martyr) was a mixed blessing. Women could escape home immurement—otherwise required in the rigidly sex-segregated Pukhtun region—to attend *majales*. Allowed to travel far afield for women's religious gatherings, they cultivated wide social networks and developed performance and managerial talents. However, these women were also more exposed to ritual symbolic messages of feminine inadequacy. Further, accompanying sermons instructed women on their innate deficiencies and service and obedience duties to males. Women attained gratifying social support, a sense of belonging, and artistic and spiritual expression, but only in exchange for submitting to their ritual companions' surveillance and social pressure. They earned performance acclaim, confidence, self-esteem, and approval or even praise from male family and community superiors, but at the cost of curbing their creativity and energy to fit into authority-designated appropriate channels for women.

In this article, I first briefly situate my Peshawar case study within the local, national, and transnational political context. I then discuss women's various ritual roles and contributions[2] and how they advance Shi'a unity as well as women's competence and confidence. Finally, I show how women's ritual community is a mixed blessing—bringing women both an empowering personal growth workshop and a strict, constricting social control unit.

POWER POLITICS AND WOMEN'S *MAJALES* IN
PESHAWAR, PAKISTAN

Ritual can be a vital instrument in the hands of people contending over power, meaning, or definition. *Majales*, rituals surrounding Imam Husein's martyrdom—focal Shi'a paradigm, provide a striking embodiment of such possibilities. Imam Husein, Third *Imam* or Shi'a leader, and some seventy of his male followers were killed on the Karbala plains, south of Baghdad in present-day Iraq, in their 680 A.D. battle against the reigning Caliph's much larger forces. The captive womenfolk were then taken to Damascus, the Caliph's seat of power. On '*Ashura* (the tenth) of the Arab lunar month of *Muharram*, Shi'a commemorate the death of Husein, their consummate martyr. Adherents recall Husein's and his followers' martyrdom through story recitations, passion plays, processions, chanting and singing verses about Imam Husein's and his family's suffering, and weeping and self-flagellation indicating participation in Imam Husein's struggle.[3] According to tradition, Imam Husein's enslaved sister Zaynab's courageous lamentations and Karbala martyrdom recitals initiated these mourning commemorations, which evolved into the *majles* (pl. *majales*, meaning gathering or meeting in Persian) practiced among Peshawar Shi'a.

The 1979 Iranian Revolution, brought about through utilizing Shi'a rituals, paradigms, leaders, and organizations, had facilitated greater awareness of Shi'a identity. Encouraged by growing Shi'a religious transnationalism, Pakistani Shi'a were gaining self-consciousness. Many believed the Pakistani Sunni Muslim government and majority population mistreated and discriminated against them, a religious minority including about 15 percent of Pakistanis. Shi'a remained angry about the still-unpunished 1988 Peshawar assassination of Arif al-Hussaini—highest ranking Pakistani Shi'a cleric, assuming government involvement and cover-up. Consequently, Peshawar Shi'a leaders were working to promote stronger sectarian loyalty and unite Shi'a from divergent ethnic groups into one large alliance. A stronger front could potentially pressure the Sunni government into better protection and sensitivity to Shi'a needs and demands, they felt.

Women were central in this Shi'a consolidation process. In Pakistan, where political alliances are formed mainly through personal interaction and relationships, it is not surprising that women—socialized and available for networking and social bonding—should take on much responsibility for assimilating and mobilizing disparate Shi'a groups.

In the past, women in particular had been limited to religious gatherings in their own Shi'a ethnic/linguistic enclaves: *Mohajirs* or migrants from India,[4] Pukhtun or The North-West Frontier Province dominant ethnic group,[5] and Qizilbash or the Persian speakers come long ago from the west.[6] However, during my 1991 field research[7] in Peshawar, NWFP provincial capital of some three million inhabitants not far from the Afghan border, I observed a new trend. Related to the Shi'a unification goal, both Shi'a women and men were attending other congregations' and ethnic groups' rituals. Increasingly, Urdu—Indian immigrants' language and Pakistan's national language—was used in rituals. All over the city, the format followed in Husein rituals began to mimic the Indian format characterized by extreme displays of grief and self-flagellation and a more fundamentalist world view (Hegland forthcoming b).

Modernization advantages—such as development of transportation, communication, and education—helped build a common Shi'a community, identity, and tradition and lent themselves to escalating feminine mourning activity. Because of privately owned cars and public transportation (buses, taxis, and motorized three-wheelers) in addition to the older bicycle-powered passenger cabinets and horse-drawn vehicles, women could easily get around the city or even travel elsewhere for Shi'a ceremonies accompanied only by other women, without male escort. Improved communication systems, printed material availability, and use of recorders and cassette tapes all served to expedite Shi'a networking and formation of an "imagined" (Anderson 1983) Shi'a religious national and transnational community. People taped and disseminated sermons and *rozahs* or recitations about Imam Husein and his family. Young women bought, borrowed, or recorded *marsia* (mourning hymns) and *noha* (mourning chants) tapes and played them repeatedly, memorizing words and cadence. Government education in Urdu has also aided the development of Shi'a community. All educated Shi'a women, no matter what their mother tongue, could understand sermons by Urdu-speaking preachers and join in Urdu chants and hymns. Because of the common language, interaction with Shi'a of Indian background was now easy for non-Indians.

Peshawar Shi'as' sense of affiliation and loyalty to the Shi'a movement and larger community was growing stronger, while their attachment to their own smaller Shi'a ethnic and neighborhood enclaves was subsiding. Women's contributions to this Shi'a consolidation process were crucial. Women's passionate commitment, communication skills, and socialization work were necessary for the movement's success. Yet under rigid Peshawar sex-segregation rules, men could not themselves mobilize women. Women were needed to recruit other women. Shi'a movement expansion required women for religious/political work all the way from high-level leadership roles down to person-to-person and parent-child private interaction. Women must suffuse their everyday religious and social practices with movement world view, ideology, and religious/cultural markers.

Women's social skills, interaction style, and Shi'a mourning rituals were admirably suited for pulling divergent groups into Shi'a affiliation and loyalty. Peshawar women's Karbala remembrance ceremonies continued from *Muharram* through *Safar*, a third month, and even throughout the year. Particularly during mourning season, ritual activity was intense. Women commonly rose early to rush though some cooking and housework before beginning a round of six to eight neighborhood rituals with a few relatives or close friends, perhaps capping the day by attending the evening public Huseiniyyah Hall men's *majles* where they sat silently in the curtained-off women's section.

Women were more casual and possessed less dignity than men. They were thought to be more chatty and easily distracted than men and might sometimes give into their nature, even during *Muharram*—facilitating the communication necessarily for Shi'a consolidation and mobilization. Sometimes at joint mourning rituals, a low murmur wafting through the curtain divulged women's proclivity for "idle gossip." The speaker might have to interrupt his sermon and reprimand the women.

At women's gatherings, no segregating curtains were available to hide whispering worshipers from view. But women often talked quietly while waiting for the ceremony to begin. When seniors began reciting holy texts, others grew attentive. Next, several singing groups took a turn leading mourning hymns. When informal ritual leaders—senior, high-status women —signaled the hymn stage's conclusion, the day's chosen speaker left her place with other women on the sheet-covered floor. Taking the white-draped preacher's chair, she delivered a sermon outlining women's obligations as pious and pure Muslims, and ending with an emotional Karbala martyrdom account. After her final tragic crescendo, the audience that stretched from her feet to the courtyard's outside door stood again. Small chanting teams of often aggressively competitive young women then vied for the four or five chant performance slots, while all beat their chests in rhythm with the mourning couplets. As each new group started chanting, other women turned to place current chant leaders at circle center. Finally, when rituals leaders signaled women to end the chanting, a highly-respected older woman led prayers.

During these formal ritual stages, women were immersed in weeping, self-flagellation, and recitation and had little chance for conversation. But after the final prayers, women settled down again, waiting for the prepared refreshments to be distributed. While drinking and eating the offerings donated to the Karbala saints, women could visit. The relaxed, convivial atmosphere, joint partaking of sanctified food and drink, and calm fulfillment of the post-ritual setting stimulated friendly, heart-to-heart talk.

During the summer 1991 mourning season, Shi'a women's rituals of this sort were flourishing. More and larger ritual assemblies were organized. Even unmarried young women, in earlier years limited to a few gatherings on principal mourning days only, attended a far greater number of rituals and ventured off to unaccustomed ritual spaces.

For Shi'a Muslim women in Peshawar, this expanded ritual participation could be seen as a mixed blessing. On one hand, their worlds grew larger. They went out of their own neighborhoods, met many women, interacted with other ethnic groups, and even traveled to Shi'a congregations in other towns. By attending these gatherings, women could spend time outside the house in enjoyable social interaction—much appreciated by women otherwise restricted to their homes by the stern modesty code (*purdah*). They developed their social interaction skills and gained expertise and confidence from learning new mourning hymns and chants. Young women used their education to expand their repertoires of hymns and chants and join the fierce competition between chorales of several sisters or cousins to gain ritual performance fame. Some women built up citywide reputations as outstanding hymn singers, chanters, self-flagellants, preachers, or ritual hosts.

Thus, deepening involvement in ritual activity around the martyrdom of Imam Husein brought Peshawar Shi'a women many advantages. But, on the other hand, as discussed in later sections, women's furthered commitment to ritual participation meant added exposure to sermons and symbolism stressing women's spiritual, moral, physical, political, and economic inferiority and dependence. As spokeswomen for the emergent fundamentalist Shi'a movement, these women may have earned approval from male leaders and family members, but they attained this regard by operating within the confining boundaries and roles ultimately delineated by male authority figures. By limiting their personal development and social bonding work to Shi'a *majles* gatherings and personnel, women formed close social relationships and encouraging educational workshops. However, this intense interaction and positive learning atmosphere also enabled women to better supervise each other, keeping their activism and capabilities well contained and channeled.

183

SHI'A WOMEN'S RITUAL PERFORMANCES: COMMUNITY FORMATION AND INDIVIDUAL CAPABILITIES

In many cultures and communities, women carry much of the responsibility for "the work of kinship" (di Leonardo 1987) and other types of social networking. Women's work of forming and maintaining social ties can be politically crucial.[8] Enabled by better transportation, communication, and education, women helped coalesce Peshawar Shi'a into a more unified and politically effectual community through *Muharram* rituals. At the same time, through the opportunities opening up to them because of the wish to knit Shi'a from various ethnic backgrounds into closer cooperation, women could develop themselves—within certain constraints. The *majles* was a central vehicle for Shi'a unification and also for women's accomplishments.

Bridging Ritual Groups through Marriage

Women contributed to community consolidation through many activities. Those who formed bridges between locations through marriage were particularly well situated to reinforce linkages during the mourning period. Brides were brought from home communities in India or sent back there from Peshawar. Married women returned regularly to visit their mothers and other relatives. For example, a preacher went back to India to see her mother every year. In 1991, this preacher with two of her daughters and her sister-in-law—her mother's close relative, also brought as a bride from India—spent the mourning period in India, heavily involved with ritual gatherings. In this manner, women born into a Shi'a Indian community in one country and married into another country could hone social and performance skills and accrue personal power while strengthening Shi'a international ties.

Reaching Out

Women's actions in reaching out socially to include more women in their circles and rituals were critical for blossoming common Shi'a identity and community. Women were friendly to newcomers, invited them to their own rituals, and notified them of rituals elsewhere. I benefitted from this tendency and shortly knew of more rituals than I could possibly attend.

Women welcomed all who came to a *majles*, no matter what their social station. Although urban, well-to-do *Mohajirs* and Qizilbash considered rural Pukhtun women to be beneath them, when Pukhtun women were present, they were sure to make them feel at home with one or two Pukhtun language mourning chants. Even professional singing girls, regarded as low-class and lacking moral constraint, were not turned away.

Informal *majles* leaders tried to ensure each circle of aspiring ritual performers the chance to lead a chant, incorporating all comers. At the huge gathering held in the Old City Huseiniyyah, my student Shahida's group prevailed in competition with another group for a performance slot. After Shahida's chorale finished their lengthy *noha*, several women pointed toward the group who had lost out, and they were given the next turn. Women practiced their own skills of tact, diplomacy, and affiliation while contributing to Shi'a consolidation.

Raising Up

As part of their incorporating behavior, women refrained from noticeably criticizing others, choosing rather to influence by example and praise. Women extended an overtly uncritical attitude to all who performed at a *majles*. Even

184

when a woman stumbled while reading the Qor'an, there were no raised eyebrows or words of reproach. Performance seemed to be fail free; one received only encouragement with no danger of criticism. Children were especially praised for contributions. At one *majles* a little girl boomed out in a loud and deep voice, "*Na'rah-i Haideri!*" All gave the response "*Ya, Ali!*" An older women sitting close to her hugged her. Others exchanged pleased glances.

Women served as instructors, guides, and prompters for their daughters. They started teaching them at home, singing and chanting to them at a tender age. A mother celebrated with sweets for the whole assembly when her daughter first soloed leading a chant or song, usually between the ages of four and eight. Several times I saw a mother nod or nudge her daughter to begin a song before someone else beat her to it. Mothers were sometimes leaders of a singing group consisting of their daughters and perhaps nieces. Women enjoyed mentoring and apprenticing rewards at the same time as they conducted crucial Shi'a socialization.

Surveillance and Supervision

All women were part of the ritual managerial structure in that they assisted in controlling themselves and others during ritual meetings. By following proper form throughout a ritual's course, women hoped to earn respect and avoid disapproval. The women who spent so much time together for two and a half months every year formed an effective social control network. These women watched each other carefully and pressured each other to attend *majales* and behave appropriately. Women were sensitive to observational glances from ritual associates. At one *Mohajir majles*, Shahida's mother and her best friend exchanged a knowing, amused look after the mother gave a bellowing call for response during another woman's sermon. Then they noticed my eyes on them (although I certainly had no intention of hinting that they were behaving inappropriately), and immediately and automatically retreated into their roles of serious mourners.

Through activities discussed above, women enhanced Shi'a unity but also built up their own confidence, competence, feelings of self-worth, and prestige through their valuable social and guidance capacities. Such activities were open to a wide range of women, although those women with higher status could more effectively engage in them. Other activities, such as ritual administration, hosting, preaching and teaching, performance, and innovation, allowed women to shine more openly as individuals while furthering Shi'a causes and promoting allegiance to the Shi'a community. Only a few women could avail themselves of these opportunities. Success in such endeavors was limited by age, marital status, economic situation, and family connection with male leaders, as well as personality and talent.

Majles *Administration*

Among both Qizilbash and *Mohajirs*, I noted, older, more experienced women, higher level managers, regulated the ritual by beginning and ending it. These senior women quietly made decisions from the back rows of the group circled around the current performers. Through hand signals and glances, they expressed their judgements to each other. Quietly self-assured, they knew the value of their behind-the-scenes administration and realized others respected them. They seemed to feel no need to take center stage through leading the assembly in ringing choruses accompanied by reverberating blows to the chest. To the younger, unmarried women they left opportunities to compete for performance time and *noha* chanting fame.

Majles *Hosts and Helpers*

Among the Shi'a, hosting a *majles* was an individual's and her family's primary means of building prestige. Mahreen, the *Mohajir* preacher, held many large *majales* in her courtyard and the public Sadar Huseiniyyah Hall. Many other Indian-Pakistani women held *majales* in their Sadar homes, some sponsoring a scheduled yearly ritual series. In the Old City as well, Qizilbash women hosted *majales* in their shrine rooms or courtyards. Wealthy Shi'a families constructed buildings specifically for *majales*. Women could also arrange a supplementary donation for a *majles* hosted by someone else or help with post-ritual hospitality: spreading the long, narrow tablecloths on the floor, distributing food and drink, and cleaning up afterwards. A core of women and their unmarried daughters generally served and then gathered up dishes and tablecloths after people had eaten. Their work finished, the servers sat and ate together in a companionable circle.

Preaching and Teaching

Female preachers spread a common, more fundamentalist understanding of Shi'a Islam through *majles* sermons in the many home shrines and the public Huseiniyyah Halls. Mahreen, an unmarried woman in her forties, was Peshawar's most renowned female preacher. An Indian-Pakistani *Mohajir* preacher from Sadar, she was frequently invited to other parts of Peshawar. As honored speaker, she would deliver one of her fire and brimstone sermons, ending with a heartrending rendition of Imam Husein and his family's suffering. Demand for her services kept Mahreen busy throughout the two and a half month mourning period and, at a slower pace, the rest of the year as well.

Women preachers, especially Mahreen, brought women from the different Shi'a groups together by weaving back and forth between them to give sermons. As it was becoming fashionable among the Old City Qizilbash to invite Mahreen to preach, she was exposing more women there to the *Mohajir* type of sermon delivered in Urdu. Some Indian-Pakistani Sadar women started attending *majales* held in the Old City when Mahreen spoke. Because they grew to appreciate her performances, some Old City Qizilbash women then came to *majales* in Mahreen's courtyard and at the Sadar Huseiniyyah Hall where she frequently delivered the sermon.

Besides reaching women within and beyond the Indian-Pakistani *Mohajirs* of her own background, Mahreen worked with the younger generation. She was training several little *Mohajir* girls in sermon delivery. At a *majles* in her courtyard, one of her small students delivered an impassioned if brief sermon before Mahreen took her place in the preacher's chair. Through teaching and preaching among their own Indian-Pakistani people and also reaching out to Qizilbash and Pukhtun, Mahreen and the other *Mohajir* women preachers practiced public speaking and leadership, while disseminating their hell-fire and damnation sermons and extreme grief and self-flagellation, pulling more and more women into the hegemonic, fundamentalist Shi'a community and world view.

Piety and Modesty Exhortation

Mahreen and two younger women of Indian background, students at the women's Zahra University in Qom, Iran—center of Shi'a learning, wore the all-enveloping black veils common in Iran. Conscious of their righteousness, they hoped to earn religious merit through inspiring other Shi'a women to wear stricter *hejab* (veiling or covering) and more somber clothing. The two younger women were not content with the *dupata*, a long, rectangular scarf always worn as part of Pakistani female dress. Even at women's *majales*, where men were generally excluded, they cloaked themselves entirely in black. These two virtuously kept their hair carefully covered at rituals. Other women and girls covered their hair when praying at a *majles's* conclusion, but otherwise let their *dupatas* slip from their heads to lie around their shoulders. A few women even let their *dupatas* fall to the ground for greater freedom of movement during chest beating. But my Qizilbash friend Shireen and her daughters wore "Islamic" dusters, following the more conservative cover modeled by Mahreen. Possibly other Qizilbash and *Mohajir* women will take on heavier veiling as well. Through more stringent modesty, these pious women elevated their own status while promoting Shi'a movement religious/cultural markers and attitudes.

Performance and Preeminence

My student Shahida's mother presided at her sister Mahreen's home. To begin a *majles*, Shahida's mother, sitting in a circle with her sisters, daughter, and best friend, put her glasses on and read the words from the notebook resting on a black cushion in front of her.

Women could also gain acclaim by becoming outstanding at the *marsia*, the singing during the early part of a *majles*. Three or four circles of women took a turn leading *marsia* singing while sitting on cloth spread in a courtyard or

187

on the floor in a home. Shahida's mother always started the first *marsia* at her sister Mahreen's *majales*, and then her circle added their voices to hers.

Opportunities for singing *marsia* and *noha* during rituals were mainly relegated to younger, unmarried women. This strategy seemed to effectively attract young people. No other paths to eminence were open to girls, but they could attain stature through ritual complex involvement. Small choruses of sisters, cousins, or neighbors competed for performance slots and reputations.[9] Their competitiveness and thirst for eminence helped draw them into the heavy round of ritual engagements. When I asked Shahida, my M.S. student from the University of Peshawar, why she was so active in ritual performance, she unabashedly declared, "I do it for fame!"

Borrowing and Innovating to Construct Tradition

Women also derived personal satisfaction, self-esteem, and recognition through modifying ritual practices. Their literacy allowed young women to transcribe, learn, and perform the latest *nohas* and *marsias*. Combing shops and social networks for new tapes from India and elsewhere, the more ambitious young performers competed to accumulate the largest and most up-to-date repertoire.

Once I saw my friend Shireen lift both hands high and shout "*Hey*" with each blow as she then flung them down to smash against her chest. I had seen young men do this when practicing self-flagellation, but it was an innovation for females. As a special offering, Shireen also practiced a more severe form of self-flagellation than other women—the formidable face flagellation. Face flagellation was commonly practiced by Pukhtun women, but was an innovation for Qizilbash and *Mohajir* women.

Once we went by bus to the town of Nowshera for a *majles*. We chanted and beat our chests as we disembarked to enter the Nowshera Huseiniyyah. Hands hitting simultaneously in time to the chanting, Shireen beat herself on the cheekbones as she led our Peshawar group to the Huseiniyyah Hall. The Nowshera women came out to meet us. Upon seeing our *rozahkhwana* (Qizilbash Karbala story intoner) beating her face, the Nowshera leader began to strike her face in the same manner. Later I asked Shireen about it. She had seen Pukhtun women doing cheek-beating. It was better to practice this taxing self-flagellation, she explained; it showed greater devotion to Imam Husein. She was hoping others would follow her example. The other leader had imitated her arduous face-beating, she pointed out.

Shireen was pleased with herself for initiating the cheek-beating and the tradition of visiting the Nowshera Shi'a congregation. Last year, she commented, one bus load of women had gone to Nowshera. This year there were two buses, and next year, God willing, three buses would make the trip. Through introducing new chants and hymns and initiating novel mourning modes, women developed self-definition and pride. They gained social recognition as they injected novelty, friendly rivalry, and excitement into the Shi'a movement and mourning practices.

Provocateurs: Emotional Work

Women commonly take most responsibility for movements' and social groupings' emotional work. For Shi'a Muslims, ritualized grieving is a main religious/cultural/political marker. Peshawar women handled the greater share of this emotional work. In 1991 women donated their usual *Muharram* emotional work to the Shi'a movement as well as to Imam Husein. They applied it toward uniting all Shi'a ethnic groups through joint mourning sessions—*majales*—symbolizing their incorporation as Husain's spiritual heirs and a powerful political group. Further, they carried on Zaynab's example—keeping the memory of martyrs alive through mourning and relating—with outraged sorrow and distraught recapitulations after deaths of fresh Shi'a martyrs.

Those few women born to one ethnic community and married into another could pull the two closer together through their emotional bonds with each. A Qizilbash woman from the Old City was married to a Pukhtun man from The North-West Frontier Province town of Parachinar. She and her daughter were active in both Qizilbash and Indian migrant rituals. With the mother's sister, they sponsored a huge women's gathering at the large Old City Huseiniyyah Hall. Women from Pukhtun, Indian immigrant, and Qizilbash backgrounds all attended. This mother-daughter team helped foment grief and rage among Pukhtun, *Mohajir*, and Qizilbash women after Shi'a *Muharram* casualties. For example, on August 30, 1991, some four mourners were killed and 26 wounded by the (Sunni) police sent to guard the Pukhtun Parachinar Shi'a procession. This woman and her daughter furiously discussed the incident with associates during *majales*, helping to whip up fury among all Shi'a ethnic groups. Displaying sorrow for early martyrs and kindling wrath about current martyrs earned women spiritual credit and social approval as well as stirring up communal memory and anticipation of mistreatment and martyrdom.

189

SHI'A MOVEMENT AND *MAJLES* ACTIVISM: WOMEN'S MIXED BLESSING

Peshawar Shi'a women were not prepared to pursue social status, self-assertion, career, competence, or eminence through means considered illegitimate for women in religious and cultural discourses. In Deniz Kandiyoti's useful and provocative terminology, the women—at this point in time anyway— were not prepared to jeopardize their "patriarchal bargain." (Kandiyoti 1988) Given their existential situations, they had good reason for this stance. Shi'a women thus appropriated the authorized *majles*, framing their ritual performances with their own interests and goals.

Involved through greater time commitment to ritual attendance with the rising Shi'a movement—an alternative power structure offering them entrance into a wider world, Peshawar Shi'a women more often encountered the androcentrism permeating *Muharram* ritual symbolism and organization. With escalating *majles* attendance, women listened to Indian-Pakistani female preachers more often. *Mohajir* women preachers taught women their Islamic duties, such as seclusion, modesty and *hejab* or covering, separation from un-related men, and absolute obedience to husbands. The Shi'a were honoring a male saint, who through his Karbala martyrdom opened the possibility of in-tercession and redemption for believers. In addition, the two main *majles* sym-bolic complexes were masculine. The horse representing Imam Husein's steed Zuljinnah, who had returned empty-saddled from the 680 A.D. Karbala bat-tlefield to the waiting women—thus announcing Imam Husein's martyrdom and arousing their distraught grief, was brought into the women's *majles* after every Peshawar male procession, with similar effect. At other *majales*, an *alam* or standard representing the battle flag held by Imam Husein's younger half-brother Hazrat-e Abbas, martyred with him at Karbala, was brought out to the assembly to frenzied demonstrations of grief. As they did with the horse Zuljinnah, women reached out their hands, kissed, and tearfully clung to the *alam* in hopes of intercession and succor (Hegland forthcoming a).

Although women themselves organized, administered, and performed at women's *majales*, if attending male rituals, they must remain silent and out of male sight behind curtains. Women spent far more time in ritual performance than men, yet the most dramatic and extreme demonstrations of anguish and devotion were denied them. At the conclusion of men's rituals, some men, stripped to the waist, swung chains with knives attached to final links rapidly around their bodies, slashing their backs into raw, red pulp. Women were not qualified[10] to enact this sensational self-mortification, or to offer themselves as martyrs, a readiness which the male blood-letting self-flagellation symbolized. *Majles* symbolism forcefully confronted women with their inferior natures and ultimate spiritual, social, and economic dependence on males (Hegland forthcoming a).

The affirming camaraderie available through *majales* was likewise a mixed blessing. While providing a supportive developmental environment, the warmth and sense of belonging women received from fellow mourners made their insistence on attending faithfully and participating devoutly all the more efficacious. Even surveillance and supervision were mixed blessings for women. Managing this task effectively helped women build up and demon-strate respected *majles* positions. And, of course, scrutiny and coercion from other women helped women to be successful in the only way open to them within their existential parameters. At the same time, the social pressure set limits. Sometimes women experienced the cajoling negatively. Students felt torn and anxious no matter what they did when *majales* conflicted with ex-ams. I remember a woman, who obviously didn't feel well, urged by her co-resident in-laws to attend an all night *majles*. She gave in to their exhorting,

190

but looked listless and uncomfortable the whole night. More pious, modest women and informal ritual leaders were just as restrained as those whom they sought to guide; others watched them too, and they had to live up to and within their exalted positions.

Outstanding performers were greatly sought after. They gained mobility, a busy social schedule, prestige, gustatory delights (*majles* offerings), and perhaps even a fulfilling career. But they could only access these advantages if they lacked husband and children—Peshawar women's foremost goal and highest responsibility. The energetic, high-level *noha* chanters—young and well-displayed to *majles*-attending, prospective mothers-in-law—could expect good proposals and then, with marriage and child-birth, declining performance distinction. But young females who were *too* good at preaching or reciting might be in danger of having a religious career—and not marrying. Their guardians, if aspiring Shi'a politicians, might judge them too valuable to turn over to a husband. Single female preachers, especially those who had never been married, attained ritual freedom, mobility, and prominence at the cost of domination by their male guardians.

Mahreen, the most successful female preacher in all of Peshawar, although middle-aged, was unmarried. Although Mahreen was always treated with respect, her single status created some internal ambiguity and discomfort in how people regarded her. At the surface level, we pretended not to consider her unmarried state, but women discussed the issue at length privately, speculating over possible reasons behind this aberration. Another *Mohajir* preacher was also single, and others were widows with grown children. One woman, much requested for *majles* appearances, whose singing voice was so exquisite her solos brought tears to my eyes, was childless. Her *majles* singing was her career, her vocation, other women explained, and helped to fill her otherwise empty days. It seems that only women lacking responsibilities to husband and family—highly desired and valued among these Peshawar women—could turn their ambitions toward outstanding *majles* achievement. For young, famous *noha* chanters, ritual renown likely accompanied their pre-marriage life stage. For feisty, independent widows who had come into their own, influencing grown children and controlling resident daughters-in-law, a preaching career was just the thing to further garner personal power, acquire additional status, legitimize extensive socializing and travel, and amass spiritual remuneration. But for the never-married and childless, religious performance preeminence granted a substitute—a poor substitute—for all-important marital position and reproductive success.

CONCLUSION: PESHAWAR SHI'A WOMEN'S *MAJALES*—A MIXED BLESSING

As we have seen, ritual contributions to Imam Husein and Shi'a consolidation brought Peshawar Shi'a women a mixed blessing. On the one hand, *ma-*

191

jles gatherings provided women with expanding opportunities for expression, social interaction, performance, prestige, leadership, mobility, meaningful religious involvement, and emotional comfort. They were assertive and aware of their contributions' value. From ritual engagement and *majles* social interaction, women gained competence, confidence, and self-esteem.

On the other hand, women's increasing involvement in Shi'a rituals made them more accessible to conservative preachings about women's Islamic duties, such as strict *purdah* (seclusion and modesty), obedience to husbands, and women's pollution. In turning to the wider Shi'a movement's alternative power structure, they were more often in contact with limiting symbolic representations of femininity and confining fundamentalist values and expectations regarding women's place. Women were extremely sensitive to the social pressure of female ritual companions, their social control unit. In ritual—either directly by males, or indirectly through other women's surveillance and supervision—women were subject to patriarchal authority, an authority increasingly colored by fundamentalist values and expectations regarding women's place.

Nevertheless, in the summer of 1991, the benefits of women's greater religious involvement seemed to outweigh the disadvantages. They were traveling, attaining mobility without male escort, meeting many women, achieving ritual and social competence, and making significant spiritual and political contributions to their religion. Both Indian-Pakistani and Qizilbash women appreciated *majles* opportunities for gaining fame and status, or at least approval and social interaction, and did not pay much attention to *majles* gender lessons. They did not take sermon admonitions very seriously. Women laughed quietly in their curtained-off rooms during the men's *majles* sermon when the visiting cleric from Karachi rebuked them for their *purdah* lapses.

At the time of my research, women's freedom seemed to be expanding with their ritual activity. As women were kept from many other opportunities by gender expectations and the *purdah* system, they were naturally eager to take advantage of *majles* socializing, self-expression, personal growth, status, and fame. However, their wider-ranging mobility and performance competence were allowed and encouraged by men. Because their dynamic 1991 ritual activity was channeled by forces above and beyond their own decision-making, I wonder if Peshawar Shi'a women's ritual work will continue to be at the discretion of those male supervisors—when and if the men decide to change their tactics and again tighten female parameters.

NOTES

1. Sunni (the majority in most Muslim countries) and Shi'a are the two main subgroups of Muslims. Shi'a, with their belief in intercession between God and humanity through the Family of the Prophet, *Imams* (successors to the Prophet), and *imamzadeh*

192

HEGLAND

(descendants of the *Imams*), are roughly analogous to the Catholic branch of Christianity. Similar to Protestant Christians, orthodox Sunnis do not accept intermediation or spiritual hierarchy, although many among the Sunni masses do.

2. Unfortunately, scholars working with Shi'a rituals have largely neglected woman's participation. Among the few sources on Shi'a women's rituals are Anne Betteridge (1985, 1989); Robert and Elizabeth Fernea (1978); Mary Hegland (1995, forthcoming a, forthcoming b); Ursula Sagaster (1993); and Azam Torab (forthcoming). Several other publications include some information on Shi'a women's mourning rituals. See Bauer (1983); Betteridge (1983); Cole (1988); Fernea (1989); Friedl (1983, 1989); Hegland (1986, 1990, 1991); Pinault (1992); and Waugh (1977).

3. Nakash (1993) has studied the historical evolution of rituals surrounding Imam Husein's martyrdom.

4. Most *Mohajir* Shi'a had come from India to live in the newer Sadar area of Peshawar during the 1947 partition and exchange of populations, with Hindus migrating east to India and Muslims west to Pakistan. Many *Mohajir* Shi'a families lived comparatively well, often on proceeds from commerce centered in the Sadar bazaar area. Their homes were on upper stories over street level shops.

5. Shi'a among the Pukhtun (also called Pushtun, Puxtun, or Pathan) are a religious minority, as most Pukhtun are Sunni Muslims. British colonial administrators, challenged by the "unruly" tribal Pukhtun, initiated Western scholarly work among them. Several outstanding anthropologists have since conducted research among the Pukhtun, who populate Pakistan's North-West Frontier Province and also are one of the two main ethnic groups in Afghanistan. See, for example, Ahmed (1976); Barth (1986); Grima (1992); Lindholm (1982); and Tapper [Lindisfarne] (1991).

6. Originally of Turkish background, their forebears had been brought by the Persian shahs from Anatolia in the west to serve in their administration and military. The Qizilbash had become Persianized during their long residence in that country. Qizilbash fought for the Safavid state of Persia (present day Iran) and then were employed by Nadir Shah during his invasion of India in 1739 (Cole 1988:41, 45). Because of traveling further east in Persian service, Qizilbash had become scattered all along the way. Many lived in Afghanistan, and a sizeable group, still speaking an older version of Persian, lived in Peshawar, often in close proximity to each other in the Old City. Most Qizilbash women who attended *Muharram majales* lived comfortable lives, supported by the profitable occupations of male family members who might be rug merchants or bankers.

7. Additional ethnography and analysis from my Peshawar research can be found in Hegland (1995; forthcoming a; forthcoming b). For funding my research in Pakistan, I am grateful to the Fulbright Commission. For their generosity in allowing me to take a year of leave and providing me with supplementary research funds, I thank the administration and the members of my department at Santa Clara University. I owe much to my students at Peshawar University, where I taught as part of my Fulbright fellowship, and other Pakistani Shi'a friends in Peshawar for their generous assistance and fellowship. Their names have been changed to protect their privacy. For creative, constructive comments on several drafts, I am grateful to Michelle Brunet, Maria Cattell, Diane Dreher, Sima Fahid, Marilyn Fernandez, Dorothea French, Erika

Friedl, Shahla Haeri, Jean Hegland, Pat Higgins, Diane Jonte-Pace, Seyyed Vali Reza Nasr, David Pinault, Nayereh Tohidi, and George Westermark. To my wonderful research assistants, Michelle Brunet and Caprice Scarborough, many thanks!

I dedicate this article to my parents. My mother, Mrs. Margaret Hegland, endowed me with her interest in people and her observation and perception skills and, through her dedicated work as a minister's wife in Montana, South Dakota, Alaska, and Oregon, first alerted me to women's vital religious ritual and community contributions. My father, Rev. Norval Hegland, inspired me to intellectual interests and sent me to Iran and thus a career in anthropology and Middle East Studies with his words when I was a college junior, "If I were your age, I would go into the Peace Corps."

8. For other examples where women's work of forming and maintaining social ties was useful for political purposes, see, for example, Hegland (1986; 1990; 1991), Joseph (1982; 1983), Kaplan (1981); and Peteet (1991).

9. For an entertaining account of the strategies of one aggressively competitive chorale determined to capture a performance opportunity at a major *majles* of the 1991 season, see M.E. Hegland, "Fundamentalism and Flagellation: (Trans)forming Meaning, Identity, and Gender through Pakistani Women's Rituals of Mourning," forthcoming a.

10. As one reader commented, "Thank goodness for that!"

REFERENCES

Ahmed, A. S. 1976. *Millennium and Charisma among Pathans: A Critical Essay in Social Anthropology.* London: Routledge & Kegan Paul.

Anderson, B. 1983. *Imagined Communities.* London: Verso.

Barth, F. 1986. *Political Leadership among Swat Pathans.* London: The Athlone Press.

Bauer, J. 1983. "Poor Women and Social Consciousness in Revolutionary Iran." In *Women and Revolution in Iran.* ed. G. Nashat, pp. 141–169. Boulder: Westview Press.

Betteridge, A. 1983. "To Veil or Not to Veil: A Matter of Protest or Policy." In *Women and Revolution in Iran.* ed. G. Nashat, pp. 109–128. Boulder: Westview Press.

———. 1985. *Ziarat: Pilgrimage to the Shrines of Shiraz.* Unpub. Ph.D. dissertation, Dept. of Anthropology, University of Chicago.

———. 1989. "The Controversial Vows of Urban Muslim Women in Iran." In *Unspoken Worlds: Women's Religious Lives.* eds. N. A. Falk and R. M. Gross, pp. 102–111. Belmont, California: Wadsworth Publishing Company.

Cole, J.R.I. 1988. *Roots of North Indian Shi'ism in Iran and Iraq: Religion and State in Awadh, 1722–1859.* Berkeley: University of California Press.

di Leonardo, M. 1987. "The Female World of Cards and Holidays: Women, Families, and the Work of Kinship." *SIGNS* 12:440–453.

Fernea, E. W. 1989. *Guests of the Sheik: An Ethnography of an Iraqi Village.* New York: Anchor Books, Doubleday.

Fernea, R. A. and E. W. 1978. "Variation in Religious Observance among Islamic Women." In *Scholars, Saints, and Sufis: Muslim Religious Institutions since 1500.* ed. N. R. Keddie, pp. 385–401. Berkeley: University of California Press.

Friedl, E. 1983. "State Ideology and Village Women." In *Women and Revolution in Iran,* ed. G. Nashat. pp. 217–230. Boulder: Westview Press.

————. 1989. "Islam and Tribal Women in a Village in Iran." In *Unspoken Worlds: Women's Religious Lives.* ed. N. A. Falk and R. M. Gross, pp. 125–133. Belmont, California: Wadsworth Publishing Company.

Grima, B. 1992. *The Performance of Emotion among Paxtun Women.* Austin: University of Texas Press.

Hegland, M. E. 1986. "Political Roles of Iranian Village Women." *MERIP, Middle East Report,* No. 138, pp. 14–19, 46.

————. 1990. "Women and the Iranian Revolution: A Village Case Study." *Dialectical Anthropology* 15:183–192.

————. 1991. "Political Roles of Aliabad Women: The Public-Private Dichotomy Transcended." In *Women in Middle Eastern History: Shifting Boundaries in Sex and Gender.* eds. N. R. Keddie and Beth Baron, pp. 215–230. New Haven: Yale University Press.

————. 1995. "Shi'a Women of Northwest Pakistan and Agency through Practice: Ritual, Resistance, Resilience." *PoLAR: Political and Legal Anthropology Review* 18(2):65–79.

————. forthcoming (a). "Fundamentalism and Flagellation: (Trans)forming Meaning, Identity, and Gender through Pakistani Women's Rituals of Mourning." *American Ethnologist.*

————. forthcoming (b). "The Paradoxical Power in Women's *Majles* Rituals: Freedom and Fundamentalism, Community and Coercion." *Signs, Journal of Women in Culture and Society.*

Joseph, S. 1982. "The Family as Security and Bondage: A Political Strategy of the Lebanese Urban Working Class." In *Towards a Political Economy of Urbanization in Third World Countries.* ed. H. Safa, pp. 151–171. New Delhi: Oxford University Press.

————. 1983 "Working Class Women's Networks in a Sectarian State: A Political Paradox." *American Ethnologist* 10:1–22.

Kandiyoti, D. 1988. "Bargaining with Patriarchy." *Gender & Society* 2:274–290.

Kaplan, T. 1981. "Female Consciousness and Collective Action: The Case of Barcelona, 1910–1918." In *Feminist Theory: A Critique of Ideology.* eds. N. Keohane, M. Rosaldo, and B. Gelpi, pp. 55 -76. Chicago: University of Chicago Press.

Lindholm, C. 1982. *Generosity and Jealousy: The Swat Pukhtun of Northern Pakistan.* New York: Columbia University Press.

Nakash, Y. 1993. "An Attempt to Trace the Origins of the Rituals of Ashura." *Die Welt des Islams* 33:161–181.

Peteet, J. 1991. *Gender in Crisis: Women and the Palestinian Resistance Movement.* New York: Columbia University Press.

Pinault, D. 1992. *The Shiites: Ritual and Popular Piety in a Muslim Community.* New York: St. Martin's Press.

Sagaster, U. 1993. "Observations Made during the Month of Muharram, 1989, in Baltistan." In *Proceedings of the International Seminar on the Anthropology of Tibet and the Himalaya.* eds. C. Ramble and M. Brauen, pp. 308–317. Zurich: Ethnological Museum of the University of Zurich.

Tapper (Lindisfarne), N. 1991. *Bartered Brides: Politics, Gender and Marriage in an Afghan Tribal Society.* Cambridge: Cambridge University Press.

Torab, A. forthcoming. *Piety as Gendered Agency: A Study of Women's Rituals in an Urban Quarter in Iran.* Unpub. Ph.D. Dissertation, Anthropology, University of London.

Waugh, E.H. 1977. "Muharram Rites: Community Death and Rebirth." In *Religious Encounters with Death: Insights from the History and Anthropology of Religions.* eds. F.E. Reynolds and E.H. Waugh, pp. 200–213. University Park and London: The Pennsylvania State University Press.

PART THREE

WOMEN OPPRESSED
BY FUNDAMENTALISM

LOST RITUALS
Sunni Muslim Women in Rural Egypt

Judy Brink

THE MEDIA teaches us to associate Egyptian Islamic fundamentalism with the assassination of political officials, attacks on tourists and the bombing of the World Trade Center in New York. Journalists focus on the activities of a small militant minority while scholars studying the phenomenon also tend to focus their attention on the men in groups with names such as The Holy War, Soldiers of God, The Muslim Group and Repentance and Holy Flight (Rubin 1990; Ibrahim 1988). The same scholars speculate on the causes of the men's dissatisfaction with the government of Egypt and the reasons they seek solutions in Islam. With the increased veiling of young women in Cairo, however, some scholars (Zuhur 1992; El-Guindi 1981; Macleod 1991) have widened this narrow focus and explored the reasons why middle and working class urban women don the religious dress that identifies them as fundamentalists. This paper widens the focus yet further by exploring the effects of fundamentalism in rural Egypt. More specifically, I will relate the effect of fundamentalism in one village, which I refer to by the pseudonym Sadeeq.

In 1983 and 1984 I lived in Sadeeq studying the effect of employment and education on the status of women.[1] Sadeeq is located in an area of Giza considered to be a hotbed of fundamentalist activity, and several young men who lived in the neighboring town were arrested in the roundup after the assassination of Sadat in 1981. The people of Sadeeq dismissed the fundamentalists as radicals and extremists. This prevailing attitude became apparent to me when a family in our neighborhood was visited by their fundamentalist relatives from Cairo. The visitors' clothing clearly proclaimed their religious affiliation. The man wore loose-fitting white pajamas, a skull cap and beard, and the women wore long, loose-fitting dresses in drab colors, waist-length *hi-gaabs*[2] (a modest head covering), *niqaabs*[3] (face veil), gloves and socks, thus covering their entire bodies. The reaction in the neighborhood was one of amusement, and it was made clear to me that this was an aberration of the urban educated that had no relevance to the village.

Imagine my surprise then, when I returned to the village in 1990[4] to find that it had been literally transformed by fundamentalism[5]. The village market, previously located in the center of town, had been moved to the outskirts. I was astonished at this change because many of the richest and most influential families in the village sold goods from shops in their homes, shops that formed the nucleus of the market. Thus, moving the market would cause them a great deal of inconvenience and perhaps financial loss. When asked the reason for such a drastic change, the reply was that it had been done at the request of young male fundamentalists who objected to the market being close to a mosque on the same street. This was my first clue as to how influential the formerly ridiculed fundamentalists had become in Sadeeq.

Very soon the increasing religiosity of Egypt as a whole, as well as the village, became apparent. One television channel was devoted solely to religious programming, and increasingly people listened to religious sermons on the radio and on cassettes. A nearby video store was bombed because of its offensive movies; and soon reopened, stocking only carefully selected Islamically correct films. Attendance in the village's summer Islamic school for children soared, and some of the little girls begged their mothers to make them *hi-gaabs*. which they proudly wore to school in imitation of the many young village women wearing them. Even in my adopted family profound changes had occurred as several of the young men, including my "brother," identified themselves as fundamentalists.

Every night we would wait for my "brother" to come home from fundamentalist discussion groups held at the mosque. Once the bastion of the older men of the community, the mosque was now the place where fundamentalists would preach to the young men. As the summer progressed, my "brother" spent more and more time at the mosque, and reading the Koran. His conversation became filled with Koranic sayings, rantings against Israel, and praise for young martyrs who sacrificed themselves while protesting the injustice of the Mubarak government. The experience of male fundamentalists in urban areas seemed to have reproduced itself and become firmly rooted in this rural environment.

I found, however, that fundamentalism does not affect rural women in the same way as urban women. When questioned about why they veil, the *muhaggabat* (women who wear religious dress) in Cairo say that it is a personal and moral decision made after a religious conversion (Zuhur 1992: 76; Fernea 1982; Macleod 1991: 109). They maintain that their families did not convince them to wear religious dress, and some, in fact, veil despite opposition from their siblings, parents and husbands. For support in their decision and their new lifestyle they rely on a community of like-minded women who hold discussion sessions to study the Koran (Zuhur 1992: 98; Fernea 1982; Macleod 1991:110).

When I asked *muhaggabat* in Sadeeq why they wore the veil, they never spoke of a personal moral decision but always referred to the wishes of a male relative. Women said they veiled because their brother or husband was "sunni" (fundamentalist). The long religious *higaab* or the *niqaab* was a symbol of the husband's or brother's religious conviction, not that of the woman. In the village, for example, women are not able to wear the veil when their husbands object. One women who wore the *niqaab* at the request of her brother married a farmer. When she began to work in the fields people were amused to see a fully-veiled woman working like a peasant. Humiliated by his neighbors' teasing, the husband forced his wife to take off her *niqaab* despite her wish to keep it in accordance with her brother's beliefs. It is important, therefore, for fundamentalist men to arrange the marriages of their sisters to fellow fundamentalists who will allow their wives to wear the *niqaab*. I knew of several cases where brothers successfully arranged the marriage of their sisters to fellow fundamentalists even over the opposition of their parents. These men considered it important to have both their sisters and their wives wear the veil as testimony to their own religious convictions. Unlike Cairo, in the village becoming *muhaggabat* is not a woman's personal decision.

Village *muhaggabat* also have no community of like-minded women with whom they can study or discuss the Koran. A few young educated women told me that they wanted to learn more about Islam but were prevented from doing so because they lacked books and opportunities to study with colleagues. Women in the village, especially young women who are the ones most likely to be interested in fundamentalism, have very little autonomy and are able to visit only the homes of close relatives. Village women are forbidden to enter the mosque, and so there is no place for unrelated women to meet and study.

But most village *muhaggabat* are illiterate and cannot read the Koran. These

201

BRINK

women have little opportunity to learn about Islam as they cannot study any written material. However, their lack of knowledge of fundamentalism is not due just to lack of autonomy and education. In the village women have always been excluded from formal public Islam. As mentioned above, women can not attend the mosque; however, the sermon which the men hear on Friday is broadcast so that women can hear it in their homes. But they do not pay any attention to the sermon, and they are not a relevant part of their religious experience. Thus it was not surprising to me that village *muhaggabat*, as well as other village women, showed little interest in the sources of formal fundamentalist information which were available to them— religious sermons on the television, radio and cassettes. Young fundamentalist men spend hours listening to and debating these sermons, but the women ignore them.

Other public Islamic rituals also occur in a strictly male environment. Only male villagers gather in the desert to pray together during the holy month of Ramadan[6]. Only men participate in the reciting of the Koran that solemnizes marriage contracts. As the standard of living rises in the village more and more men are able to make the pilgrimage to Mecca— but very, very few village women get to fulfill this important religious duty. In the village formal public Islamic ritual is restricted to men.

A reason for the lack of women's interest in the sermons is that their religious behavior has never been dominated by formal Islam. The religious ceremonies and rituals that women participate in—*sabou'a, zar,* mourning at the cemetery, and the consulting of *sheiks* and *sheikas*—have long been considered to be "unIslamic" by scholars (Eickelman 1981: 202). These religious behaviors are part of the "Little Tradition" and represent pre- and non-Islamic behavior which is merely tolerated by the "Great Tradition" or formal Islam. Young educated men in the village agree with this analysis and condemn the women's rituals as unIslamic. In 1984 I noted that these men were unhappy that women participated in these rituals but that they were unable to prevent it. In 1990, with the authority of powerful fundamentalist doctrines, men were able to force women to stop what they considered to be unislamic activities.

Sabou'a is a ritual which is performed on the seventh day after a child is born. In the village women give birth at home in their bedroom. For seven days, the mother and child remain secluded in this room. The *sabou'a* is a ritual that cleanses the house of evil spirits and makes it safe for the infant and mother. Close female relatives of the mother and their young children attend the ceremony which is presided over by the midwife who delivered the child. The midwife throws a mixture of salt and grains around the home and calls upon the evil spirits to leave. Then she sews an amulet for the child that includes the grain mixture and a coin. Worn by the infant on a string which fastens his or her swaddling cloth, the amulet is believed to magically protect the infant from harm.

This ceremony is of major importance to women but is little valued by men. Some of the young fundamentalist men in Sadeeq have forbidden their wives and sisters to participate in the ceremony since they regard it as unislamic magic. Despite the wishes of their female kin to have the ceremony, they have been successful in stopping it. Nonfundamentalist women still perform the ritual, however, and even those who give birth in hospitals engage the local midwife to perform the ceremony when they return home. But because of the objections of their men, fundamentalist women are denied participation in this important women's religious activity.

Another forbidden women's ritual is *zar*, a possession trance cult. *Zar* spirits are pre-Islamic spirits which possess people, usually women, and make them ill. Symptoms of possession include headaches, chest pains, depression and infertility. In 1984, over a hundred women would gather every Friday for a *zar* ritual at a saint's shrine near the center of Sadeeq. This particular *zar* ceremony was well known and women came to participate not only from Sadeeq, but also from neighboring villages. The women who participate believe that some types of illness and misfortune are caused by possession by mischievous and malicious spirits. Each spirit is identified by a name, color, personality and an associated dance. A woman who suspects she is possessed attends a *zar* ceremony where a small band of musicians performs each of the spirits' songs in turn. A possessed woman falls into a trance when her spirit's song is played and begins to dance. While in this trance, the spirit takes over the woman's personality and a *zar* spirit specialist questions the spirit to find out how to get the spirit to leave the woman's body and thus cure her. The cure usually involves acquiring a necklace, a special *zar* dress, or a meat sacrifice to placate the spirit and convince it to stop harming the woman. In addition to the benefits of curing one's illness, attending *zar* ceremonies is an enjoyable activity and is one of the few times that unrelated women can meet and interact with one another.

In 1984, village men, especially educated young men, saw *zar* as superstition and did not approve of it; but they were unable at that time to prevent women from attending. By 1990, however, the *zar* cult had been driven out of town by the young fundamentalists who objected to a saint shrine being used for this purpose. With their objections now supported by the powerful ideology of fundamentalism they were able to stop, not just the women in their own families, but all women in the local area from attending *zar*. The nearest *zar* ceremony was now too far away for women to attend.

Another wholly female religious activity in the village is visiting the cemetery. On Thursdays small parties of women visit the graves of their deceased relatives to weep, pay for verses of the Koran to be recited, and leave food on the graves of their loved ones. Women say they gain a great deal of emotional release and satisfaction by paying their respects in this manner. As in the case of *zar*, young educated men disapproved of this women's ritual as unislamic

203

BRINK

because it shows an unwillingness to accept death, which must be accepted as God's will. But in 1984 young men were unable to stop their female relatives from going to the cemetery. As in the case of the *sabou'a*, young fundamentalist men are now successful in forbidding this activity to the women in their families.

The final example of loss of women's rituals is their use of *sheikas* (holy women) for help to solve problems of infertility or illness. *Sheikas* heal by reciting verses of the Koran or by making protective amulets consisting primarily of verses of the Koran written with special ink on paper. Fundamentalists object to healing of this sort if it is done for profit, but, they will grudgingly permit it if the *sheika*. accepts no money for her services. One *muhaggabat* told me that the *sheikas* are now so fearful of censure by the fundamentalists that they will only help close relatives. She said she believed in the efficacy of the *sheikas'* power and disapproved of the fact that women were prevented from seeking this help but she accepted it as just one more male restriction on women's behavior.

With the increased religiosity prevalent in Egypt, young fundamentalist men are admired and respected by their families for their beliefs. This new respect has given them added power within their families, and they use this power to change the religious behavior of their wives, sisters and mothers towards a more pure, more formal version of Islam. Thus village *muhaggabat* are forbidden to attend women's rituals and forbidden to join the men at the mosque. At present the religious participation of fundamentalist village women is limited to three behaviors: solitary prayer in the home, fasting during Ramadan, and avoiding or wearing the veil in front of any unrelated man.

It is ironic that the women who, to the casual observer, would appear to be the most religious in the village, the heavily veiled *muhaggabat*, have in fact been stripped of most of their religious rituals. They are forbidden to attend *zar*, and *sabou'as*, mourn at the cemetery or consult *sheikas*, and they have nothing with which to replace these lost rituals. Urban *muhaggabat* can pray in mosques and are literate and thus able to study the Koran and other religious literature. They can also attend meetings and discuss their faith with other like-minded women. Rural women, however, are forbidden to enter the mosque, are illiterate, and so unable to read or study the Koran.

I was, in fact, quite shocked one day to see the depth to which some women are ignorant of Islam. One of my informant's sons is a fundamentalist and the entire family admires his convictions and is attempting to live up to his standards. His oldest sister is *muhaggabat*, and he arranged her marriage to a fundamentalist friend, thus ensuring she would remain veiled. His younger sister, who was only ten, desperately wanted to become *muhaggabat* herself. To this end she nagged her mother to teach her how to pray. As the mother tried to teach her daughter the words to the prayer, which she has performed five times a day since she was a girl, it quickly became apparent that she did not know the words well enough to teach them to her daughter. Because she is illiterate and unfamiliar with written Arabic, the words of the prayer had become over the years a jumble of meaningless sounds.

This incident was representative of the dilemma that faces village *muhaggabat*. Fundamentalism prevents them from participating in the religious rituals that are most meaningful to rural women, but village custom and illiteracy blocks them from fully participating in the rituals that are condoned by the new fundamentalist ideology. In the village these rituals are available only to men. And so it is the village *muhaggabat*, who outwardly appears the most religious of women, who has the least space to practice religion.

CONCLUSION

The chapters in this book all testify to the fact that we must consider gender when studying fundamentalism because this phenomenon does not affect men and women in the same way. This article also cautions that it can not be assumed that fundamentalism will stay the same as it diffuses from urban to rural areas; we must therefore be sensitive to the fact that it can be a very different phenomenon in a rural environment. Over time will fundamentalism for village women become more like the experience of urban women? For this to happen there would need to be two major changes in village life. First, more village women need to become literate. Only through the study of the Koran and other official religious texts can women claim the knowledge they need to be true converts to fundamentalism. Second, to achieve this knowledge, women need to gain the autonomy to leave the house and meet in a public place such as the mosque. Perhaps sometime in the future the village mosque will no longer be off-limits for women and it will be considered appropriate for women to pray and meet in the mosque. With these abilities women would be able to gain the knowledge which would make conversion to fundamentalism a personal experience, not just as validation of the religious status of their husbands and brothers.

As it is today, for women, fundamentalism in the village is following a much older pattern of behavior known as the honor and shame code (Brink 1985:41; Antoun 1968; Dodd 1973). The honor of men depends on the virtuous conduct of their female relatives. A woman who engages in premarital sex stains the honor of her father and brother; an unfaithful wife stains the honor of her husband. Today male fundamentalists no longer mark their status with special clothing. I believe that the practice of wearing the white pajamas and skull cap has stopped because as fundamentalists engage more often in anti-government activities and the police are making more and more arrests, it is too dangerous to publicly call attention to fundamentalism in this way. Some of the young men still grow beards to mark their religious status, but otherwise they dress in the same way as other village men. Now, a man's religious status is marked by his sister and wife becoming *muhaggabat*. This requires some sacrifice on a woman's part as *muhaggabat* are expected to strictly avoid unrelated men—much more so than ordinary village women. This means that when an unrelated male visits the house, the *muhaggabat* must leave the room; similarly, in public when veiled with the *niqaab*, *muhaggabat* cannot speak to any unrelated man unless it is absolutely necessary. The *muhaggabat* with whom I spoke accepted these restrictions, and some even adopted them with pride, as proof of their love and loyalty to the men in their family. However, the price for this display of loyalty is loss of autonomy and the inability to attend women's ceremonies.

Why then do women accept the restrictions which come with fundamentalism? There are two levels of explanation which can be examined-the emic and etic. As already stated, the emic or informant's explanation for adherence to fundamentalism differs for urban and rural women. Urban women say they wear the veil as a result of religious conversion while rural women say they veil to express loyalty to fundamentalist male kin—usually their brothers.

Etic explanations by outside observers focus on the practical advantages which fundamentalism provides women. In urban areas these include increases in autonomy because *muhaggabat* are assumed to be pious and thus that they will behave modestly. This frees women, especially working women, from sexual harassment on the streets and at work, alleviates the jealousy of husbands and provides protection against the gossip of neighbors (Macleod 1991: 139–140).

There is also a practical etic explanation for the veiling of rural women. In the village, women are subject to the authority of their husbands. When they are being mistreated the only protection that women have is to run away[7] to their natal homes. While a woman's father lives she will run away to his house, and after his death she must rely on her brothers for protection. In recognition of the importance of a brother's protection it is a common practice in the village to arrange marriages of women to close relatives who live in the village. This is done for the express purpose of keeping women nearby so that brothers can more easily check on their welfare. Brothers are also obligated to care for their sisters in case of divorce. Thus it is very much in the best interests of women to establish and maintain good relations with their brothers. One way that village women do this is to forego inheriting agricultural land (Rosenfeld 1960). Women turn over their lawful share of their inheritance to their brother with the expectation that he will be an advocate for his sister and provide her a place of refuge.

Today, as the economy of the village becomes increasingly less agrarian, young educated men, some of whom are fundamentalist, are likely to see ownership of agricultural land more as a burden than an advantage. Women must therefore find another way to ensure the support of their brothers. For sisters of fundamentalists, the best way that they can ensure the support of their brothers is for them to accede to their wishes to become *muhaggabat.*[8] Which also means that they must give up participation in women's rituals.

Village men are accustomed to validating their status by the conduct of the women in their family. A man maintains his honor by the sexual purity of his wife and sister. In the same way a fundamentalist man validates his status as a fundamentalist by the veiling of his wife and sister. In return for her compliance to this request the sister can expect her brother's support in case of separation or divorce. The village is a world which is dominated by kinship obligations. Women can not live alone and are highly dependent on their male kin— be it father, brother or son. Under these circumstances it is likely that village *muhaggabat* believe that the loss of women's rituals is a price that they must pay in order to gain the support of their male fundamentalist kinsmen, support which is necessary for their security.

NOTES

1. This research was made possible by grants from the National Science Foundation and Mellon Predoctoral Fellowships.

2. A *higaab* is a modest head covering which is associated with Muslim identity. There are two basic types of *higaabs* which I will refer to as fashionable and religious. Fashionable *higaabs* cover the hair, neck, and shoulders and are usually made of a sheer, pastel shaded fabric. These *higaabs* are often decorated with braiding and jewelry, or expose the ears to display earrings. Most middle-class, Muslim women in Cairo wear this type of *higaab* and it is increasingly being worn by young women in the village. This type of *higaab* is worn by some women as a fashion statement and is not necessarily associated with fundamentalism. The religious *higaab* is made of white or drably colored cotton, is never decorated, and is associated with fundamentalism. In 1984 religious *higaabs* (which resemble nuns' coifs and veils) covered a woman to just below her breasts. In 1990 the *higaabs* had been lengthened and covered a woman's fingertips.

3. A *niqaab* is a face covering associated with fundamentalism. In Cairo the niqaab. has eye slits, but in the village three layers of sheer black cloth cover the entire face. If a woman wears a *niqaab* she will also wear socks, or special shoes which cover her feet and ankles, and gloves, so that her entire body is hidden from the eyes of men.

4. This research was completed with a grant from the Pennsylvania State System of Higher Education Professional Development Council, whose support I gratefully acknowledge.

5. Women fundamentalists are referred to as *muhaggabat* which means they pray regularly, and wear a religious *higaab* or a *niqaab*. In the village male fundamentalists are referred to as "*sunni.*" This means their sisters and wives are *muhaggabat*, they pray regularly, read, recite and study the Koran, both on their own and in meetings which are held nightly in the mosques.

6. This ritual takes place in order to emulate the pilgrims in Mecca who pray at Mount 'Arafa.

7. When a woman becomes *za'alaan,* or angry, she leaves her husband's house with her children, bringing with her none of her possessions, to seek refuge with her father,

207

BRINK

or if he is dead, with her brother. After ten days her husband comes to the house to negotiate for her return. This is often a humiliating experience for the husband as he is taken to task for his behavior and must promise to treat his wife better in future before she is returned to him. Consult Rosenfeld (1960) for more information on this practice.

8. One of my informant's fundamentalist brothers asked his sister, who wears a short *higaab* which covers her to her breasts, to wear the longer *higaab* which today is considered by fundamentalists to be more appropriate. She confided in me how worried she was because inflation was making it difficult to feed her family and she could not afford the additional expense of new *higaabs*. She did not feel that it was possible for her either to not obey her brother, or try to persuade him to withdraw his request, because she is in great need of his support. Her husband has a bad temper and occasionally beats her and throws her out of the house, forcing her to seek refuge with her brother.

REFERENCES

Antoun, R.T. 1968. "On the Modesty of Women in Arab Muslim Villages: A Study in the Accommodation of Tradition." *American Anthropologist.* 70(4): 671–697.

Brink, J. 1985. *The Effect of Education and Employment on the Status of Rural Egyptian Women.* Ann Arbor: University Microfilms.

Dodd, P.D. 1973. "Family Honor and the Forces of Change in Arab Society." *International Journal of Middle East Studies.* 4: 40–55.

Eickelman, D.F. 1981. *The Middle East An Anthropological Approach.* Englewood Cliffs, New Jersey: Prentice Hall.

El-Guindi, F. 1981. "Veiling Infatah with Muslim Ethic: Egypt's Contemporary Islamic Movement." *Social Problems.* 28(4): 465–487.

Fernea, E. 1982. *A Veiled Revolution.* New York: First Run Icarus Films.

Ibrahim, S.E. 1988. "Egypt's Islamic Activism in the 1980s." *Third World Quarterly.* 10(2):632–657.

Macleod, A. E. 1991. *Accommodating Protest Working Women and the New Veiling and Change in Cairo.* New York: Columbia University Press.

Rosenfeld, H. 1960. "On the Determinants of the Status of Arab Village Women." *Man.* 60: 67–70.

Rubin, B. 1990. *Islamic Fundamentalism in Egyptian Politics.* New York: St. Martin's Press.

Zuhur, S. 1992. *Revealing Reveiling: Islamist Gender Ideology in Contemporary Egypt.* Albany: SUNY Press.

FUNDAMENTALIST POLITICS AND WOMEN IN INDIA

Ilina Sen

THIS PAPER attempts to discuss the evolution of the democratic women's movement and the rise of fundamentalism and communalism as two important and contradictory tendencies in the modernization process in India. The tensions and conflicts produced in the course of this parallel development are discussed, as well as the implications for women of recent events associated with the growth of Hindu fundamentalism in India. For convenience, the discussion is structured into the following sections: (1) the evolution of democratic consciousness and secular principles in India, (2) the growth of the women's movement, (3) the chequered history of communal and religious politics on the sub continent, (4) the latest wave of fundamentalist politics, and (5) fundamentalism and women.

THE EVOLUTION OF DEMOCRATIC CONSCIOUSNESS AND
SECULARISM IN INDIA.

Liberal democracy as an ideology was born in western Europe, and was associated with major historical developments like the political separation of
church and state, and the growth of capitalism and the industrial revolution.
This is not in any way to suggest that capitalism gave birth to democracy, but
merely to point out the historical association and interrelationship in a chain
of historical processes. In the third world, this relationship is manifested in a
peculiarly contorted way.

The history of capitalist colonization has destroyed from mainstream consciousness traditional cultural, educational, and sociopolitical norms. This has
led to the imposition, among the intelligentsia, of Western thought patterns,
including the adoption of secular democratic ideology. However, the very basis of capitalist colonization, was the merciless rape of the human and material resources of the third world, and thus, the growth of secular democratic
consciousness was accompanied by systemic denial of the democratic rights
of large sections of the population. This was also the case with India.

Apart from this, the secular democratic ideal had other problems to con-
tend with. India has always been a multireligious, multicultural country, and
one of the major problems of Indian nationalism has been coping with this
plurality. Contrary to popular supposition, there have been several versions of
Indian nationalism. The dominant version has been the Nehruvian one,
which believed that the spirit of nationalism which won our country independence from British rule, would also lead to progress, greater rationality in
the conduct of our politics, and an all Indian identity which would erode local ethnic and religious identifications. Although the diversity of communities
was acknowledged, this modernizing nationalism emphasized the unity ("We
are Indians first") of all Indians as a political community and down played
cultural particularities as almost an embarrassment. This understanding of nationalism formed the basis of a consensus among almost all political parties,
except the professedly fundamentalist, on the eve of independence, and in the
years to follow. This was obviously based on the European model of the nation state (Menon 1993).

This secularist version of Indian nationalism grew in competition with at
least two other versions. One was the Gandhian, which famously rejected the
separation of politics and religion. Gandhi used religious idiom to mobilize
people, and at the same time did not accept religious prescriptions uncritical-
ly. The idioms primarily used by Gandhi were the ones familiar to him, viz
the Hindu, yet he conceptually had space for other idioms too.

The other competing version of nationalism was the militant Hindu nationalism, led by V. D. Savarkar, Swami Shraddhanand, and M. S. Golwalkar.
Like the Gandhian, it also rejected the separation of politics and religion, and
in fact, viewed the religious and political identities as converging 'naturally' in

SEN

the identifications of all Indians as Hindus. The mirror image of this version of nationalism was the Muslim nationalism to which Jinnah gave voice in the pre-independence years, and which demanded separate geographical and political space for Muslims, for whom, by definition, there was no place in India. The creation of Pakistan took the mirror image out of the terms of political discourse in India. The militant Hindu nationalism too, following the assassination of Gandhi, went underground and only emerged into blaring limelight in the sequence of events leading to the destruction of the mosque at Ayodhya in December, 1992.

THE GROWTH OF THE WOMEN'S MOVEMENT IN INDIA

One of the major fallouts of the growth of democratic consciousness has been the rise of the women's movement. In the nineteenth century, the attention of many of those with 'modern' education and outlook was drawn to the problems of women in our society, and to the extremely degraded position that women occupied in many traditions. The early work of Raja Rammohan Roy, Ishwarchandra Vidyasagar, and the Brahmo Samaj in Bengal (Majumdar 1967) attacked practices like *Sati*[1] and promoted women's education. The work of Jyotiba Phule in Maharashtra had similar dimensions, and it is correct to generalize that improvement in the condition of women was one of the priority items on any agenda for social reform.

Women, although only from educated families, began to be drawn to the nationalist movement in the twentieth century, and in the 1920s and 1930s organizations like the All India Women's Conference became well known. These organizations maintained a close link to the nationalist movement, and also worked on a relatively small scale for the economic empowerment of less privileged women through income generation programmes. Gandhi's movement drew many women into the nationalist struggle, and although the nationalist movement did not at all stages raise specific demands for the empowerment of women, for many women who took part in the events of the period, the experience of participation in political struggle was itself an empowering process.

The liberal democratic principles on which the post-Indian constitution was based had a major contribution to make to guarantee to women, at least in law, equal rights as free citizens of a free country. This legal equality, something for which women in the West had had to struggle for many long years, was a major gain for women in the post independence period, and gave obvious political space to more conscious women to struggle to fill up the gap between the reality and the promise. During the 1960s and 1970s, a strong movement to fight against the violation of women's rights grew up in many metropolitan centers, and these played an important role in highlighting cases of violation when they happened, in campaigning for legal change needed to ensure full equality, and in providing support to women victims of oppressive social norms.

211

SEN

As examples of the kinds of issues that the new women's movement took up, we can quote the campaign against dowry, wife beating, and for the change in laws related to the evidence about and prosecution of rape. As societal and economic pressures created newer manifestations of the degradation of women under patriarchy, newer fronts were opened. For example, the growing physical elimination of middle-and lower-middle class brides for having brought in insufficient dowry led to a growing campaign against these dowry murders, at the same time as the development of a structure, however insufficient in relation to the need, of support for victims of these happenings. When the technology of amniocentesis began to be widely misused in India as an instrument for sex selective feticide, this became another major front for the movement, and ultimately, regulatory legislation to control this practice was passed under the pressure of the movement. The outreach of these issue based campaigns cut across all communal boundaries, since women of all communities were equally affected by them.

The women's movement also responded to the sociocultural and communal currents of the time. In the late 1960s and 1970s, one of the major demands of the newly articulate movement had been for a common civil code. This was derived from the fact that in the matter of personal laws, Indians continued to be governed by the laws of the religious communities to which they belonged, and this is the situation to this day. In the 1980s, with a growing realization of the plurality of cultures in the country and of majority fundamentalist forces seeking to subsume all cultural diversity under its aegis, many women's groups dropped this demand for the reason, as they put it, that a patriarchal society was capable of giving a patriarchal civil code only (Gandh 1993).

The late 1970s and 1980s witnessed also major economic crises, and political upheavals. Inflation, growing prices, unemployment, caste tensions flared up in many parts of India, and the failure of the mainstream political structures and parties to provide any solutions threw them up in a poor light. A new wave of peoples' movements swept the country, under different ideological and political banners, but all seeking basic structural changes if current crises were to be overcome. Among the most important characteristics of this new wave of protest movements, were the strong participation of women, and the integration of these movements into the framework of a political agenda for women. (Sen 1990)

The actual issues and demands addressed by these movements showed a lot of variation, and have included: the issue of land rights for women, as in the case of the Bodhgaya land struggle of the 1970s, preservation of fragile ecosystems, as in the case of the Chipko movement and the insistence on women's right to public production in the face of mechanization and retrenchment (both of which have historically affected women unequally), as in the Chhattisgarh movement in the 1980s (Sen 1990). Despite problems of

SEN

women's lack of political experience and consequent problems about emerging into conscious political leadership in many of these movements, these examples do clarify a few things. One is that for a large number of women, their participation in these movements has been an empowering experience. And another is that it is perhaps no longer possible to open a political agenda without integrating women's issues actively into it. This is quite independent of the fact that the mass movements do not often raise classical women's issues, and are not thus recognized as women's struggles by the specifically women's groups.

The mid-1980s were thus, a period of enormous hope, strength, and looking ahead for the entire women's movement in the country, and even the government began, with all its structural limitations, to initiate in many parts of the country, large programmes of women's empowerment and women's development. The different political parties too, ranging from left to centre to right, began active programmes for women's mobilization and initiated political programmes for women.

COMMUNAL RELATIONS AND FUNDAMENTALIST POLITICS IN INDIA

India has been a multireligious society for long historical years. The modalities of relations among different religious communities are still a matter of debate and discussion among historians, but we have examples both of religious tolerance and peaceful coexistence, as well as strife and intolerance. The majority religion in India is Hinduism, and unlike the semitic religions it is not codified. The historical practice of Hinduism is thus a large determinant of its ground reality, and historically it has been a highly stratified religion. This has always encouraged conversion to more egalitarian faiths from among its disadvantaged sections, and we have several examples of the dominant religion attempting to cope with this "onslaught" on its well being with strident militancy. Buddhism and Jainism have faced such attacks on the subcontinent in the past, and today Hinduism has entered a new phase of militancy in response to the perceived threat of Islam.

In contrast to this, we have also centuries of evidence of harmonious coexistence of different faiths on Indian soil, and particularly small groups of followers of certain threatened religions, like the Jews and Parsis, have enjoyed in India a security not known in other places. However, it is the relationship of Hinduism with the next most numerous community, the Muslims, that is the most complex of all. Although in small regional pockets, like Punjab, Hindu Sikh relations, or in pre-partition days, Muslim Sikh relations, have been a central concern of communal relations, normally when we speak of communal relations in India, we are talking of Hindu Muslim relations.

The history of Hindu Muslim relations on the subcontinent are long and complex, and the details are beyond the scope of this paper. There have been

213

SEN

phases of heightened tension, and phases when integrational processes have been at work. The most notable examples of the latter have been during the sixteenth-century Bhakti movement, when the teachings of Kabir, Surdas, Raidas and Meera stressed tolerance, love, and faith in each other (Manushi 1991). The "popular" cults deriving from the teachings of these saints still have many adherents in the rural areas of India, and there is on the ground a history of living in peace and harmony. More modern versions of these teachings are to be found for example in the adherents of the Baul faith in Bengal, who cutting across political frontiers, practice an amalgam of the two faiths that appear at times so irreconcilable.

Colonial administration and historiography saw the interests of the Hindus and Muslims as irreconcilable, and actively promoted discord through measures like the "Communal Award" and separate electoral seats even prior to the idea of partition was born (Sarkar 1991; Pandey 1990). "The Communal Award" is the name popularly given to the provisions of the Government of India Act which came into force in 1935, and provided that there would be separate electorates for Hindus (with reservations for certain weaker sections), the Muslims, and other religious minorities (Sarkar 1991). They were aided and abetted in this by adherents of the militant Hindu view of Hindu nationalism as well as followers of the Muslim League who claimed that the Muslims were a separate nation and as such would have no place in a Hindu dominated India once the colonial masters left. Through active propaganda and political work, support was built up for these ideas, and socioeconomic realities also helped to make them acceptable. Over large parts of north India, a class of Muslim landlords and rich peasants looking for new opportunities saw greener pastures in a newly created nation. Millions of oppressed Muslim peasants saw in the idea of the new homeland a way out of the crushing domination of the Hindu landlords. And thus, in 1947, along with independence, erstwhile India was divided into India and Pakistan to the accompaniment of one of the worst communal killings known until then. Almost a quarter of a century later, internal contradictions forced the division of Pakistan into Pakistan and Bangladesh.

After a period of relative stability, while independent India attempted to fulfill its promise of a better life for all citizens in a free country, communal clouds again gathered in India in the late 1980s. By this time, severe economic stress had already led to the growth of chauvinistic organizations like the Shiv Sena in Bombay and the rest of Maharashtra. Beginning with the targeting of non-Maharashtrians as eating up all the scarce jobs, the Shiv Sena switched its attention to Muslims as the main source of the malfunctioning of the economic system and the main hoggers of scarce economic opportunities that rightly belonged to Hindu youth. The realities of the socioeconomic crises, a stagnant economy, rampant inflation and unemployment combined with the failure of established political structures to provide any solutions

must be seen as a major determinant of the rise of chauvinistic and fundamentalist forces in the country (Heuze 1992). European history has seen parallels in the pre-Second World War years. In 1990, the party of the Hindu
rightists, the Bharatiya Janata Party (BJP) even managed major successes at the
elections in several states in north and central India.

The Ram Janmabhoomi movement erupted on this scenario in the mid-
1980s. The ground was prepared by the anti-Muslim propaganda of organizations like the Shiv Sena and the Sangh Parivar (group of organizations belonging to the family of the Rashtriya Swayamsevak Sangh, or National Volunteers Organization, a wing of the Hindu Nationalist Bharatiya Janata Party). Among the kinds of images used to whip up popular sentiment against
the Muslims were generalizations like those stating that the Muslims bred
much more prolifically than the Hindus, and that if this trend continued, they
would soon overtake Hindus as the majority community in India. A story going around in the 1980s was that a family planning slogan for the Hindus was
"ham do hamare do" (we are two and we will produce two) whereas an appropriate slogan for the Muslims was *"ham panch, hamare pachchis"* (we are five,
i.e. a man is legally allowed four wives, we will produce twenty-five). This
kind of propaganda cleverly exploited the insecurities of Hindu youths and
the resentment among many, including sections of the women's movement,
about the existence of communal personal laws in a professedly secular country.

The emergence of new organizations like the Vishwa Hindu Parishad
(VHP) has to be seen in this context. VHP as an organization thrived on the
support of expatriate Indians, and in the country the main plank of VHP's organizational efforts and country wide mobilization efforts was that the Ram
Janmabhhomi (birth place of Ram) should be liberated from the clutches of
the infidels. The reference was to a folk belief in the Gangetic Valley, that the
site of a temple built where Ram, the hero of the Ramayana, one of the two
major epics of ancient India, and a major peg on which the sociocultural belief systems of the Hindus rests, had been destroyed by the conquering armies
of Babur, the first Moghul emperor of medieval India. Worse still, Babur was
supposed to have built a mosque on the site of the destroyed and desecrated
temple. The controversy had flared up in the past, and in the communally
charged atmosphere of the immediate pre-partition days, an image of Ram
had "miraculously" appeared inside the mosque leading to communal tensions in Ayodhya , the site of the mosque. There was a subsequent legal ban on
worship by either community in the disputed building until a solution could
be found.

The VHP successfully worked to increase its support base during 1989,
1990 and 1991 through countrywide Ramshila *pujas,* in which individual villages or groups were encouraged to consecrate and send bricks to Ayodhya
with which to build the new temple to Ram on the sacred site once the

215

SEN

mosque was destroyed and the site was liberated. The political instability of the times prevented the government from defending the secular traditions with any degree of success. The Hindu fundamentalist party, the BJP, was a partner in the coalition that ruled at the center, and the Congress party was faction ridden and ineffectual. The left was supremely confident that communalism was an imperialist construct, and the political vacuum was filled with admirable success by fundamentalist groups like the BJP, the RSS, the VHP and the Shiv Sena. The destruction of the mosque finally took place by an army of frenzied *kar sevaks* (religious volunteers) on December 6, 1992, plunging the country into one of its darkest periods of violence and distrust.

The immediate aftermath of the destruction was communal disturbances and riots in many parts, not only of India but also Pakistan and Bangladesh, showing both that the cultural and emotional roots of the people of the subcontinent were one, and that on the subcontinent it is difficult to delink fundamentalism and communalism. Hindu property and religious places were destroyed in several places. In reaction, Muslim homes and property were attacked in many towns across India, and in yet further reaction, a chain of bomb blasts destroyed life, limb and property of thousands in Bombay in January 1993. The latter event was supposedly triggered by the efforts of international destabilization agencies, and much of the property destroyed in prime locations in cities was grabbed by builders for the construction of high rise buildings. This shows that vested interests are quick to take advantage of any situation. The mood of pessimism lasted for a long time, and has only now begun to lift a little with the defeat of the fundamentalist BJP in the elections in several states in which they were in power.

216

FUNDAMENTALIST POLITICS AND WOMEN

The women's movement has long pointed out that the control of all religious establishments in a patriarchal world order is in the hands of patriarchal forces. As such, establishment interpretations of any religion are bound to be anti-women. This is true of all religions and within the Hindu tradition. We have Manu's notorious dictum that low caste people, animals, and women all deserve derogatory treatment. Hindu traditional law allows women unequal control over property and even child custody is traditionally a male preserve. Since Hinduism is not an officially codified religion, there is no book to fall back on for ultimate authority, and it is sometimes difficult to distinguish what is religious dictum and what is common law practice. Even today, a controversy rages about whether women are entitled to read the Vedas or not, with three of the four Shankaracharyas insisting that they are not. In practice of course such fundamentalist controversies mean little, since, with the Vedas written in Sanskrit, which few can read, not many women or men read the Vedas anyway. It is sufficient to remember that women are discriminated against in Hindu society as a general rule.

SEN

Evidence is not lacking that fundamentalist organizations work in support of a derogatory image of women. In 1987, Mrs.Vijaya Raje Scindia, the president of BJP's Mahila Morcha, led bands of women in protest against the anti-*sati* legislation and for the preservation of past cultural glories of India.

In 1992, also there was total silence among BJP women on the issue of the gang rape of 13 Muslim women in Surat, Gujerat which was led by a BJP politician. Quite possibly the silence was accompanied by admiration for the vindication of Hindu machismo. This kind of evidence is not difficult to deal with in a secular framework, it is with other kinds of evidence that is harder to cope.

There are several important aspects to the present round of fundamentalist politics as far as women are concerned. The most important of these is that fundamentalist forces have co-opted the vocabulary and style of the women's movement and have made a conscious attempt to mobilize women for their programmes. Statistics released by the VHP tell us that over 50,000 women took part as *kar sevikas* in the programmes at Ayodhya during 1991 and 1992, and that the demolition squad that worked on the mosque included many women. The Rashtriya Swayamsevak Sangh in the 1990's acquired a sister organization, the Rashtrasevika Vahini, to channel women's energies into the construction of the Hindu nation. Similarly, the VHP has a mass front for women as for men, the Durga Vahini and the Bajrang Dal (Sarkar 1991). The kind of terms used by these women's organizations are interesting. They speak of the rousing of *matrishakti* (mother energy) in the same breath as they speak of mobilization. Interestingly, they never speak of empowerment of women, but only of channeling the female energy in a public cause. Whatever be the content of the professed purpose of the organizational process, in form and content, there is little to distinguish this kind of militant political participation from women's participation in the mass political action that we earlier talked about.

This throws up very disturbing questions for the women's movement as a whole. On the one hand, we have seen the devastation of the legend put out by the women's movement throughout the 1960s and 1970s that since women were the worst sufferers of communal disturbances, women were essentially acommunal. The women's movement, it was said, was a natural bulwark against communalism . Not only has this myth been demolished, but certain other questions as disturbing, and without any comforting answers have surfaced.

While it is possible to argue that the upper middle class and relatively better educated women have dominated the more professedly feminist, urban women's groups, we have earlier argued that women from poorer backgrounds have played a major role in India in pro-social justice mass movements. If as is said, participation in mass organizations and mass movements as happened during the 1970s and 1980s, was an empowering process for the

217

SEN

women who took part in them, how are we to look at the participation of women in fundamentalist mass action? Is this to be seen as an empowering process as well? And if so, how does one look at a kind of (possible) empowerment that is totally devoid of what is, in liberal, secular terms, social concerns?

A similar difficulty is faced when we look at the practical problems faced in dealing with secular or communal articulation. One should take note of the fact that one of the leading demagogues of the VHP, whose audio cassettes were played at countless public meetings throughout the country in the year or two before the Ayodhya events, was a woman. Sadhvi(woman saint) Ritambhara's strident speeches are difficult to forget by anyone who has heard them. This woman was responsible more than anyone else for whipping up anti-Muslim hysteria in India. Her shrill voice calling on Hindu manhood to destroy the Islamic demon or else face castration is easy for feminists to reject. Although spoken by a woman, this is obviously the voice of patriarchal Hindu fascism. It is true that her public meetings are attended largely by men, but the minority of women who do attend also do not reject her appeals. The fact that ordinary Hindus, some not necessarily ogres in private life, attend her rallies is not to be taken lightly. Obviously, she touches a deep chord in them somewhere,when she appeals to their manhood. Is it that the sense of impotence in the face of socioeconomic realities is so great, that they jump at an attempt to prove themselves against soft targets?

If this is an unsolved puzzle, more difficult are the issues of the response generated on the Shah Bano or the Tasleema Nasreen episode. Shah Bano, an elderly Muslim woman of Indore, challenged the nonprovision of maintenance by her husband who had divorced her. The specific circumstances of the case allowed this in accordance with Islamic personal law, but Shah Bano challenged the Islamic laws in secular court on the grounds that this violated her rights as a citizen. The court gave a verdict in her favour, and then the fireworks started. While women's organizations welcomed this judgment, intense pressure was brought to bear on Shah Bano by her community leaders to withdraw from her position. Ultimately she was forced to do so. The government, rendered anxious by the signs of minority unrest, introduced a bill in parliament that effectively ensured that Muslim women would be governed in future by the personal laws of their own community and be beyond the reach of secular courts. By this time, (mid- 1980s) women's groups with one or two exceptions, had grown extremely touchy on the question of uniform civil rights. The BJP had emerged as the main champion of one law in one country, and in view of the communal and fundamentalist undertones to this, women's groups had withdrawn from their previously held position. The upshot was that a retrogressive bill as far as women were concerned, went through parliament on the pretext of safeguarding minority rights.

The Bangladeshi writer Tasleema Nasreen wrote "Lajja" after communal disturbances had engulfed Bangladesh following the destruction of the mosque at Ayodhya. The book drew attention to the demonization of the minority Hindu community in Bangladesh, and Tasleema drew the wrath of the Islamic religious establishment upon herself. Surprisingly, in India the main champions of "Lajja" were not the women's organizations, or the progressive intelligentsia, but the Hindu communal organizations, whose purpose it suited to have attention drawn to the threats faced by Hindus in an Islamic country, to be able to play the communal card at home.

In general, communal women's organizations have not struggled on platforms specific to women, but some recent evidence contradicts this trend. The BJP's Mahila Morcha has taken up issues of dowry deaths in Bombay and agitated for a social boycott of the families of husbands of dowry victims (Setalvad 1994). The Shiv Sena Mahila Aghadi (Women's front of the Shiv Sena) similarly has adopted the use of brute force in securing women in need of maintenance or legal redress. In a society where legal means of redress are in a state of permanent paralysis and collapse, this kind of rough and ready social justice cannot be without appeal. But once again, they pose very tough questions of even issue based cooperation or alliance for other women's organizations.

The confusion and bewilderment of women's groups is shared by all progressive Indians today. The limitations of the Western concept of secularism in our society are obvious. The fundamentalists' success has demonstrated that, if nothing else. The only way, it appears, of coming to terms with and then dealing with the communal and fundamentalist reality seems to be to develop new moorings for the secular terms of discourse rooted in our own soil that can take account of our indigenous traditions of togetherness, our differences, and the common bases of our struggles.

219

NOTES

1. *Sati,* the practice of self-immolation of Hindu widows on the funeral pyres of their deceased husbands, was common in historical India. However, there is no clear knowledge about the universality of the practice. The practice was legally banned by the British administration, but has been defended then and now in the name of cultural relativity. In recent years, the most infamous incident of *Sati* took place in Deorala, Rajasthan in 1988.

REFERENCES

Gandhy, A. 1993. *A Critical Evaluation of the Women's Movement in India,* Paper presented at the conference the Women's Movement, Patna, Bihar, India.

Heuze, G. 1992. "Shiv Sena and National Hinduism," *Economic and Political Weekly,* XXVII: October 3 and 10.

Manushi (pub).1991. *Special Issue on Women Bhakta Poets.* Manush: New Delhi

Majumdar, B.B. 1967. *History of Indian Social and Political Ideas—from Rammohan to Dayananda,* Calcutta.

SEN

Menon, P. and Sen, G. 1993. "What is Wrong with Secularism?," *The Radical Humanist*, April.

Pandey, G. 1990. *The Construction of Communalism in Colonial North India*. Oxford University Press: New Delhi.

Sarkar, T. 1991. "Women as Communal Subject," *Economic and Political Weekly*, XXVI: August 31.

Sen, I. (ed). 1990. *A Space Within the Struggle: Women's Participation in People's Movements*. New Delhi: Kali for Women.

Setalvad, T. 1994. "Women and Communalism," *Frontier*, August 27.

CONCLUSION. THE MIXED BLESSINGS OF WOMEN'S FUNDAMENTALISM[1]

Democratic Impulses in a Patriarchal World

Janet L. Bauer

chapter 13

THE PLACE OF WOMEN AND GENDER IN RELIGIOUS FUNDAMENTALISM

"*Women*" and "*gender*" are used by both secularists and religionists to define, characterize, and politicize the currents of our times, as Sondra Hale, Ilina Sen, and others have pointed out.[2] This is strikingly so for the religious forms we call "fundamentalist."[3] Gender roles and the situation of women have become the focus of concern for both observer-critics and member-participants of so-called fundamentalist religions.[4] Indeed concern with women's roles and sexuality may be the one common feature of the varieties of resurgent or reformist religions represented in this volume. None of this means, however, that women in such groups, or work about them, have had a prominent place in the study of fundamentalisms.

That women's activities have been omitted is not surprising. Women have until recently been left out of discussions of public politics and religion cross-culturally. From a distance, politicized religious movements may appear male-dominated but upon closer scrutiny, congregations are filled with women. In those cases where we have demographic reports, women participants often outnumber men (e.g. Bendroth 1993; Cucchiari 1990; Willis 1985); certainly women have always been important in the maintenance of religious observances (Holden 1983; Castelli and McBride 1991). In late ninteenth century Christian America, the feminization of evangelicalism (with increasing numbers of women participating in church work) was considered a threat to male dominance in religious organizations. Ironically while women accepted the eventual transformation of their roles in the church, they also resisted in various ways.[5] This is underscored in Stocks' accounting here of the historical experiences of women in the denomination she studied.

Consequently some associate male-dominated fundamentalism with historical periods when perceived increases in women's independence and changing family relations result in a subsequent backlash against women's participation in the public sphere (cf. Faludi 1991; Bendroth 1993; Riesebrodt 1993). This accentuates the portrayal of women as victims of fundamentalist belief systems rather than active participants, even fighters, and ignores the evidence that nonfundamentalist men may also feel this "challenge" from women but respond in different ways (cf. Faludi 1991; Brusco). If contemporary fundamentalisms can be seen, as I will argue, to be in part a reflection of "democratic" urgings for identity, meaning, and voice within specific sets of circumstances, and if restrictions on women's roles are seen as emblematic of the fundamentalist path to either moral purity or national autonomy, then one must ask how women, especially women who are active in religious groups, can find a place for themselves? Is fundamentalism a "male" movement or set of practices? Where do women stand in this view?

To add to the complexity of the phenomena, revolutions in media technology and the global reach of various religious sects have made possible, on the one hand, the spread of numerous varieties of the "fundamentalist word" as well as the impetus to standardize them (through television, radio, cassette recorder and personal travel as Brink, Hegland, Pang and Eiesland have described). But, they have also created alarmist (and anti-modern) images about the political repercussions of fundamentalism and its victimization of women and conflated "fundamentalisms" across different traditions. This objectification, as Brusco details, has made it even more difficult to assess fundamentalism and it's meaning for women, especially since fundamentalists are often portrayed as uneducated, poor, and distinctly unmodern.

This is especially true for many of what I will call "men's studies" of fundamentalism, in which women are viewed as objects or symbols rather than actors (cf. Hawley 1994 or the Fundamentalisms Project volumes). I don't mean to imply that these studies are written only by male authors or that we can completely distinguish between the styles and approaches of male versus female studies. However, these "men's studies" of fundamentalism have given high-profile attention to explaining the creation of political movements and activism, charismatic male leaders and the authoritative ideologies (or interpretations of traditions) they fashion, the class backgrounds of followers, and state level or "public" politics.[6]

Despite some, more detailed studies which contradict the stereotypes, these studies continue to accentuate what I call the *metaphor of "reaction"*. In this view, religious fundamentalists are characterized as seeing the modern, secular world as morally decadent and as rejecting, fighting or opposing it—as members of the "traditional" or poorer classes or individuals alienated by the pace of change.[7] The language of these studies accentuates this—"beleaguered believers," "threat," "revolt," and "oppositional"[8]—as does generalizing from written texts and secondary accounts, put together by other researchers. These studies often take a more distanced stance, focusing less on individual commitment and ethnographic insight and more on the structural characteristics of groups and movements or the central representatives and authors in the movements.[9] The farther removed, the easier it is to construct those essentializing categories (categories which reduce variation to a few generalized characteristics) by which to measure attraction to fundamentalisms and the more readily we overlook the role of spirituality and commitment on the part of both men and women.

Although we are told that additional articles on women are forthcoming in the Chicago Fundamentalisms Project, whose volumes have set the standard for defining and observing fundamentalisms cross-culturally, the initial volumes reinforce a "male studies" approach. Even those articles on or by women have primarily explored the potential impact of state policy or fundamentalist rhetoric on women, especially nonfundamentalist women.[10] Likewise in *Fundamentalisms and Gender* (Hawley 1994), attention is given to the place of gender, rather than women, in fundamentalism. While gender policy at a state or movement level is clearly important, women have also been active participants in fundamentalist groups (and radical religious movements) historically.[11]

By contrast an increasing number of studies about women and fundamentalism, what I call the "women's studies,"[12] as represented in this volume, employ a *metaphor of "agency,"* that is, of active engagement, integrating involvement (rather than reaction or *negative* agency). They study actual women involved in conservative religious groups, not just impute some impact of fundamentalism to their lives. The increased interest in feminist life history and ethnographic methods also support an agency approach (cf. Gardiner 1995). One picture emerging from this research is that within specific locales relatively better-educated women are often the first to reenter or return to active religious life in what are, ideologically-speaking, patriarchal religions. They are not reacting but struggling to create and find something for themselves through fundamentalist religion.[13] They engage the circumstances and challenges in their lives within these religious traditions.

These distinctions between men's and women's studies, as noted above, do reflect differences between existing studies of male and female experiences in contemporary fundamentalism, indeed a general absence of attention to women's religious activities in many treatments of fundamentalism cross-culturally. This is reminiscent of the public/private divide, where women are relegated to the household and kept out of sight. But as these authors reveal, and as theorists in the past have argued, it is an illusion to think that women, even women in fundamentalism, don't constantly step into the public world.[14] From Brink's and Friedl's focus on primarily rural women dealing as individuals with new restrictive measures encouraged or demanded by fundamentalist men, to Hegland's and Eiesland's look at women's use of communal rituals for personal empowerment and Bennion's and Brusco's examination of women who are using community membership and extended family relations to improve social and economic positions, to Stocks' and Goonatilake's analyses of women challenging church hierarchy, to Pang's Utsat women who are able to use and maintain their strong socio-economic position and even accentuate it with the new, more conservative forms of religion, to Hale's, El-Or and Aran's, and Sen's accounts of women doing battle in the public political sphere—these women are having an impact across private and public domains, constantly renegotiating their status, and engaging their worlds.

To characterize approaches as "male" versus "female," public versus private, or "reactive" versus "active" in focus is, of course, to overgeneralize the differences between these studies and to risk falsely problematizing the study of fundamentalisms. In the past, such dichotomization lead to the failure to look beyond "public" spheres of activity where men predominate to the domestic or "private sphere" of women's activities (cf. Nelson 1974; Holden 1983). However, by contrasting "men's" and "women's studies," I seek to highlight what's been *missing* from studies of fundamentalism: (1) not only concentration on women's roles and lives within these religious organizations and groups, but also (2) significant attention to the nuances, to the negotiations and accommodations beneath the "rules," which are sometimes referenced or footnoted but not often explored, and (3) the use of ethnographic approaches to achieve this. As Nelson pointed out for the political domain, by not focusing enough on women's sphere of activities we fail to understand something about the larger phenomenon of politics—or religion—in general. The authors in this volume enrich the study of fundamentalism, perhaps rewrite it, by looking at fundamentalism from the perspective of women involved in it, as Joan Mencher stresses in the introduction. Using cultural and ethnographic/life history methods, they give some "balance" as it were to an unbalanced field. This would be one way of reading this volume. However, these case studies also provide additional insights and raise important questions about

the complexities and comparativeness of the phenomena of (men's) fundamentalisms in the contemporary (and capitalist) world, beginning of course
with the enigmas assumed to be reflected in women's (or anyone considered
forward-looking's) participation in patriarchal, fundamentalist religions.

STUDIES OF WOMEN IN FUNDAMENTALISM: PARADOX UNDONE?

When fundamentalists are described as "secondary male elites" (Lawrence
1989) and fundamentalism, as a kind of "radical patriarchalism" (Riesebrodt
1990), women's participation in fundamentalist religion may seem to be a
"paradox." As Riesebrodt, who has written on women's involvement in fundamentalism, contends, "from a modern western view" these women are contributing to their own oppression (1993:244). Of course it's relevant to reiter-
ate that patriarchy (in various forms of social, cultural, political, i.e. institutional, domination) persists across religious and secular organizations and societies—democracies and dictatorships. Religious fundamentalism becomes
equated with "radical patriarchalism" because an integral feature of its acknowledged ideology or "traditions" has been support of different roles for, as
well as protection of, women within a patriarchal family.[15]

Although he does advocate looking more closely at gender relations in
fundamentalist groups, Riesebrodt admittedly does not have the data to examine them specifically. He must resort, therefore, to what others have also
done—focus on the treatment of gender issues in fundamentalist writings and
texts, texts which often seem preoccupied with "restoring" moral authority
to the family and circumscribing women's behavior outside of it. Riesebrodt
allows that women "must have their reasons" for belonging to patriarchal religious groups, but he analyzes their "mobilization" in terms of paradox, largely inferred from structural conditions. That is, the complexities of mobilization—whom, for what purpose, public or private activities—are not stipulat-
ed in specific terms. The reasons he offers are similar to those offered for
men—wanting to defend or purify a traditional way of life in the face of
changes in family and gender roles or being disappointed by a modern life
style. Such explanations attribute to women the kind of anger and disen-
chantment represented by male fundamentalism.

As the authors in this volume suggest, despite an image for limiting
women's options, fundamentalism offers mixed blessings, as Hegland calls
them, for many women. The recognition that both benefits and burdens
might be imposed or provided by fundamentalism contrasts significantly with
explanations of "paradox" or contradiction—which suggests lack of rationality or "false consciousness" on the part of women who participate and reflects
a label imposed from outside by others, encouraging "either/or," dichotomization (cf. Hale; El-Or 1993). Often assumptions are made about
men's preference or choice to be fundamentalist, while fundamentalism is imposed upon women through social, economic and cultural conditions beyond

225

BAUER

their control. Perhaps, those who categorize women's fundamentalism as an enigma, have not been able to look closely at the interplay between the official positions of fundamentalism, the immediate circumstances in women's lives and their own perspectives to understand the "trade offs" that women (most women for that matter) have to negotiate in their lives, or have taken too seriously the textual interpretations of key male leaders as the source of authority.

The agency metaphor allows us to presume and take into consideration these nuances or variations in women's position and to reconsider the importance of beliefs or ideology in women's choices. Each of the articles in this volume explores, as much as possible from inside (or the "emic" perspective as Brink refers to it), something about women's search for spiritual satisfaction, community, personal social status and empowerment, or more control within different "patriarchal" religions, under varying economic, political and cultural conditions. They provide new insight into conventional notions about the role of fundamentalism by highlighting, with selective emphasis, (much as other studies of women's status do) the role of different factors in women's involvement in fundamentalisms, as outlined below—social and family relations, religious ideology and ritual, local culture, personal background (rural/urban location, class background, mobility or migration, and ethnicity), as well as the importance of the state or external events:

1. *Social relations and support*—explored as social networks, family life, and conjugal relations—figure prominently in debates about fundamentalism and more generally in studies of the status of women, where both the benefits and limitations of family life, women's community and gender segregation have been much examined (cf. Nicholson 1986; Collier and Yanagisako 1987; Sered 1992,1994; Abu-Lughod 1986; diLeonardo 1987). Fundamentalist groups or associations not only emphasize the benefits of family relations and responsibilities but also provide enduring social relations and roles for their members. In fact some women "return" or come to these groups in search of social support and fellowship.[16] Of course, family life and community relations can also constrain women's options within the larger world, as many articles here also illustrate (cf. Held 1993; Bauer 1994).

In this volume, we see women engaged in negotiating family and community relations, creating women-centered activities, and establishing their positions vis a vis others, with differing results. In rural Egypt, where women have their traditional community relations challenged (Brink), newly fundamentalist male relatives expect women to conform their behaviors in order to enhance the well-being of the family's social (and fundamentalist) status. On the other hand, Mormon polygynous women's female networks (especially ties with co-wives) facilitate the creation of their own organizations, providing them with more latitude (Bennion). Eiesland explains that many Crossroads Pentecostal women don't live in traditional family households or, having been mobile, don't have so much contact with extended family—Crossroads Assembly's prayer group provides those meaningful relations. In Peshawar, Muslim women build women's community across ethnic groups (Hegland). In Colombia, Pentecostal women have been able to transform gender relations in family and community through evangelical conversion (Brusco). El-Or describes a similar occurrence for ultra-Orthodox women in Israel (not Gush Emunim) who despite the extension of men's religious patriarchy are able to interject non-Orthodox discourse about love and conjugal relationships into their marriages (1993). Pang finds that women in Hainan even enjoy the support of their male relatives in conducting their independent economic activities.

2. *The ritual events of religious communities* in particular can provide opportunities for women's social interaction and self-realization, even contestation of male dominance. In Eiesland, Pentecostal women find ways to put their life testimonies in context through the women's prayer group they have organized. It is "as much (or more) about emotional release and ritual practice," she says, "as it is about ideas of God and the Bible." Women's rituals also provide the context for women's community building and for giving individual women a chance to excel at chanting and singing in Pakistan (Hegland). Utsat women find empowerment through religious (Koranic) education (Pang). Fundamentalist Mormon women take an active role in healing and in religious services (Bennion). Stocks and Eiesland's evangelical and Pentecostal women use relationships in their religious communities to enhance their own. Evangelical women have a place as deacons and Sunday School teachers (with some limitations) but not as elders or pastors, a situation that leads some "feminist" women to challenge the notion of headship in their congregation (Stocks).

Women not only reinterpret religious ideology (below), but also reconstruct or emphasize women's rituals in ways that celebrate womanhood (cf. Kaufman 1991). Hegland reports that Muslim women ritual specialists engage in individual innovation. In fundamentalist Mormon communities, females must be present with males for any creation to take place (Bennion). In some cases women-centered activities are used to redefine women's role toward political ends, as among the Gush Emunim women in Israel (El-Or and Aran). Brusco also reports that, in contrast to expected practice, Colombian Pentecostal women take on public roles in prayer meetings.

On the other hand, deritualization (in this case, removal of approval for women's traditional rituals which are deemed "unIslamic") in Egyptian villages decreases women's sources of status and personal satisfaction (Brink). The rituals, feasts, and ceremonies women have traditionally taken part in come to be viewed as not rational or in need of rationalization (cf. McAllister 1992). Buddhist nuns also face opposition in their struggles to revive *Bhikkhuni Sasana,* on the grounds of established "textual" traditions.

227

BAUER

3. Religious/patriarchal ideologies provide the specific guidelines (Kaufman 1991) or boundaries (Brusco) and role models (Friedl) for living one's life. These beliefs can be both liberating and restricting depending upon women's circumstances, although the general tendency is to emphasize the limiting aspects of fundamentalist thinking for women.[17] While most cultures are patriarchal, fundamentalisms across religious traditions place special emphasis on differences in men and women's (sexual) natures, God-ordained, separate roles for men and women, and women's place in the domestic sphere.[18] In some situations these work to limit or decrease women's options, as for Egyptian rural women where fundamentalism is newly arrived (Brink) or in India, as Sen describes. Yet other women either find strength and power in these positions or they find ways to "subvert" or use the ambiguity of the ideals to challenge restrictive ones and create spaces for themselves in personal life, sometimes contesting religious authority in wider public debates.

Women, as Friedl demonstrates, can find multiple possibilities in the Islamic Republic's invocation of ideal images and, as Hegland reports from Pakistan, manage to avoid the more restrictive religious messages; Utsat women, whose social/economic position is already quite secure, find additional strength in Islamic "renewal" messages about the importance of women's participation in ritual and in education (Pang); Pentecostal women use conversion (and the religious asceticism it encourages) to fight the type of machismo that alienates men from their households (Brusco). In Brusco's words they find "a format for living" in its "explanatory power." In Goonatilake, Buddhist women are presenting reinterpretations of historic texts to reestablish convents of fully-ordained nuns, although the original texts suggest that the Buddha had to be persuaded in first admitting women to the order[19]. In Stocks, women use biblical texts to challenge limitations on women's roles of authority in textual debates. In Bennion, fundamentalist women rely on earlier Mormon traditions allowing women to have priestly duties (particularly in the periodic absences of men) and emphasize the mother goddess more than nonfundamentalist Mormon women.

Some women are in a position to use the religious texts or official interpretations of them in more public debates over various issues to the benefit of women. Muslim women from the Sudan to Pakistan and Malaysia have challenged the "new" application of Islamic thinking to legal codes. Hale has shown how professional women with the Sudanese National Islamic Front are critical of persistent male dominance, by which men try to deny women their rights due under Islamic law and Islamist women in the Iranian parliament challenge male implementation of religious law.[20]

If we can indeed distinguish between religious and cultural worldviews, *local cultural ideals* previously unattainable for some may be supported in the views advanced by fundamentalist religions, as Friedl suggests here. The behavior which fundamentalists expect Egyptian village women to adopt invokes ideals of family loyalty (Brink). For some women there may be a sense of finally being included in that traditional ideal.[21] In Eiesland, Pentecostal women's ideas of southern traditional culture are reaffirmed in the face of work-force sexism.

4. *Variation in women's involvement* and degree of empowerment (versus constraint) from fundamentalist thinking or groups depends upon interconnected *contextual and personal circumstances.* These factors, explored differently in the different papers here, further explain women's personal motivations: from seeking personal meaning or identity, to finding solace or relief in personal or social life, to resisting general patriarchy and sexism at work, to offsetting a lack of other options in education and social status:

Urban/rural residence affects the availability of religious alternatives, and other options. For example, fundamentalism seems to have emerged first as an urban phenomenon.[22] Pakistani women in Hegland and Utsat women in Pang are urban or have contact with urban areas; in Eiesland they are "suburban," while in Brink, it's women's male relatives, who have more "contact" with urban places or sources, who encourage fundamentalism in the village. While television is an important source of some religious information, even if *muhaggabat* village women want to study the texts, they lack occasions and materials (Brink). Gush Emunim who live on the frontier, however, take part in national debates (El-Or and Aran).

Class, social mobility, prestige or status are associated with interest in fundamentalist religion. A degree of class variation is evident in these studies, although additional studies suggest that the relatively better-off, among the poor, the lower middle, or middle classes, are more involved in fundamentalist activities, at least initially.[23] The Crossroads Pentecostal congregation, writes Eiesland is "primarily white, upper-middle class, college-educated," from suburbia, and generally mobile. The feminist Grace was able to devote time to challenging male authority in the church because of her husband's ability to support the family (Stocks). On the other hand, Utsat women who are acquiring an Islamic education live in a society that has promoted classlessness in the recent past. A number of authors here have also established a relationship between participation in fundamentalist activities and increased social prestige for the individual or her family (Hegland; Brink; Brusco). In La Paz, Gill (1990) reports working class, immigrant Pentecostals come to view themselves as among the "elite."

Women's work status and experiences also provide different opportunities and resources to draw on. Some fundamentalist women view work outside the home as degrading and sexist—in principle or from experience. For them, leaving the work world provides status and opportunities to engage in religious activities. Eiesland's professional women—middle class women—"retire" early to devote themselves to home life (cf. Kaufman 1991; Davidman 1991; Stocks). However, the control that other fundamentalist women maintain is reinforced by their economic roles. In Pang, Utsat women's work opportunities, the nature of Chinese development and communal organization and the high valuation on women's labor provided the backdrop for women's ability to pick and choose Islamic practices. This is also the case in McAllister, where Negeri Sembilan women's economic roles and matriliny mean that women have tools at their disposal to rework Islam; still revival affects the holding of traditional rituals and matrilineal practices (1992). A high percentage of Bennion's Mormon fundamentalist women, unlike other Mormon women, work outside the home (in the community) due partly to rather remote locations and partly to the absence of men working away from home to support their large polygynous families.

Mobility (refugee, migrant) or ethnic status, especially contact with urban centers or international travelers, affects interest in and access to fundamentalism or religious activity, as Hegland describes in Peshawar. Middle Eastern visitors heighten Utsat awareness of Islam elsewhere and urban relatives often bring fundamentalist ideas about women's roles to villagers (Bauer 1983). Their immigrant, as well as ethnic and religious (Shi'a), statuses affect the positioning of individuals in women's religious communities in Pakistan (Hegland). In fundamentalist Mormon communities, however, the migrant status of men affords women more opportunities to run community affairs and assume roles in "vital priesthood religious and social rituals."

Minority/majority identity or the status of a religious or ethnic group in the wider culture, particularly where religious identity coincides with ethnic minority status, can accentuate the importance of religious identity and take on an oppositional quality, with specific implications for women, as Sen and El-Or (1994) demonstrate. The minority status of Utsat women in Hainan may also enhance the importance of Islam (as an identifier) in their lives (Pang). For Pentecostals in Colombia, becoming born-again or fundamentalist within the larger Catholic society becomes a source of meaningful pride (Brusco), while selecting "Muslim" over "Arab" identity registers Sudanese women's displeasure with the sexism they associate with Arab men.

Literacy or education (often correlated with class) is an important part of contemporary fundamentalism, where researching the textual traditions becomes a priority. Without literacy, reading and reshaping the authoritative texts and traditions would be difficult; in rural Egypt women, who have little literacy, show little interest in formal Islamic information. Some knowledge for reading the Imams' stories and being able to copy the latest *nohas* are important to Shi'a women (Hegland). In Hainan, learning to read the Koran is very important to enhancing women's religious status (Pang) and Bible study is an important activity in all of the Christian fundamentalist women's groups here. The evangelical Grace is in a position to research Bible passages for her book and newsletter, debating the place of women and women's authority in the Church (Stocks). Certainly the well-positioned women that Hale interviews, as well as those El-Or studied in her book-length study of ultra-orthodox women in Israel, place great emphasis on their studies of the texts. Buddhist women are searching out legends about the Buddha, particularly through written texts, to build their case for reinstituting *Bhikkhuni Sasana* (Goonatilake). At one extreme, as already noted for some women (as in Eiesland and in Kaufman 1991), higher education and professional experiences make fundamentalism attractive to women because of their failures to achieve the kind of life they sought through these other means.

Life cycle circumstances or the history of local fundamentalisms—cohort or generational differences—may affect how fundamentalism appeals to women, what effects it has on them, and what kind of role they can play. It is sometimes suggested that the young (college students or the unemployed), having reached a point in life where they question existing society, are more likely to be attracted to fundamentalism.[24] Brink reports that *muhaggabat* women in the village are primarily younger women. Some of the outstanding Peshawar Shi'a chanters are young, unmarried women, although some ritual leaders are older. As Hegland says, senior women managed the *majles* rituals while younger women competed as speakers. Goonatilake also reports that the majority of the novice nuns enter religious life before even undertaking any family obligations (in their early 20's), but about one-third enter after already fulfilling their family obligations. In Eiesland, Pentecostal women are largely middle-aged (or "late life" converts) and have experienced disappointment in the lack of equality in workplace and professional life, as have the *ba'alot teshuva* (returnees to Orthodoxism) in Kaufman (1991). Grace, the evangelical feminist challenging women's place in her denomination, is also in her 50's. The fundamentalist Mormon women who take on active community roles seem to be of childbearing age but also span the life cycle.

Conversion experiences often mean a different level of commitment to fundamentalist religion in contrast to being born into the religions, a distinction made by Eiesland. As Kaufman (1991) pointed, out those who chose to become Orthodox (or fundamentalist) consciously commit themselves to a way of life (although as Davidman (1991) and Kaufman point out they may not be totally accepted in Orthodox communities). For these converts—as in Brusco's case—the content and behavioral codes of religious ideology may be especially significant. Goonatilake notes that in contrast to monks, Sri Lankan women who become Buddhist nuns have generally chosen this way of life. On the other hand, Grace's position may be slighty enhanced by her family's deep roots in her evangelical denomination (Stocks).

Additional levels of personal commitment and individual spirituality are important and they are seen here most vividly in the unique, individual women highlighted in these articles. It is clear that "leaders" and "ordinary partici-

231

BAUER

pants" often have different experiences in fundamentalism and may bring different backgrounds to it. Some authors have focused on the way ordinary women receive or challenge fundamentalism (Brink, Friedl, Eiesland, Bennion, Brusco, Goonatalike, El-Or and Aran); others have highlighted or at least described some unique individual activist women (Stocks, Hegland, Hale, Pang, Sen and Eiesland) and differences among them. The women who take leadership roles (often the more educated or experienced) and other women of moral standing or reputation in the community have the "opportunity" to transgress some of the rules applied to others and derive a great sense of personal power (cf. Faludi 1991; Hardacre 1993; El-Or 1994).

5. *Certain structural and historical factors* including the role of the state (it's organization, policies and ideologies), long standing cultural traditions, and events like revolutions and economic conditions also contribute to variations in the benefits and limitations of fundamentalism to women. State legal structures and policies encourage or support particular behaviors and treatment, as outlined for both secular and religious regimes in the Sudan by Hale.[25] This has different impacts on women of different classes and locations (Hale; Friedl). Although women may figure prominently in the ideology that states and other political groups use to legitimize plans and policies, their ideals of womanhood might not be articulated in monolithic terms or have the desired effects on all women, as Friedl makes clear for Iran. Extralocal events—like the Iranian revolution or prior economic collectivization in China—can create situations where women come to value their public and economic roles in ways that may prevent them from succumbing to some forms of gender restriction. In the cases of Pang and Brink, local economic conditions and cultural traditions help shape the current effects of fundamentalisms which come from outside the communities, with different results; in Goonatilake, external groups bring pressure in assisting local groups of women seeking to restore the order of nuns.

This intersection of state plans with economic conditions and cultural traditions often necessitates accommodations in official policy and ideology (cf. Abrahamian 1993; Obermeyer 1994). The irony for the "fundamentalist" states (and fundamentalist organizations) is that women can "use" state apparatus and ideology to challenge male dominance. The nonfundamentalist nature of some states may also expand the public opportunities of religious women. Utsat women clearly maintain their position by relying on secular, state courts; their traditional economic roles also sustain them, as is the case for fundamentalist Mormon women. El-Or and Aran suggest that the roles of Gush Emunim women beyond the community are, in part, made possible by the "open cultural market and the democratic state within which the women live." Even where the state supports restrictions, women may still exert some leverage on its leaders, as Hale illustrates in interviews with Sudanese women activists.

6. Of course, *drawing conclusions about patterns* across fundamentalisms from this evidence is made difficult by the variety of factors discussed and the fact that each of the authors here specifically highlights different aspects of women's fundamentalism. In addition, various authors suggest caution in interpreting the importance of any one factor—Hale and Sen have pointed to the difficulties of separating the religious and the secular (in beliefs and traditions); Brusco warns against simple economic reductionism and points to a need to look across the individual's life cycle of conversion in trying to explain women's attraction to Pentecostalism—economic and social benefits alone cannot explain the joy and satisfaction that women derive from religious activities.[26] Friedl also makes reference to what she calls the failure to look at the existential side of women's experience.

Cross-culturally, women are associated with fundamentalism, and have different degrees of engagement with fundamentalist groups and organizations, for a variety of reasons which are not done justice by Riesebrodt's explanations for women's involvement. Fundamentalism, as a set of "rules" and religious practices and a social support system, affects women's lives differently, sometimes providing increased social status, even improved standards of living, and an oppositional position vis a vis the dominant majority; other times, imposing new or additional constraints that some women find irritating and limiting. Fundamentalism can clearly provide something for some women in the current climate of economic hardships when gender and gender roles are hotly contested in most societies. We might call it a sense of greater efficacy over their lives or a kind of personal empowerment. This is especially so for those women who choose to join or participate—for those without family, for the working class or migrants without status or economic security, for unmarried or infertile women, for those desiring to make their lives more meaningful or in search of some measure of control over their lives they have not found through life outside. The *paradox* of women's fundamentalism especially for those who elect it as a way of life may be in the eye of the beholder.

What does emerge at this point, in light of the theoretical discussions offered in "men's studies," contrasting structural/material and ideological factors, is the importance of women's communities and the social negotiation of the different factors entangling them. Perhaps this reflects that women in most societies are constantly placed in the position of doing "balancing acts" in their ordinary lives (Johnson 1992) or called on to make what Kandiyoti terms "patriarchal bargains" (1991). According to Gill (1990), women Pentecostals in La Paz focus on the positive things they derive from existing (albeit patriarchal) relations and Klatch's activist conservative women find no paradox in their activity (1994).

We begin to see how individuals deal with ambiguities and complexities in their own lives, instead of only presuming causation from the presence of certain factors. Despite encountering some restrictive ideals and facing difficul-

233

BAUER

ties in assuming authority, fundamentalist women are engaging, incorporating, questioning—a different metaphor from that of rejection or reaction, which is seen more clearly in "men's studies" because of their lack of comparable attention to "agency" and to the methods of ethnography and participant observation as research tools for studying fundamentalism. Women fundamentalists even provide a kind of model for this; in Eiesland women's biographies (as testimonies) become an integral part of religious conversion and personal transformation in prayer group. Women are creating a space for themselves within fundamentalism in ways that intersect, even collide, with men's worlds and that may have implications for conclusions drawn about (men's) fundamentalism and in particular, for feminist concerns about gender equality. But before we can consider the relevance of these findings for the comparative study of fundamentalism, more generally, we have to consider whether there is anything to compare.

THE IMPLICATIONS OF WOMEN'S STANDPOINT FOR RETHINKING COMPARATIVE FUNDAMENTALISMS

As typically used, "standpoint" theory references the difference women's views can make in theoretical assessments or, in Hale's terms, the project of putting women at the center. For El-Or and Aran, feminist standpoint is a vision that is different from the dominant one.[27] Taking this view involves both methodological and substantive adjustments (cf. Reinharz 1992) and typically involves questioning existing structures of power. One might ask why women's "voice," viewpoint, or methodologies are important. An example of the difference women's standpoint makes is seen in the use of the following terminology in studies of fundamentalism: anomie (or alienation)[28] in "men's studies" is typically used to convey emotions of dissatisfaction and displacement, presumed from particular external conditions, often with little reference to actual individuals' perceptions, while "women's studies" more frequently talk of "life crises," with a focus on personal responses to those conditions. Like the metaphors of reaction or rejection versus engagement and incorporation, this language reflects the attitude or views of the researchers and the methodologies they employ. Ethnographic and life history approaches further encourage the kind of focus on agency in which the authors here actualize individual negotiation of their life circumstances, although, as Gardiner points out women's agency does not insure their autonomy (1995).

Because "men's studies"—and predominately Western male points of view—have set the content, definitions, and language in studies of fundamentalism, women's standpoint brings us something about the perspective of the others in it—the "underside of fundamentalisms"—the nonmale-secondary elite, the marginal, the followers. A look at women not only sheds light on variation within fundamentalism but also challenges the general focus and conclusions of these studies, addressing what A. Ahmed (1992) calls a failure to link fundamentalisms with the larger issues of fragmentation and the search for identity and inclusion perceived to lie behind the religious resurgence in the postmodern world. It is perhaps a reconsideration of these "voices" that will make clearer the democratic impulse in the processes of fundamentalism.

Fundamentalism: By Any Other Name Is It the Same?

Joan Mencher introduces this volume with the definition of fundamentalisms offered by Marty and Appleby in the Fundamentalisms Project. In general, however, the authors here have been reluctant to use "fundamentalism" as an unqualified category, and general dissatisfaction with the term has been expressed by others considering non-Christian forms of "fundamentalism" or noting the inherent bias against religion in the negative descriptors attached to it.[29]

Lawrence (and much of anthropology) hails comparative studies as important for understanding what is both common and unique about different fundamentalisms (1989: 6). On what bases can we establish a comparative study of the phenomena? It is not easy to address this question for the reasons already touched on above: *first,* different types of information are provided in each of these articles; not everyone provides distinctions between converts and born-into-members, or the role of ideology and women's engagement with it, for example, and "men's studies" haven't usually provided the rich detailed experiences of the "women's studies"; *second,* the authors themselves argue strongly against essentializing the experience of women in terms of the summarizing categories typically used in discussing fundamentalism, focusing instead on women's actual experiences; but *thirdly,* and most importantly it's just not clear how women (and certain varieties of resurgence or reformism, Pentecostalism and non-Christian varieties) fit into the larger study of fundamentalisms. In its very construction, "fundamentalism," defined as an "exclusionary" phenomenon, has excluded a variety of "others" engaged in very similar projects.

The "family of resemblances" conceptualized by Marty and Appleby to make it possible to compare fundamentalisms is patriarchal. Fundamentalism, they suggest, is a "habit of mind and pattern of behavior—found within modern religious communities and embodied in representative individuals and movements" (1992:34).[30] In practice, these representatives have been men, in particular, leaders, writers and thinkers in politically vocal groups (cf. Lawrence 1989; Davis 1984). "Resemblances" which include "drawing on the full resources of the tradition," "fighting back with the world in a politically active way," and the "retrieval of beliefs and practices from the past" to mention only a few, ignore many women in fundamentalism, who rework or reinterpret the texts or traditions, who subvert (or seek to alter) as it were the texts and goals officially selected by males, and who may not be as visible as men in attempts to reform society with religion. In other words, women must conform to pre-

235

BAUER

viously established defining characteristics, as set out in the Fundamentalisms Project and by "men's studies," which gauge fundamentalism by male behaviors and by textual traditions, as opposed to nontextual ones.

When fundamentalists are defined by reaction, active struggle with the secular, and "secondary male elite" positions, and women, by the ideals of passivity, motherhood and family roles, then by definition, most women cannot fit the category. Some women (leaders) may demonstrate those "male" qualities but do not encourage them in other women (cf. Faludi 1991). Although ordinary women fighting for a place within fundamentalism may be seen as oppositional, they do not seem preoccupied with defeating the secular. In many ways they come to rebel as much against the structure and elements of fundamentalist traditions as against "the modern world."

The debates about qualifying terms affect the inclusion of a host of "others" who are caught up in religious revivals but who are characterized variously by those who write about them. This is the case for varieties of fundamentalist tendencies within the same tradition—like evangelicals and fundamentalists in the Protestant tradition, as Eiesland explains here;[31] and reformers, modernists, and fundamentalists (cf. Esposito 1984) or the traditionalists and the fundamentalists (Peacock 1978), the traditional versus the textual (Riesebrodt 1990), or fundamentalists and revivalists (Lawrence 1989) in the Islamic tradition. In other instances differences are elaborated between those who propose social programs and those who have a political agenda (Klatch 1994).[32] Thus, Juergensmeyer favors distinguishing between religious nationalists (with a political agenda), whom he considers more antiwest than antimodern, and fundamentalists who stress religious principles (1993b). This may be a useful distinction, particularly since women do not seem to figure as prominently as men in the visible political activity of fundamentalisms. Bounded or seclusive groups that withdraw from the material/secular world around them, like the Amish and Ultraorthodox Jewish groups, are often not included either.

Despite the disagreement over whether the key characteristics attributed to fundamentalisms by the Fundamentalisms Project are appropriate for one or another religious tradition or inclusive enough given the apparent variety of contemporary fundamentalisms within any one tradition, what seems to remain as *common general features* are (1) first, a *specific concern with gender roles, women's behavior and sexuality*[33]—although it is not clear whether this concern is an expression of moral conviction, cultural traditions, a reflection of working- or middle-class men's loss of prestige and control, disillusionment with change, or a symbolic way of asserting cultural autonomy for the nation or culture; (2) second, *location in a global capitalist economy* and culture— although local historical conditions vary and greatly determine the trajectory of fundamentalisms, contemporary world economy and the globalization of cultural/media forms mean that in very general terms varieties of fundamentalism

236

are operating in or responding to the same broader context of concerns for improving the world. As Bernal (1994) points out for her village in the Sudan, it is capitalism which has helped to separate the religious realm from everyday material life in ways that provoke a recognition of this reality and, through technological advances, has made available new forms of religious and secular knowledge, which are no longer the property of any one group or class;[34] and (3) third, *attempts to conceptualize, agree on, and privilege certain religious guidelines* in order to find meaningful places, even justice, for themselves, improving their lives, and flourishing in the modern world— even if there is no agreement on central texts within a body of traditional practices as in Hinduism (Sen), there are attempts to search for, draw on, recreate, and standardize a set of beliefs and practices, at least at an official level (cf. Swearer 1991; Wei-ming 1991; Gold 1991). Perhaps Stacey and Gerard (1990) put it most succinctly, fundamentalists believe in the authority and truth of the text but there is disagreement on what the text says.

Fundamentalist women's relationship to the text is more problematic but adhering to *religious* guidelines remains important in their lives. Moreover, since women are located within (*not separate from*) these more general fundamentalist climates, it is not inappropriate to also compare women in fundamentalisms across different societies, applying some caution. Even though women may not accept the "inerrancy" of texts, traditions, and interpretations that deprive women of opportunities and choices, they still work within these traditions and within this context. Thus, despite the difficulty (even inappropriateness) of fitting their subjects' religious affiliations and experiences into the category of "fundamentalist" as currently understood, and despite their hesitations about constructing comparative categories that distort, the authors here have come to terms with how women's religious participation in the groups they studied can be viewed as "fundamentalist."

Still, there is something in a name. As Brusco reminds us, when referencing Harding, fundamentalism doesn't simply exist, it is created by the way we talk about and study it, and as these women's ethnographies remind us, the media has played a large role in this complicated process by both propagating difference and contributing to sameness. So much so that if the current descriptors of fundamentalism were to be applied to Khomeini of Iran, Abrahamian suggests he would not qualify as a fundamentalist.[35] At least in raising questions about women's exclusion, we are made to consider some of the advantages in opening up the category to include more of those who participate—challenging received definitions and assumptions, blurring lines between types of fundamentalism, yet making us more conscious of differences.

The Processes of Fundamentalism and the Democratic Impulse

Beyond questioning the category, what these women's cases suggest for comparative study of the processes of fundamentalisms is also instructive. The au-

237

BAUER

thors in this volume certainly do not encourage drawing any conclusions of the "typifying" sort found in many "men's studies," focusing instead on the rich detail of women's lives in fundamentalist traditions. As Susan Waltz (1985) points out, in many ways "fundamentalism" is over-determined—there are so many variables that contribute to the motivations of individuals to join (or "be mobilized") and to the construction of groups or organizations.

In many quarters, however, the debate rages on over what these variables mean, what patterns emerge, and what kind of theoretical framework they suggest for capturing the processes of fundamentalisms or of "becoming fundamentalist." In addition to those previously mentioned theoretical discussions over the competing importance of *material, social and structural* factors versus *ideological* factors (relying heavily on textual assessments), another set of concerns over more explicitly connecting local fundamentalist choices with historical, economic, and political conditions has emerged (cf. A. Ahmed 1992). Indeed there is probably now some agreement that studies of fundamentalism must consider the intersection of a number of factors at the individual and extra-individual levels, in historical perspective. Eric Davis has expressed this concern in his work on Egyptian male fundamentalists (1984). The difficulty, however, as Davis points out in the case of beliefs, is not in seeing some kind of correspondence between background and the appeal of Islamic "radicalism," but in explaining the way "such thought mediates reality for its followers" (cf. Ammerman 1987).

238

At the risk of bringing too much attention back to those bothersome, essentialized terms associated with fundamentalism (i.e., those that collapse characteristics to a few model ones), let me explain briefly how women's standpoint (via its methodology, assumptions, and focus on relationships) speaks to these concerns and what it suggests, once and for all, toward rethinking current generalizations and reordering research tactics in the study of fundamentalism. I do this in the form of four interrelated (counter)claims: (1) First, the dichotomies forged between modernity (as secularism) and fundamentalism (expressed as tradition, religiosity, reaction to or failure of secularization, or opposition to change in traditional social organization and values) are uninformative and their continued use obscures both the efforts of fundamentalists to engage conditions around them and actively become part of the "modern" world and the impact that fundamentalism has on women (and others) who do not enthusiastically choose to participate; in many ways these terminologies grow out of an academic search to name explanatory linkages (or causative relations) between personal background and motivation in "men's studies," without necessarily explicating the relations or the deliberate choices that are presumed to lie behind them; (2) second, the primacy of (and easier access to) the fundamentalist group and public political activity over individual variations in participation and nonpoliticized religious communities is dubious, oversimplified, and

BAUER

misleads us in determining what explains people's interest in fundamentalisms—what they might be dissatisfied with in their lives, whether they do perceive women's opportunities to be a threat, whether they are experiencing "crisis" or "anomie"; (3) this leads to the third counterclaim, the historical trajectory of fundamentalisms (and gender) in relation to various structural conditions is neither unilineal nor uniform with respect to what causes it (or motivates individuals to become fundamentalist or organize groups) or what impact it has on those in its path. That is, if we investigate beyond the stereotyped characteristics and the group focus described above, to reassess the linkages between individuals and the conditions that affect them, we will find it difficult to construct any single, satisfactory pattern for fundamentalism, over time or in different historical periods, across different classes, and in different places. (4) And, establishing the importance of women and gender for analyses of fundamentalism leads to the last (counter)claim—fundamentalism has mixed effects for women (oppressive to some, liberating to others), and the struggles of some women within fundamentalism to improve women's situation challenge both men's authority in religion and the primacy of (secular) feminist discourse about women's liberation— it offers a vision of liberation that is both similar to and different from secular feminism.

Following the lead of women's studies of fundamentalism means adopting methodologies and assumptions that focus more on the conditions and relationships underlying what we characterize as traditional and modern behaviors; going beyond analysis of the beliefs or texts as interpreted by noted group leaders or conditions of economic hardship, to understand what, if any, valuative impact fundamentalist creed has on individual participants who are making choices in specific situations. The means or messages (including resentment of women's behavior) used by public religious figures to appeal to and organize groups or movements may not reflect precisely the economic circumstances or personal reasons that explain why other individuals take action, nor capture the impact of fundamentalist thinking in their lives. Indeed women's experience suggests that public religious leaders and ideology may not be as important as other factors in explaining participation in, or even impact from, fundamentalism and that the lives of leaders or organizers may not conform to their espoused ideals.

Further, it is not enough to investigate how religious beliefs are meaningful or appealing. Women's relationship to fundamentalism, and how it affects women's autonomy and position historically, has depended upon preexisting traditions as well as specific circumstances in which women are found—the class location of individuals, local culture, personal factors, social relations and household economic circumstances, as well as larger political structures (government deployment of religion as a legitimation of restrictive policies or nonrestrictive ones), as demonstrated in the second section above. As noted there, the impact of the message may be tempered by circumstances—an idealized message may encourage either higher status or equality for women or restrictions on women. Yet, the position that women have enjoyed or enjoy after encountering a new religion or fundamentalism depends upon the historical moment at which women encounter it, their class background (and how the religious messages are interpreted there), and whether they choose it or not.[36] Attention to the interplay of historical, local and international factors can be seen, for example, in Hale who highlights the preceding impacts of development on the rise of the fundamentalist impulse in the Sudan or Bernal (1994) who accentuates the intersection of external factors like world economy and communications with the internal dynamics of Islam in rural Sudan.

Class or urban/rural background are frequently used to assess the connections between personal crises and historical factors or "crises" (like broad-based economic or social changes associated with the expansion of capitalism) in the development of fundamentalism. Since women's experience attests to a variety of class backgrounds, "personal disruptions," rather than "calamity culture" (Eiesland), personal choices, cohort specific events like the Iranian revolution, and life cycle events like youthfulness, unemployment or widowhood that enhance the salience of religious solutions or practice, drawing the connections between women's lives and fundamentalism in the larger social, economic, and political world does not easily support the patterns previously put forward—for instance, the idea that traditional, backward, poor, rural-born migrants or even lower-(working-) class individuals are the backbone of fundamentalism—nor do they allow us to otherwise insinuate some kind of straightforward causal relations between either background characteristics or economic crisis and specific emotional states that induce fundamentalist inclinations or activity. It would be difficult to categorize professional women in Eiesland or in Kaufman (1991) as clearly traditional rather than modern or as disenfranchised migrants or primarily members of certain classes.

Gradually, conceptions of "rural" religious traditions invading the city are giving way to the contemporary picture of fundamentalism as more urban, middle-and lower-middle-class in origin, perhaps drawing on other classes or areas—suggesting the interaction of historical and personal circumstances over time.[37] Several authors, like Hale for the Sudan, have noted a class shift in time, from the "radical lower middle classes" to the "newly educated urban middle class support of cultural nationalism." Emancipation for women followed similar class lines, with the upper and upper middle classes favoring a liberation of the liberal western sort and the lower middle classes stressing opposing models they saw as based in "cultural traditions". Brink reports Cairene women were observant by moral choice, while rural women are beginning to veil at the behest of male relatives. Urban migrants or villagers may find participation in these activities an indication of social status and modernity, an opportune locus of affiliation.[38] As Brusco points out, women's experiences suggest that fundamentalism is a way for some to embrace and go forward in the modern world. It can be a part of becoming modern, especially for those who have few, or reject other, alternatives.[39]

The apparent "class shift" is significant first, in light of presumptions about the relationships between class background and fundamentalism and second, because relatively little attention has been given to the relationships between classes in the development of fundamentalism or the process of becoming fundamentalist.[40] The exact class location of religious fundamentalists varies by historical moment, across different geographical locations, and over time. This class shift, then, becomes important in understanding the trajectory of fundamentalisms and their impact, which can change over time, with changing conditions and government policies.

In parts of rural Malaysia traditional practices supporting strong economic roles for women are still in the process of being accommodated to notions from the Islamic revival (McAllister 1992). Egyptian women in Brink's study may experience an initial loss of traditional status and ritual participation with development and with the onset of fundamentalist thinking/ideology in the villages (as Friedl has argued for Iran); this same loss of previously more expansive options affected professional, middle-class women in Iran and the Sudan with the Islamization of those governments. Will Egyptian rural women experience increased status later as circumstances and options associated with fundamentalism change? Will Brink's women find some empowerment in fundamentalism, while Hegland's and Pang's go on to find more restraint? Iranian women in the Islamic Republic, where fundamentalist ideologies (as opposed to religious/cultural traditions) were imposed on, not chosen by, much of the population, have found ways to negotiate their places at both official and personal levels (Friedl; Ramazani 1993; Haeri 1993). In other words, as supported in the cases here, we cannot state categorically that fundamentalisms are good or bad or have a specific impact on women's status, behaviors, alternatives, or gender relations everywhere.

If there is *a* process or pattern to becoming fundamentalist or to the course of fundamentalisms, it seems to differ for leaders of groups and individual followers, to be historically unpredictable in terms of general structures, certainly not explained in terms of traditional and modern, and to have different consequences for men and women because of "woman's" position as object as well as agent in fundamentalisms. It takes different forms and routes for different people. It changes over time in response to many things—movements are made and institutionalized, groups become politicized and agendas change. In the contemporary instance, however, especially among ordinary participants, it is associated as much with, or appeals as much to, a desire to participate in the fate of one's life or the well-being of the community as it does to reinstitute the past.

We've seen that fundamentalist groups offer some women the only means available to them for controlling their lives, finding social acceptance or middle-class status, and expressing themselves (Gill 1990; Brusco). If the renewed and "scientific" interests in exploring dimensions of one's faith textually has origins among the urban and educated, then interest in or association with reformism or fundamentalism can be seen as entry into the modern world. In any case it represents the desire to be counted—whether within groups that enter into discourse with the larger political world, or those who withdraw into themselves—a kind of democratic urge—spawned or made possible by the life it is said to oppose. Therefore, it is more productively pursued as an integrative impulse, rather than as opposition or reaction. However, in this search for justice and inclusion, religious reformers have seriously neglected to examine fairness in gender relations (cf. McNeill 1993). Men's studies of fundamentalism have not addressed the concerns of women and fundamentalist women's struggles to be reckoned with have, subsequently, become a challenge for feminism and for the study of fundamentalisms more generally.

(a) Cross-cultural Feminism or Antifeminism: The Religious (Women's) Challenge to Secular Feminism

Those politically active fundamentalist women, as described in Hale, El-Or and Aran, Sen, Goonatalike and Stocks, who are working to assert themselves or advocating changes in communal ideologies[41] for the benefit of women, challenge not only male authority but also the primacy of feminist views on women's liberation. At times there seem to be, as Hale and Sen allude to, two women's movements, a fundamentalist, religious one and a secular one. The positions taken by fundamentalist feminists or womanists, pose the ultimate questions for feminists—what is emancipation and how is it achieved? Should women seek control over choices and can they do this through perspectives of "difference" as advocated by most fundamentalist groups, with their focus on God-ordained biological and social differences that separate men and women, or through secular feminist perspectives that focus on transformations of power to achieve individual rights and equality within democratic communities?

Despite feminists' attempts to open up discussion of women's oppressions to multiple voices, the applicability of definitions of feminism to some forms of fundamentalist women's activity (cf. Humm 1990:74; Jagger 1983), and the use of the term to describe fundamentalist women here by Pang, Hale, and Stocks,[42] there is considerable reluctance to include fundamentalist women or to use the term "feminist" for activist fundamentalist women, as Eiesland points out. Secular feminists (like those working with WAF, Women Against Fundamentalism, an international organization based in London) are alarmed by the implications of religious resurgence for those who do not elect to join and the ultimate limitations its patriarchy imposes on the pursuit of women's equality seen, for example, in attempts to restrict women's occupations in cases where fundamentalists enjoy political power (Friedl; Hale; Lesselier 1992/93). It is often fundamentalist women, with more education or of better means, who can choose to become more active and find ways to empower themselves or fight for others; when they do it's often outside of formal authority structures or legitimized in terms of their role as mothers and caretakers (Klatch 1994; Hegland; El-Or and Aran).

Whatever the limitations of ideology, however, some women do find in fundamentalism strength, social status, public position, or power in personal and marital relations—a kind of "liberation," as Islamist women would say. It is even suggested that this route might be more accessible to the poor than secular alternatives (Sen). Given that secular feminists have not yet successfully challenged cultural patriarchy (the ethos and structures that support male advantage and control in various spheres of activity), that they are often no more successful in putting gender issues before communal (ethnic or national) ones (cf. Sen, El-Or and Aran, Gill 1990), that they recognize the variety of women's circumstances may require different strategies for liberation or justice in different situations, and that religious communities have traditionally offered women some cultural/religious power at different moments in their life cycle (cf. Sered 1994)—perhaps we should take a closer look at religious feminism, particularly its successes in transforming women's personal or familial relationships (as described earlier).

In fact both Western and nonWestern feminists see interesting, though problematic, intersections (cf. Bauer 1993;1994). Sen observes that fundamentalist groups in India have "co-opted the vocabulary and style of the women's movement and [made] a conscious attempt to mobilize women for their programmes," and Judith Stacey finds that evangelical feminism has begun to reflect some influences of feminist thinking (1990). Out of the considerable disagreement between them over what constitutes liberation and equality for women and the best ways to achieve it (sameness or difference) comes a semblance of convergence between secular and religious feminists, as secular feminists attempting to recenter individual rights within the community, take up the "difference" theme focusing either on motherhood or common oppressions (cf. Fox- Genovese 1991; Held 1993; Dietz 1985; Coontz 1992;Young 1995). El-Or and Aran note that Gush Emunim women are able to see some common bond between Palestinian mothers and themselves, in the midst of much difference, in their concerns over "motherhood".

Moreover, in the face of enormous public anxiety about political fundamentalism, there is increasing recognition that the ability of fundamentalist religions to impose their moral guidelines on others in the long run is tempered by both political and practical considerations, as Friedl and Hale demonstrate (cf. Moghadam 1993; Juergensmeyer 1993a; Marty and Appleby 1994).

REWRITING FUNDAMENTALISM AS IF WOMEN MATTERED: THE PROMISE OF INCLUSION

From the vantage point of ethnographic cases which highlight women's active negotiations of their circumstances, however, it's easy to lose sight of the structural limitations on women's power, the "etic" explanations that Brink identifies. Sered, for example, specifically conditions the beneficial aspects of women's religious associations upon the presence of supportive social and economic conditions (1994). As women, even some fundamentalist women, reclaim a little space for themselves, rewriting the language and ritual of women's practices, or find room for more equal participation in public; religious and societal authority remains vested in men, demonstrated in the cases here (cf. Castelli and McBride 1991; Kaufman 1991). While the idealized religious expectations for women's behavior in Iran may not be "fixed," in Friedl's words, the fundamentalist (as well as the secular) patriarchy remains suspicious of women's autonomy over individual choice. This has lead Pang and Hegland to wonder what impact the fundamentalist oratory of separation and difference might eventually have on the women they interviewed.

As Sen's analysis at the end of this volume reminds us, the ultimate challenge facing both secular and religious feminists is existing patriarchy and finding ways to challenge economic and political structures of power. However emancipation is defined and whatever is required to achieve it, confronting the ultimate limits of authority and power over women at various levels becomes the issue. As Hale conjectures, despite accommodations by the state, it is unlikely that men in the Sudan will relinquish control over women's "access to power and privilege."

Perhaps this holds the ultimate potential for sisterhood. Historically women have not been able to rely on men to do the right thing when it comes to equality of opportunity or justice for women, regardless of the patriarchal bargains they make (Kandiyoti 1991). But if Roy and others are correct, religious fundamentalism contains the seeds of its own dissolution. Fundamentalism, he suggests, by operating within and accommodating to capitalist processes, has deprived itself "of its value as a place of transcendence, refuge and protest" (1994:199). If so, perhaps religious and secular women can, at that point, reclaim the democratic impulse to recognize, discuss, and confront the common forms of patriarchy that will, most certainly, remain (cf. Cucchiari 1990).

Religious feminists may be able to broaden their nascent challenge to celestial patriarchy, raising the crucial questions about power—through either bringing men back to religion (as they do in Brusco) or questioning the ultimate authority of men to interpret God's wishes (as in Stocks). Is it self-interest or religious texts that legitimize inequalities for women or control of their sexuality in fundamentalism? There are, as women have found, textual bases for challenging inequality in religion (cf. Grob, Hassan and Gordon 1991).

Doing this will require delicately separating cultural patriarchies from the religious—never an easy, sometimes impractical, task. They will also need to look beyond family relations to seriously examine connections with the larger world, which Kaufman suggests fundamentalist women have been less concerned with (1991, 1994).

Even when women live in religious communities that wish to seclude them or the whole community from the world, the larger society still shapes the circumstances under which these communities exist. Until women have obtained the power to penetrate structures of economic and political power and the authority to assert their interpretations they are likely to remain, in Stocks' words, "voices on the margins." In this regard, secular feminist thinking already encourages more open challenges to social, economic and political structures of power and the analysis of broad sets of relations, especially those beyond the local group (cf. Young 1990a).

Often both women in fundamentalism and women writing about fundamentalism seem to occupy marginal, gender-specific spaces (cf. Strathern 1987). Many of their experiences and their influence in or with fundamentalism are distinct and certain notions (about sexuality for example) affect them differently than men. But as these studies show, one thing is certain: women and gender are essential factors for understanding the broader phenomena of fundamentalisms—both because fundamentalists make women central to their concerns and because we can more realistically understand fundamentalisms in the contemporary world by adopting some of "women's standpoint."

245

Some scholars may prefer to restrict the definition or category, "fundamentalism," to a narrow set of religious behaviors and traditions represented by nineteenth-century Protestant fundamentalism. However, investigating varieties of reform and resurgence which are not publicly visible, individuals who are not affiliated with or not prominent in specific groups, women, and groups which are considered nontextual (like religious movements with some animistic roots, in simpler societies)[43] provides greater comprehension of contemporary revival and resurgence and the desire to be included—perhaps, illuminating why, as Bendroth says of nineteenth-century fundamentalist men and women, they chose religious fundamentalism to "simplify the daunting range of choices in a secular lifestyle" (1993)—or why US soldiers in the Gulf War, attracted to its "total" explanation for life, converted to Islam (Utne Reader 1994).

The articles in this volume have provided us with the challenge and the basis for rethinking fundamentalisms. The use of methodologies, like life history and ethnography (despite the controversies of feminist ethnography), and assumptions (like a focus on "agency") represented by women's "standpoint" in fundamentalism leads us to reexamine terminologies, to explore underlying relationships, and to reconsider a variety of factors not fully developed in

BAUER

"men's studies." For example, the studies here highlight the importance of re-considering spirituality and the connections between religious texts and the beliefs of individual participants and between personal and historical circum-stances; as well as the distinctions between individual practitioners and mem-bers of groups, between those who are affected by fundamentalism and those who enthusiastically participate, between those who observe privately and those who use religion in political activity, and between different classes over time.

In particular, the consideration of a "religious feminism" brings into sharp-er focus two critical points which confront the future of cross-cultural funda-mentalisms in an age marked by the desire of others to participate and be heard: (1) the inviability of male authority and power (over women and women's sexuality) and (2) the trials of multiculturalism or pluralism in com-munal relations, the one thing, as Ammerman says, that fundamentalists have not been able to confront (1987). The issues of relations between different ethnicities within fundamentalism and choosing between communal ideolo-gies are raised by Hale and Hegland.[44] Although debates among feminisms have hinted at different (as well as common) interests among Western and nonWestern communalisms (and between different classes), feminists like Sen ideally envision multicultural societies as places where political structures are transformed to allow women (and others) equal participation (cf. Young 1990b). The key, as Sen describes it, is to reestablish some secular basis among/within local traditions for a common discourse, but the difficulty is in being able to distinguish the secular aspects of culture from the religious (cf. Akbar Ahmed 1992; Spitz 1993; Castelli and McBride 1991) and in avoiding reinstituting cultural traditions of patriarchy (Yuval-Davis 1994).

Most importantly these studies of women in fundamentalism direct our theoretical attention to the significance of negotiations and accommodations between individuals and their specific ideological and social circumstances which are essential to comprehending the complex patterns and processes of fundamentalisms, as discussed in previous sections. These approaches should be brought to bear on "men's" as well as "women's studies" of fundamental-ism. The *Fundamentalisms Project* itself seems to have become transformed so that by volume four, *Accounting for Fundamentalisms* (1994), Marty and Apple-by come to agree, more or less, with the first three (counter)claims I listed earlier.

NOTES

1. The use of "mixed blessings" in the title of this book is borrowed from the phrase used by Mary Hegland in her article to characterize the impact of fundamentalism on Shi'a women practitioners in Pakistan.

2. Cf. Yeganeh (1993); Sanday (1981); Thapar (1993); Yuval-Davis (1993; 1994); Brown (1994); Lesselier (1992/3); El-Or (1993); Thaiss (1972); Ong (1990) and many

others. While other volumes, in particular, Moghadam's excellent collection, *Identity Politics*, have explored the repercussions of using "women" as emblems of culture and identity in national and partisan politics, including religious politics, this is the first anthology to look exclusively at women in fundamentalist groups and movements.

3. In this volume we focus on religious fundamentalisms; "fundamentalism" as a stance connoting narrow faithfulness to a particular set of beliefs is applied at least colloquially to other spheres of activity, including leftist politics.

4. Cf. Hawley (1994); Riesebrodt (1993); Brown (1994) and many popular sources like "The Stealth Crusade," *The Washington Spectator* (March 15, 1993); "Tearing off the Veil" (*Vanity Fair*, August, 1993); *Zeit-Punkte* Nr. 1, 1993, special issue, "Der Islam Feind des Westens?"

5. See Bendroth (1993) and Hill (1985) for excellent discussions of women, evangelicalism and fundamentalism in turn-of-the-century America. Other recent volumes continue to examine the complexities of women and evangelical history in the United States, for example Juster (1994). See Tucker (1990); Briggs (1995); Holden (1983); Kirkpatrick (1985); and Kephart and Zellner (1991), on the limitations faced by women in more liberal, nonfundamentalist US religious communities historically.

6. This can be generally seen in the Fundamentalism Project volumes and other volumes cited here, Juergensmeyer (1993a), Arjomand (1984), and Lawrence (1989), among others.

7. Some studies indicate that fundamentalists, especially the central characters, come from relatively better circumstances, with more education or resources than others [e.g. Riesebrodt (1993); Munson (1988); Ibrahim (1980); Davis (1984); Lubeck (1981); Nagata (1979)], but there is no shortage of studies that continue to characterize the poor, migrant masses as the source of fundamentalism and "opposition" to modernity (cf. Dekmejian 1985). Other studies remain unclear. Marty and Appleby (1991a and b) portray fundamentalists as demonstrating "religious reaction to secular modernity" while also emphasizing their being able to choose between tradition and modernity. Wuthnow suggests motive in the dissatisfaction between lower strata and upper strata (1987).

8. For a fuller list of examples see discussion below.

9. For exceptions see Heilman's ethnography among ultra-Orthodox couples (1992) and Loeffler's study of Muslim men in rural Iran (1988).

10. See Shahla Haeri's and Andrea Rugh's fine pieces in Marty and Appleby (1993), which, although based on ethnographic research projects, do not utilize ethnography of women's religious practice or individual lives in these particular articles.

11. See Reeves (1989); Yuval-Davis (1993); El-Or and Aran; and Klatch (1994) for examples from different religious traditions.

12. Again, I do not mean to imply that all of these studies are authored by women.

13. For examples beyond this volume, see Kaufman (1994; 1991); Davidman (1991); Stacey and Gerard (1990); and Hatem (1988).

14. In fact, Sered suggests that women's religions also make less distinction between religious and nonreligious or secular activities (1994).

15. For more discussion, see Riesebrodt (1993); Juergensmeyer (1993a); Lawrence (1989); Stacey (1983); Klatch (1994) and any number of primary fundamentalist sources, like Falwell (1981).

247

16. See examples in Gill (1990); Davidman (1991); and Kaufman (1991).

17. This is reflected in the debates about Muslim women's veiling, which are briefly summarized in El-Or (1993) and other sources. As Brink has described here, educated or middle class fundamentalist women describe veiling as liberating them from the negative influences of male behavior, the pressure to keep extensive wardrobes and so forth, while other women may see this clothing as restrictive (cf. Bauer 1983 for the Iranian case).

18. See for example, Lesselier on Catholic revival in France (1992/3), Hardacre on the new Japanese religions (1993); Bendroth (1993) and Hill and Owen (1982) on Protestant evangelicalism, as well as articles in this volume.

19. See Willis (1985) and Leslie (1983); See Findly (forthcoming) regarding debate over Buddha's being tricked into admitting women.

20. For other examples of women's challenges to fundamentalist authority, see Shaheed (1988–89); Mernissi (1988); Tabari and Yeganeh (1982); Ramazani (1993); and McAllister (1992).

21. See Gill (1990) for examples from Bolivia.

22. See Ong (1990); Doumato (1991); and Beck and Keddie (1978).

23. See footnote seven. Women fundamentalists are variously described as better-off migrants, sometimes lower middle class, or more middle class, as in Crossroads Assembly [cf. Kaufman (1991); Hatem (1988); Faust et al. (1992) and Bauer (1983)].

24. Differential participation by women of different ages suggests possible generational or life cycle variation. It has been suggested that the young generally (college students or the unemployed, for example) are more likely to question existing conditions and are often attracted to both leftist groups and religious fundamentalism (cf. Elizabeth Fernea's film, "Veiled Revolution" or Ibrahim 1980; Dekmejian 1985; Waltz 1985; Verges 1995; and Ong 1990). On the other hand where women are expected to marry young, they are often able to assume more authority at later stages in their life cycle (after childbearing).

25. For example, also see Shaheed (1988-89); Yuval-Davis (1993); Hecht and Yuval-Davis (1984); and works in Kandiyoti, ed. (1991); and Afshar, ed. (1987).

26. The latter comments do lend credence to Lawrence's criticism that not enough emphasis is given to the importance of religious ideologies (1989).

27. Hennessy provides a more specific theoretical definition, "Standpoint refers to a 'position' in society which is shaped by and in turn helps shape ways of knowing, structures of power and resource distribution" (1993: 67); since a feminist standpoint, a way of viewing the world from women's experiences, would be "different," El-Or and Aran's use of standpoint in this volume is consistent with Hennessy's description.

28. This typical usage contrasts with the technical meaning of alienation in Marx, which does not carry the emotional connotations that might be associated with structural changes.

29. Cf. Juergensmeyer (1993a and b); Harris (1994); Hardacre (1993); and Marty and Appleby (1991a).

30. See Marty and Appleby (1991a and b) for a complete discussion of their fundamentalist traits.

31. See Falwell (1981); Spittler (1994); and Bendroth (1993) for more on historical and contemporary distinctions between Christian evangelicals and fundamentalists.

32. Even current typologies of fundamentalism seem to ignore women. Riese-brodt's categories of social movements and secret societies within fundamentalism still don't fully capture women's involvement (1993); Dekmejian's typology (1985) does include active and passive types of fundamentalisms which might encompass some of women's activities.

33. See previous descriptions and footnote references suggesting that most fundamentalists support a separate but equal approach to gender equality. See also Nielsen (1993). Whether this is integral to the religion or an influence of cultural tradition is irrelevant here, if it is currently incorporated into religious belief or practice.

34. Cf. Spitz, " . . . this ideal of an autonomous secular category of life activities has no roots in any of the major Indian religious-cultural traditions" (1993: 258).

35. Abrahamian's book, Khomeinism lays out nicely why the standard understandings of the term "fundamentalist" are problematic when applied to Khomeini or to any religious group (1993).

36. Cf. Hammami and Rieker (1988); Leila Ahmed (1992); Doumato (1991); and Peacock (1978).

37. See previous footnotes on the nondiscreet class position of fundamentalists across cultures, which perhaps suggests increasingly religiously conservative attitudes among those lower middle class or middle class women of more education or longer residence in urban places in contrast to poorer migrant populations. There have also been suggestions that fundamentalist women are middle class and more educated (as in Faust et al. 1992) while men are more often lower middle class and less educated (as in Davis 1984).

38. See Andezian (1986) and Mandel (1990) for examples of religion as a source of identity for immigrants.

39. See Hill and Owen (1982) on the "rising" working-class background of much of the religious right in the United States.

40. See Bauer (1983) for discussion of the impact of cross-class contact on women's participation in "fundamentalist" religious activity in Iran.

41. That is, those supported by "groups" of various kinds to which one can be said to belong and to which values can be ascribed—ethnic, national, religious, political.

42. A number of other authors apply the term to fundamentalist women (cf. Riese-brodt 1993; Bendroth 1993; Reeves 1989; Bauer 1993; Kaufman 1994). Hale and Stocks note that the women they interviewed applied the term to themselves, while El-Or and Aran mention that Israeli-born women are reluctant to designate themselves as "feminists." Others are dubious that a so-called religious feminism can bring any meaningful change to women (cf. Friedl; Mazumdar 1994). The feminist category itself is problematic and carries many negative connotations, particularly in its association with western culture (cf. L. Ahmed 1992; Bauer 1993).

43. Like "fundamentalist" religions, "messianic" or nativistic religions in simpler societies were seen as responses to cultural change, involving a degree of innovation (Lanternari 1963) and demonstrate many of the characteristics attributed to fundamentalist groups. For contemporary examples of "fundamentalisms" in simpler societies, see Gewertz and Errington (1994).

44. For example, see Haddad and Smith (1994) for articles on relations between African-American and other Muslims in the US.

249

REFERENCES

Abrahamian, E. 1993. *Khomeinism: Essays on the Islamic Republic.* Berkeley: University of California Press.

Abu-Lughod, L. 1986. *Veiled Sentiments: Honor and Poetry in a Bedouin Society.* Berkeley: University of California Press.

Ahmed, A. 1992. *Postmodernism and Islam: Predicament and Promise.* London: Routledge.

Ahmed, L. 1992. *Women and Gender in Islam: Historical Roots of A Modern Debate.* New Haven: Yale University Press.

Afshar, H., ed. 1987. *Women, the State and Ideology: Studies from Africa and Asia.* Albany: State University of New York Press.

Ammerman, N. 1987. *Bible Believers: Fundamentalists in the Modern World.* New Brunswick: Rutgers University Press.

Andezian, S. 1986. "Women's Roles in Organizing Symbolic Life: Algerian Female Immigrants in France." *International Migration: The Female Experience.* eds. Simon and Brettell, pp. 254–265. Totowa, N.J.: Rowman and Allenheld.

Arjomand, S. 1984. "Introduction: Social Movements in the Contemporary Near and Middle East." In *From Nationalism to Revolutionary Islam,* ed. S. Arjomand, pp. 1–27. Albany, NY: State University of New York Press.

Bauer, J. 1983. "Poor Women and Social Consciousness in Revolutionary Iran." In *Women and Revolution in Iran.* ed. G. Nashat, pp. 141–170. Boulder: Westview Press.

———. 1993 "Ma'ssoum's Tale: The Personal and Political Transformations of a Young Iranian "Feminist" and her Ethnographer." *Feminist Studies* 19(3):519–548.

———. 1994 "Conversations on Women's Rights Among Iranian Political Exiles: Implications for the Community-Self Debate in Feminism." *Critique* (Spring), pp. 1–12.

Beck, L. and N. Keddie, eds. 1978. *Women in the Muslim World.* Cambridge: Harvard University Press.

Bendroth, M. 1993. *Fundamentalism and Gender, 1875 to the Present.* New Haven: Yale University Press.

Bernal, V. 1994. "Gender, Culture, and Capitalism: Women and the Remaking of Islamic 'Tradition' in a Sudanese Village." *Comparative Study of Society and History* 36(1):36–67.

Briggs, D. 1995. "Sexism Blocks Advancement of Women in Ministry, Researchers Say." *The Hartford Courant.* Saturday, May 6.

Brown, K. McC. 1994. "Fundamentalism and the Control of Women." In *Fundamentalisms and Gender,* ed. J. S. Hawley, pp. 175–211. New York: Oxford University Press.

Castelli, E. and J. McBride 1991. "Beyond the Language and Memory of the Fathers: Feminist Perspectives in Religious Studies." In *Multidisciplinary Approaches to the Study of Gender,* eds. Frese and Coggestall, eds. pp. 113–150. South Hadley, MA: Bergin and Garvey.

Collier, J. and S. Yanagisako, eds. 1987. *Gender and Kinship. Essays Toward a Unified Analysis.* Stanford, CA: Stanford University Press.

Coontz, S. 1992. *The Way We Never Were: American Families and the Nostalgia Trap.* New York: Basic Books.

Cucchiari, S. 1990. "Between Shame and Sanctification: Patriarchy and its Transformation in Sicilian Pentecostalism." *American Ethnologist* 17(4): 687–707.

Davidman, L. 1991. *Tradition in a Rootless World: Women Turn to Orthodox Judaism.* Berkeley: University of California Press.

Davis, E. 1984. "Ideology, Social Class, and Islamic Radicalism in Modern Egypt." In *From Nationalism to Revolutionary Islam.* ed. S. Arjomand, pp. 134–157. Albany, NY: State University of New York Press.

Dekmejian, R. H. 1985. *Islam in Revolution: Fundamentalism in the Arab World.* Syracuse: Syracuse University Press.

Dietz, M. 1985. "Citizenship with a Female Face. The Problem of Maternal Thinking." *Political Theory* 13(1): 19–37.

diLeonardo, M. 1987. "The Female World of Cards and Holidays: Women, Families, and the Work of Kinship." *Signs* 12 (Spring): 440–53.

Doumato, E. 1991. "Hearing Other Voices: Christian Women and the Coming of Islam." *International Journal of Middle East Studies* 23: 177–199.

El-Or, T. 1993. "The Length of the Slits and the Spread of Luxury: Reconstructing the Subordination of Ultra-Orthodox Jewish Women Through the Patriarchy of Men Scholars." *Sex Roles* 29(9/10): 585–598.

———. 1994. *Educated and Ignorant: Ultra-Orthodox Jewish Women and Their World.* Boulder, Co: Lynne Rienner Publishers.

Esposito, J. 1984. *Islam and Politics.* Syracuse, NY: Syracuse University Press.

Faludi, S. 1991. *Backlash: The Undeclared War Against American Women.* New York: Crown Publishers.

Falwell, J. with E. Dobson and E. Hindson, eds. 1981. *The Fundamentalist Phenomenon: The Resurgence of Conservative Christianity.* New York: Doubleday and Co.

Faust, K., et al. 1992 "Young Women Members of the Islamic Revival Movement in Egypt." *The Muslim World* LXXXII(1–2): 55–65.

Findly, E. 1996. "Ananda's Case for Women." *International Journal of Hindu Studies.* Forthcoming.

Fox-Genovese, E. 1991. *Feminism Without Illusions: A Critique of Individualism.* Chapel Hill, NC: University of North Carolina Press.

Gardiner, J. K., ed. 1995. *Provoking Agents: Gender and Agency in Theory and Practice.* Chicago: University of Illinois Press.

Gewertz, D. and F. Errington 1994. "First Contact with God: Individualism, Agency and Revivalism in the Duke York Islands." *Cultural Anthropology* 8(3):279–305.

Gill, L. 1990. "'Like a Veil to Cover Them': Women and the Pentecostal Movement in La Paz." *American Ethnologist* 17(4): 708–721.

Gold, D. 1991. "Organized Hinduisms, From Vedic Thought to Hindu Nation." In *Fundamentalisms Observed.* eds. Marty and Appleby, pp. 531–593. Chicago: University of Chicago Press.

Grob, L., R. Hassan and H. Gordon, eds. 1991. *Women's and Men's Liberation: Testimonies of the Spirit.* New York: Greenwood Press.

Haddad, Y. and J. Smith, eds. 1994. *Muslim Communities in North America.* Albany: State University of New York Press.

Haeri, S. 1993. "Obedience versus Autonomy: Women and Fundamentalism in Iran and Pakistan." In *Fundamentalisms and Society: Reclaiming the Sciences, the Family and Education*, eds. Marty and Appleby, pp. 181–213. Chicago: University of Chicago Press.

Hammami, R. and M. Rieker 1988. "Feminist Orientalism and Orientalist Marxism." *New Left Review* 170 (July–August): 93–106.

Hardacre, H. 1993. "The Impact of Fundamentalisms on Women, the Family and Interpersonal Relations." In *Fundamentalisms and Society: Reclaiming the Sciences, the Family and Education*, eds. Marty and Appleby, pp. 129–150. Chicago: University of Chicago Press.

Harris, J. 1994. "Fundamentalism: Objections from a Modern Jewish Historian." In *Fundamentalisms and Gender*, ed. J. Hawley, pp. 137–173. New York: Oxford University Press.

Hatem, M. 1988. "Egypt's Middle Class in Crisis." *The Middle East Journal* 42: 407–422.

Hawley, J. S., ed. 1994. *Fundamentalism and Gender.* New York: Oxford University Press.

Hecht, D. and Yuval-Davis, N. 1984. "Ideology without Revolution: Jewish Women in Israel." In *Forbidden Agendas: Intolerance and Defiance in the Middle East*, selected and introduced by J. Rothschild. pp. 179–205. London: Zed Press.

Heilman, S. 1992. *Defenders of the Faith: Inside Ultra-Orthodox Jewry.* New York: Schoken Books.

Held, V. 1993. *Feminist Morality: Transforming Culture, Society and Politics.* Chicago: University of Chicago Press.

Hennessy, R. 1993. *Materialist Feminism and the Politics of Discourse.* New York: Routledge.

Hill, P. 1985. *The World Their Household: The American Woman's Foreign Mission Movement and Cultural Transformation.* Ann Arbor: The University of Michigan Press.

Hill, S. and D. Owen 1982. *The New Religious-Political Right in America.* Nashville: Abingdon.

Holden, P., ed. 1983. *Women's Religious Experience.* Totowa, New Jersey: Barnes and Noble Books.

Humm, M. 1990. *The Dictionary of Feminist Theory.* Columbus, Ohio: Ohio State University Press.

Ibrahim, S. E. 1980. "Anatomy of Egypt's Militant Islamic Groups: Methodological Note and Preliminary Findings." *International Journal of Middle East Studies.* 12(4): 423–453.

Jagger, A. 1983. *Feminist Politics and Human Nature.* Totowa, NJ: Rowman and Allanheld.

Johnson, P., ed. 1992. *Balancing Acts: Women and the Process of Social Change.* Boulder: Westview Press.

Juergensmeyer, M. 1993a. *The New Cold War: Religious Nationalism Confronts the Secular State.* Berkeley, CA: University of California Press.

———.1993b. "Why Religious Nationalists are not Fundamentalists." *Religion* 23(1): 85–92.

Juster, S. 1994. *Disorderly Women: Sexual Politics and Evangelicalism in Revolutionary New England.* Ithaca, N.Y.: Cornell University Press.

Kandiyoti, D. 1991. "Islam and Patriarchy: A Comparative Perspective." In *Women in*

Middle Eastern History: Shifting Boundaries in Sex and Gender, eds. Keddie and Baron. pp. 23–42. New Haven: Yale University Press.

Kandiyoti, D., ed. 1991. *Women, Islam and the State*. Philadelphia: Temple University Press.

Kaufman, D. 1991 *Rachel's Daughters: Newly Orthodox Jewish Women*. New Brunswick: Rutgers University Press.

———. 1994 "Paradoxical Politics: Gender Politics Among Orthodox Jewish Women in the United States." In *Identity Politics and Women*. ed. Moghadam, pp. 349–366. Boulder: Westview Press.

Kephart, W. M. and W. W. Zellner 1991. *Extraordinary Communities*. Fourth Edition. New York: St. Martin's Press.

Kirkpatrick, F. 1985. "From Shackles to Liberation: Religion, the Grimke Sisters and Dissent." In *Women, Religion and Social Change*, ed. Haddad and Findly. pp. 433–456. Albany: State University of New York Press.

Klatch, R. 1994. "Women of the New Right in the United States: Family, Feminism and Politics." In *Identity Politics and Women*, ed. Moghadam, pp. 367–388. Boulder: Westview Press.

Lanternari, V. 1963. *The Religions of the Oppressed: A Study of Modern Messianic Cults*. New York: Alfred Knopf.

Lawrence, B. 1989. *Defenders of God: The Fundamentalist Revolt Against the Modern Age*. New York: Harper and Row.

Leslie, J. 1983. "Essence and Existence: Women and Religion in Ancient Indian Texts." In *Women's Religious Experience*. ed. P. Holden, pp. 89–112. Totowa, NJ: Barnes and Noble.

Lesselier, C. 1992/3. "France: Apocalypse Now." *Women Against Fundamentalism* 4: 15–17.

Loeffler, R. 1988. *Islam in Practice. Religious Beliefs in a Persian Village*. Albany: State University of New York Press.

Lubeck, P. M. 1981. "Class Formation at the Periphery: Class Consciousness and Islamic Nationalism Among Nigerian Workers." *Research in the Sociology of Work* 137–70.

Mandel, R. 1990. "Shifting Centres and Emergent Identities: Turkey and Germany in the Lives of the Turkish *Gastarbeiter*." In *Muslim Travelers: Pilgrimage, Migration, and the Religious Imagination*, eds. Eickelman and Piscatori, pp. 153–171. Berkeley: University of California Press.

Marty, M. and R. S. Appleby, 1991a. "Introduction. The Fundamentalism Project: A Users Guide." In *Fundamentalisms Observed*, eds. Marty and Appleby, pp. vii–xiii. Chicago: University of Chicago Press.

———. 1991b. "Conclusion: An Interim Report on a Hypothetical Family." In *Fundamentalisms Observed*, eds. Marty and Appleby, pp. 814–842. Chicago: University of Chicago Press.

———. 1992. *The Glory and Power. The Fundamentalist Challenge to the Modern World*. Boston: Beacon Press.

———. 1994. "Introduction." In *Accounting for Fundamentalisms: The Dynamic Character of Movements*, eds. Marty and Appleby, pp. 1–9. Chicago: University of Chicago Press.

253

BAUER

Mazumdar, S. 1994. "Moving Away from a Secular Vision: Women, Nation and the Cultural Construction of Hindu India." In *Identity Politics and Women*, ed. Moghadam, pp. 243–273. Boulder: Westview Press.

McAllister, C. 1992. "'It's Our Adat': Capitalist Development and the Revival of Tradition Among Women in Negeri Sembilan, Malaysia." In *Balancing Acts: Women and the Process of Social Change,* ed. Johnson, pp.88–119. Boulder: Westview Press.

McNeill, W. 1993. "Fundamentalism and the World of the 1990's." In *Fundamentalisms and Society: Reclaiming the Sciences, the Family and Education*, eds. Marty and Appleby, eds. pp. 558–573. Chicago: University of Chicago Press.

Mernissi, F. 1988. "Muslim Women and Fundamentalism." *Middle East Report* No. 153 (July-August): 8–11,50.

Moghadam, V., ed. 1994. *Identity Politics and Women: Cultural Reassertions and Feminisms in International Perspective.* Boulder: Westview Press.

Moghadam, V. 1993. *Modernizing Women: Gender and Social Change in the Middle East.* Boulder, CO: Lynne Rienner.

Munson, H. 1988. *Islam and Revolution in the Middle East.* New Haven: Yale University Press.

Nagata, J. 1979. "Religious Ideology and Social Change: The Islamic Revival in Malaysia." *Pacific Affairs* 52: 405–39.

Nelson, C. 1974. "Public and Private Politics: Women in the Middle Eastern World." *American Ethnologist* 1(3): 551–63.

Nicholson, L. 1986. *Gender and History: the Limits of Social Theory in the Age of the Family.* New York: Columbia University Press.

Nielsen, N. C. 1993. *Fundamentalism, Mythos, and World Religions.* Albany: State University of New York Press.

Obermeyer, C. M. 1994. "Reproductive Choice in Islam: Gender and State in Iran and Tunisia." *Studies in Family Planning* 25(1): 41–51.

Ong, A. 1990. "State Versus Islam: Malay Families, Women's Bodies and the Body Politic in Malaysia." *American Ethnologist* 17: 258–276.

Peacock, J. 1978. *Muslim Puritans.* Berkeley: University of California Press.

Ramazani, N. 1993. "Women in Iran: The Revolutionary Ebb and Flow." *The Middle East Journal* 47: 409–428.

Reeves, M. 1989. *Female Warriors of Allah: Women and the Islamic Revolution.* New York: Dutton.

Reinharz, S. with the Assistance of L. Davidman 1992. *Feminist Methods in Social Research.* New York: Oxford University Press.

Riesebrodt, M. 1990. *Pious Passion: The Emergence of Modern Fundamentalism in the United States and Iran.* Trans. by Don Reneau. Berkeley: University of California Press.

———. 1993. "Fundamentalism and the Political Mobilization of Women." In *The Political Dimensions of Religion*, ed. Arjomand, pp. 243–271. Albany, NY: State University of New York Press.

Roy, O. 1994. *The Failure of Political Islam.* Cambridge, MA: Harvard University Press.

Rugh, A. 1993. "Reshaping Personal Relations in Egypt." In *Fundamentalisms and Society: Reclaiming the Sciences, the Family and Education*, eds. Marty and Appleby, pp. 151–180. Chicago: University of Chicago Press.

Sanday, P. 1981. *Female Power and Male Dominance: On the Origins of Sexual Inequality.* New York: Cambridge University Press.

Sered, S. S. 1992. *Women as Ritual Experts: The Religious Lives of Elderly Jewish Women in Jerusalem.* New York: Oxford University Press.

————. 1994. "Ideology, Autonomy, and Sisterhood. An Analysis of the Secular Consequences of Women's Religions." *Gender and Society* 8(4): 486–506.

Shaheed, F. 1988–9 "Manipulating the Koran. Pakistan." *Connexions* 28:12–13.

Spittler, R. 1994. "Are Pentecostals and Charismatics Fundamentalists? A Review of American Uses of These Terms." In *Charismatic Christianity as a Global Culture*, ed. Poewe, pp. 103–116. Columbia, SC: University of South Carolina Press.

Spitz, D. 1993. "Cultural Pluralism, Revivalism, and Modernity in South Asia: The Rashtriya Swayamsevak Sangh." In *The Rising Tide of Cultural Pluralism: The Nation-State at Bay?*, ed. Young, pp. 242–264. Madison: University of Wisconsin Press.

Stacey, J. 1983. "The New Conservative Feminism." *Feminist Studies* 9(3):559–83.

Stacey, J. and S. Gerard 1990. "'We Are Not Doormats': The Influence of Feminism on Contemporary Evangelicalism in the United States." In *Uncertain Terms. Negotiating Gender in American Culture*, eds. Ginsburg and Tsing, pp. 98–117. Boston: Beacon Press.

Strathern, M. 1987. "An Awkward Relationship: The Case of Feminism and Anthropology." *Signs* 12(2): 276–292.

Swearer, D. K. 1991. "Fundamentalist Movements in Theravada Buddhism." In *Fundamentalisms Observed*, eds. Marty and Appleby, pp. 628–690. Chicago: University of Chicago Press.

Tabari, A. and N. Yeganeh 1982. *In the Shadow of Islam. The Women's Movement in Iran.* London: Zed Press.

Thapar, S. 1993. "Women as Activists, Women as Symbols: A Study of the Indian Nationalist Movement." *Feminist Review* (summer): 81–96.

Thaiss, G. 1972. "The Conceptualization of Social Change through Metaphor." *Journal of Asian and African Studies* XIII 1/2: 1–13.

Tucker, C. 1990. *Prophetic Sisterhood: Liberal Women Ministers of the Frontier, 1880–1930.* Boston: Beacon Press.

Utne Reader 1994. "Allah's GI's. The Soldier Converts of Desert Storm." After Olivier Michel in *World Press Review.* March/April, p. 81.

Verges, M. 1995. "'I am Living in a Foreign Country Here': A Conversation with an Algerian 'Hittiste'." *Middle East Reports* 192: 14–17.

Wei-ming, T. 1991. "The Search for Roots in Industrial East Asia: The Case of Confucian Revival." In *Fundamentalisms Observed*, eds. Marty and Appleby, pp. 740–781. Chicago: University of Chicago Press.

Waltz, S. 1985. *Islamist Appeal in Tunisia.* Paper presented to the Middle East Studies Association. New Orleans, November, 1985.

Willis, J. 1985. "Nuns and Benefactresses: The Role of Women in the Development of Buddhism." In *Women, Religion and Social Change*, eds. Haddad and Findly, pp. 59–85. Albany, NY: State University of New York Press.

Wuthnow, R. 1987. *Meaning and Moral Order: Explorations in Cultural Analysis.* Berkeley: University of California Press.

255

BAUER

Yeganeh, N. 1993. "Women, Nationalism and Islam in Contemporary Political Discourse in Iran." *Feminist Review* (summer): 3–18.

Young, I. 1990a. *Throwing Like a Girl and Other Essays in Feminist Philosophy*. Bloomington: Indiana University Press.

———. 1990b. *Justice and the Politics of Difference*. Princeton: Princeton University Press.

———. 1995. "The Ideal of Community and the Politics of Difference." In *Feminism and Community,* eds. Weiss and Friedman, pp. 233–257. Philadelphia: Temple University Press.

Yuval-Davis, N. 1993. "Gender and Nation." *Ethnic and Racial Studies* 16: 621–32.

———. 1994. "Identity Politics and Women's Ethnicity." In *Identity Politics and Women: Cultural Reassertions and Feminisms in International Perspective*, ed. Moghadam, pp. 408–424. Boulder: Westview Press.

CONTRIBUTORS

GIDEON ARAN is Lecturer of Sociology and Anthropology at the Hebrew University, Jerusalem. His main academic interest is religious and political radicalism. His recent relevant publications include "Jewish-Zionist Fundamentalism" in *Fundamentalisms Observed* (edited by Martin Marty). He is currently conducting a field study and comparative research of Muslim, Protestant, and Jewish zealotry in Israel and the Middle East.

JANET BAUER has a Ph.D. in Sociocultural Anthropology from Stanford University and teaches in the Anthropology, Religion and Women's Studies Departments at Trinity College, Hartford, CT. She conducted field research in Islamic societies in the Middle East and Southeast Asia and has published widely on women, family, migration and change in *Feminist Studies, Anthropological Quarterly, Critique, Women in the Cities of Asia, Women and the Family in Iran, Women and Revolution in Iran*, and other journals and edited volumes. She is completing work on a book-length manuscript on Iranian women migrants and refugees, *Liberation and the Veil: Remaking Women and Family in Iran* and a monograph on women's fundamentalism in revolutionary Iran.

JANET BENNION has a Ph.D. in Cultural Anthropology from the University of Utah, and is currently at the University of Utah teaching in an adjunct position. Her M.A. in Cultural Anthropology was obtained at Portland State University. Her field is women's studies in Mormon Fundamentalist Groups. She is completing a book on women's roles in Mormon polygyny, *Women of Principle*.

JUDY BRINK received her M.A. and Ph.D. in Anthropology from the University of Pittsburgh and is an Associate Professor of Anthropology at Lock Haven University of Pennsylvania. She has conducted research in the same village in Egypt since 1981 and has published on the changes in the extended family (*Urban Anthropology* 1987), the effect of male emigration on their wives (*International Journal of Middle East Studies* 1991) and child rearing practices (*Pre- and Perinatal Psychology* 1993; *Childhood in the Arab World Today* ed. Elizabeth Fernea, 1995).

ELIZABETH BRUSCO is Associate Professor of Anthropology at Pacific Lutheran University in Tacoma, Washington. She carried out fieldwork on gender in Colombian evangelicalism during 1982–1983. Her current research focuses on the impact of Colombian constitutional reform on the evangelical movement, as well as the early experiences of foreign missionaries in Colombia. She is the author of *The Reformation of Machismo: Evangelical Conversion and Gender in Colombia* (U. of Texas Press, 1995), and co-editor (with Laura Klein) of *The Message in the Missionary, Local Interpretations of Religious Ideology and Missionary Personality* (Studies in Third World Societies, No. 50).

NANCY L. EIESLAND was trained as a Sociologist of Religion at Emory University where she completed her dissertation on suburbanization and religious change. She conducted fieldwork at Crossroads Assembly in suburban Atlanta between March and December 1991. She subsequently carried out fieldwork in another suburban community in Atlanta during 1992–1994. She is currently an Assistant Professor in the Candler School of Theology at Emory University. In addition to her work on suburbanization and religion, she has published in the area of physical disability and social status.

TAMAR EL-OR is a lecturer of Sociology and Anthropology at the Hebrew University, Jerusalem. Her main academic interest is literacy, gender and religion. Her latest relevant publication is *Educated and Ignorant: Ultraorthodox Jew-*

ish Women and their World (Lynne Rienner, 1994). She currently studies the constitution of gender/national/Jewish identity among modern orthodox Jewish women.

ERIKA FRIEDL is Professor of Anthropology at Western Michigan University. She has done research in Iran since 1965, concentrating on a longitudinal study of a tribal village. Over the years she has become especially interested in women's philosophies and ethics. Her publications include the book *Women of Deh Koh: Lives in an Iranian Village* (Penguin, 1991) and various articles on Iran. Currently she is working on a book about children in Iran.

HEMA GOONATILAKE received her Ph.D. from the School of Oriental and African Studies, University of London in 1974 and was senior faculty member at the University of Kelaniya, Sri Lanka until 1989. She is a founding member of Voice of Women, the first feminist group in Sri Lanka. She also co-founded the Center for Women's Research (CENWOR), Sri Lanka in 1984, and became its first joint coordinator. She is also a founding member of the Sisterhood is Global Institute, based in Washington DC. and of the Women for Mutual Security based in Athens. She is currently the gender in development expert at Cambodia Resettlement and Reintegration Programme, UNDP, Phnom Penh, Cambodia.

SONDRA HALE holds a Ph.D. in Anthropology from the University of California, Los Angeles (UCLA), where she now teaches in Women's Studies and Anthropology. She has carried out six years of fieldwork in Sudan, Eritrea, and Egypt and has published many articles on Sudan and on African and Middle Eastern women, including "Gender, Religious Identity, and Political Mobilization in Sudan" in *Identity Politics and Women* (V. Moghadam, ed., 1994); "Transforming Culture or Fostering Second-Hand Consciousness?" in *Arab Women* (J. Tucker, ed., 1993); "The Rise of Islam and Women of the National Islamic Front in Sudan," *Review of African Political Economy* (1992); and "The Politics of Gender in the Middle East," in *Gender and Anthropology* (S. Morgen, ed., 1989). She is the author of *Gender Politics in Sudan: Islamism, Socialism and the State* (1996).

MARY ELAINE HEGLAND was trained in Social–Cultural Anthropology at New York University and SUNY, Binghamton. Fortuitously, she began research in Iran in the summer of 1978 and thus was able to conduct participant observation during the Iranian Revolution, prompting her interest in religion, ritual, and politics and in village women's political participation. With her field work in Peshawar, Pakistan during 1989 and 1990, she further investigated gender and Shi'a ritual as well as women in education and politics. Taking advantage

259

of the rich cultural diversity in the Bay Area of California, she is studying how women from Iran and other Middle Eastern and South Asian countries revise and represent themselves under changing circumstances. Author of a number of articles about village women and religion and local politics in Iran, she is also co-editor (with Richard T. Antoun) of *Religious Resurgence: Contemporary Cases in Islam, Christianity, and Judaism* (Syracuse University Press). She has taught at Western Michigan University and Franklin and Marshall College and is now Assistant Professor of Anthropology in the Department of Anthropology and Sociology at Santa Clara University.

JOAN P. MENCHER received her Ph. D. from Columbia University in 1958. She has lived and worked extensively in South Asia for fifteen years between 1958 and the present. Her research interests include the political economy of development, family structure, wet rice agriculture (both irrigated and rain-fed), issues of family planning, women and development, the anthropology of gender, and applied anthropology. Apart from teaching and research she has worked as a consultant for UNDP, UNFPA, UNIFEM, and USAID. Selected publications include: *Where Did All the Men Go? Female-Headed/Female-Supported Households in Cross-Cultural Perspective;* (1993, jointly edited with Anne Okongwu), *Agriculture and Social Structure in Tamil Nadu: Past Origins, Present Transformations, and Future Prospects* (Carolina Academic Press and Allied Publishers, India 1979); "Peasant and Agricultural Labor: An Analytical Assessment of Issues and the Potential for Organizing" in Srinivasan and Bardhan, eds. *Rural Poverty in South Asia,* 1989.

KENG-FONG PANG originally trained as a Southeast Asianist in Singapore, she earned her Ph.D. in Anthropology at UCLA with her doctoral research among the Muslims known as Utsat or Hui. She is currently a three-year Visiting Assistant Professor at the Department of Sociology and Anthropology at Mount Holyoke College in Massachusetts. She was a Fullbright Research Fellow (1995–96) in Malaysia conducting historical and ethnographic research among descendants of the Utsat from Hainan Island in Maylasia, focusing on migration, religious and social networks, and the process of ethnogenesis as the Utsat become known in the Malay world as the Orang Kwangtung. She was a Post-Doctoral Fellow with the two-year New Ethnic and Immigrant Congregations Project in the United States where her research focus is on the Vietnamese and Cambodian Muslim Chams in California. She recently taught Anthropology at the University of Washington, Seattle. Her other research interests include transnational religious organizations and communities, particularly in the Cham, Malay, and Chinese diaspora, gender, ethnicity, nationalism, and the nation-state.

ILINA SEN has a Ph.D. in Demography from Jawaharlal Nehru University. She

260

has been actively associated with the women's and mine workers' movements, most recently with the Chhattiagarh Shramik Sangh in Madhya Pradesh. She has been affiliated both with the Indian council for social science research and the Centre for Women's Development Studies on their women's projects, and has published widely on demography, women's work on theory and practice of the women's movement in India. She works currently with Rupantar, a social study and action Center in Raipur Central India.

JANET STOCKS received her Ph.D. in Sociology at the University of Pittsburgh. Her dissertation was an ethnographic comparative case study of two small American evangelical Christian groups in which feminist challenges were occurring. In this work she investigated how the exercise and resistance of power within patriarchal institutions changes the boundaries of those institutions and shapes gender relations. She is currently the Center Administrator at the Center for the Integrated Study of Human Dimensions of Global Change at Carnegie Mellon University.

INDEX

267

269

273